The Inspection Panel of the World Bank: A Different Complaints Procedure

The Raoul Wallenberg Institute Human Rights Library
Volume 5

The Inspection Panel of the World Bank:
A Different Complaints Procedure

Edited by

Gudmundur Alfredsson

and

Rolf Ring

THE RAOUL WALLENBERG INSTITUTE HUMAN RIGHTS LIBRARY
VOLUME 5

MARTINUS NIJHOFF PUBLISHERS
THE HAGUE / LONDON / BOSTON

A C.I.P Catalogue record for this book is available from the Library of Congress.

ISBN (hardback) 90-411-1390-8
ISBN (paperback) 90-411-1391-6

Published by Kluwer Law International,
P.O. Box 85889, 2508 CN The Hague, The Netherlands

Sold and distributed in North, Central and South America
by Kluwer Law International,
675 Massachusetts Avenue, Cambridge, MA 02139, USA

In all other countries, sold and distributed
by Kluwer Law International, Distribution Centre
P.O. Box 322, 3300 AH Dordrecht, The Netherlands

Printed on acid-free paper

Kluwer Law International incorporates the publishing programmes of
Graham & Trotman Ltd, Kluwer Law and Taxation Publishers,
and Martinus Nijhoff Publishers.

Printed and bound in Great Britain by Antony Rowe Limited.

Table of Contents

Preface

*Göran Melander**

With the adoption of extensive human rights standards and their wide acceptance by States and indeed by the international community, the time has come to emphasize the implementation of these standards at both the national and international levels. This process will inevitably take time and patience and require the input of multiple actors. International financial institutions and development agencies have a special role to play in this respect, considering the influence and the resources at their disposal. Increasingly, they are acknowledging this duty, not only as a service to human rights but more so in recognition of the contribution which human rights and democracy, and so by extension good governance and accountability, make to political stability and improved economies.

An enhanced human rights role for the international financial institutions and development agencies also lives up to the now fashionable concept of mainstreaming of human rights. The UN family of organizations should work together in the human rights field and other areas of common interest, an approach which makes perfect organisational sense and falls in line with Articles 1 and 62-64 of the United Nations Charter.

The praiseworthy initiative behind the Inspection Panel of the World Bank is very much a case in point. By allowing external challenges to an international organisation, the Inspection Panel expands on the mandates of other international complaints procedures which focus on the performance of States. AS part of the rule of law and as a model for other international endeavours, it is very important that the Panel be allowed to thrive in a manner which is independent of the Bank's management, that its recommendations be taken seriously, that the regulations and policies applied by the Panel gradually come to encompass the international human rights standards, and that the affected public and non-governmental community become aware of its existence.

* Professor of Public International Law at the Faculty of Law, Lund University and Chairman of the Board of the Raoul Wallenberg Institute

This book contains papers submitted to a Workshop about the Inspection Panel which was organised in Lund in October 1997 by the Raoul Wallenberg Institute of Human Rights and Humanitarian Law and co-sponsored by the World Bank. Ibrahim Shihata and Göran Melander co-chaired the meetings. Gudmundur Alfredsson and Laurence Boisson de Chazournes came up with the idea leading to the Workshop, and Laurence was instrumental in its elaboration and implementation. Rolf Ring and other staff members of the Institute carried out much of the organizational work. A list of participants and authors appears in an annex.

The Raoul Wallenberg Institute was happy to host the Workshop and looks forward to further opportunities of engaging the World Bank in deliberations of a constructive and friendly character. We are particularly grateful to the President of Iceland, H. E. Olafur Ragnar Grimsson, for his enlightened opening statement. We would like to say thanks to all the participants in and other contributors to the Workshop who, albeit speaking and writing in their individual capacities, represented the views of intergovernmental and non-governmental organisations, national governments and academic institutions.

The purpose of the Workshop was to look for common ground in areas of mutual interest and engage in a substantive collection of ideas which can prove useful for the future work of the Inspection Panel and similar institutions. Such undertakings must include human rights education and training for the officialdom of national governments and international organisations, as well as of the individuals and groups who stand to benefit from the implementation of the international standards. The effort must also rely on monitoring exercises, in particular judicial and quasi-judicial instances working on the basis of law, where independent and impartial experts scrutinize the conduct of national and international actors.

It is our hope and expectation that the present book will serve a useful role both in enhancing knowledge of the Inspection Panel and in underlining its contribution. The Panel has the potential not only to improve the programs and projects supported by the bank but also to strengthen the rule of law, including human rights considerations, through the external scrutiny of the work of international organisations

Democracy and Human Rights: How We Learn the Hard Way

H. E. Ólafur Ragnar Grímsson[*]

The world is undergoing dramatic transformation and the changes are fast and comprehensive. We watch with awe and admiration the advances in biology, medicine, computer science, communications and space exploration.

The progress in understanding human relations has, however, been slower. Political science, sociology, law and economics have a long way to go to catch up with the precision and sophistication of their technological counterparts. Violent conflicts and human sufferings abound, but our institutions at both national and international levels are underdeveloped and insufficient. When we succeed in resolving one set of problems, it is often by temporary or ad hoc means and other problems persist.

Still, progressive evolution in the humanities has certainly taken place. Serious efforts are underway, again in both national and international settings, to enhance democracy, good governance, human rights and the rule of law. The striving for education, legal reforms, separation of powers, independence of the judiciary, accountability of those exercising authority, transparency in legislative, administrative and judicial matters, and the prevention and elimination of corruption in both public and private sectors have indeed produced substantial results. New incentives flow from the realization that economic policies tend to fail if the people and their representatives are not involved at all stages.

Forty-nine years ago, in the Universal Declaration of Human Rights, it was stated that the will of the people shall be the basis of the authority of government. The state is to serve the people, not the other way around. Individual rights, essential for a well-functioning democracy, are firmly anchored in the International Bill of Human Rights and other legal instruments. These include the freedoms of opinion, expression, information, assembly and association as well as the rights to run for office and vote in periodic elections with a secret ballot and a free choice between political options. Furthermore,

* President of the Republic of Iceland

democracy cannot and should not be separated from economic, social and cultural rights, such as those concerning education and labour standards.

Icelandic history reflects in many ways the international developments which are being addressed at the Expert Meeting, and we are still experimenting and learning from our experience as we go along. Small states have much to learn from others, but they can also serve as a classroom or a laboratory for detecting and promoting new trends on a broader scale.

Iceland obtained sovereignty in 1918 and gained independence in 1944. The Icelanders were thus in the forefront of the decolonization wave of newly independent countries. The outcome of the referendum in 1944 showed over 95% support for independence with over 98% voter participation, clearly reflecting the will of the people and accurately forecasting the results from subsequent exercises of the right of self-determination in other parts of the world.

In half a century of independence, the Icelanders have succeeded in dramatically improving living standards. We have moved from poverty to affluence. We have made serious progress in building democratic society based on human rights and the rule of law. In so doing, we have drawn on a rich heritage and distinct cultural and legal traditions rooted in the ancient Icelandic Commonwealth so well documented in the Icelandic sagas written about 700 years ago. We have also enjoyed international encouragement and support, some of it coming through the World Bank.

Despite our success, there is as always scope for improvement. Appeals to the European Court of Human Rights in Strasbourg have not only brought about human rights corrections in individual cases but also the reinforcement of fundamental rules in our constitutional order. The European Convention on Human Rights has now been incorporated into national law. Currently we have an ongoing discussion about the separation of powers, with persistent voices claiming that the executive branch of government has gained influence beyond that of the legislature and the judiciary.

We have joined nearly all accessible international, regional and sub-regional organisations. Considering Iceland's small population, it can even be argued that we have not always been able to keep track of developments in all these forums, let alone contribute in a substantial way. It is a question of priorities, but we have been willing to learn the lessons offered by these institutions in the economic, financial, social and political sectors. In at least one field, the law of the sea, we assumed a leading position in claiming jurisdiction over and introducing conservation for the renewable resources of both coastal waters and the oceans.

In other instances, it would seem that Iceland has fallen behind reasonable demands. Our contributions to development co-operation are still below levels expected from a rich country. This may be a case of the legislature failing to acknowledge the public will since Icelandic NGO's, including the Red Cross and the Church Aid Agency, have been able to raise funds from a generous population while successive governments were caught up with balancing the annual budgets. Still, through academic training provided by Iceland in affiliation to the UN University and through other international programs and bilateral projects, we are now in a position to share our resources and expertise, mainly in fishing and geothermal technologies, with many developing countries.

Like most of you assembled here today I do not consider myself to be old. In fact I don't think it was so very long ago that I was born in the western part of Iceland. But, at the year of my birth the majority of peoples in Europe, both western and eastern, lived under military dictatorships and the cruelty of those regimes was of unpresented proportions. All fundamental freedoms were violated. During the 20th century tens of millions of Europeans have been killed and tortured; a number of European regimes have also been responsible for human rights violations in other parts of the world. No part of our continent has been spared these tragedies. We Europeans have had to learn the democratic lessons the hard way. When setting timetables for states that gained independence in the post-World War II era, especially states in other parts of the world that were ruled by the colonial powers, we should in all humility recognise the breakdown of democracy, the dictatorial rule, that occurred in many western European states during tragic periods of this century. Thus while we tend to consider our continent to be a model for others it is worth remembering that for an important part of this century European governments which violated human rights outnumbered those that could truly be called democratic.

Although many if not most European nations have now achieved fundamental democratic reforms, Europe has by no means reached perfection. Pockets of undemocratic regimes and poverty remain. Instances of "ethnic cleansing" and patterns of other discriminatory actions against national, ethnic and linguistic minorities have brought about armed conflicts while other situations may lead to violence. States have been reluctant to allow the application of the rule of law for the resolution of these conflicts; instead, political ad hoc solutions have been preferred with the consequent risk of history repeating itself.

It is useful to keep this European record in mind when discussing the situation in other parts of the world. It teaches us a degree of patience and humility vis-a-vis our partners on other continents. Our credibility is associated with our own performance. The majority of states, however, now profess democratic governance and the results are beginning to show in the work of international organisations; we can now address, promote and seek to protect democracy and democratic practices in a straightforward and forthright manner.

We all acknowledge the crucial role played by political parties and other civic organisations on the domestic scene in a democratic society. Likewise, non-governmental organisations allow the voices of the people to be heard in international forums; there the NGOs often provide contents, conscience and courage. It has been fashionable to pay respect to or at least refer to the grass roots, but we must remember that for human rights, democracy and good governance, we are not only talking about the roots. Each individual with his or her vote and opinions based on knowledge and education must have the facilities to influence the work of national and international institutions.

Opening the doors for democratically chosen representatives would further enable the people to have both influence and input at the level of international organisations. Many problems are encountered and resolved by diplomats and national and international civil servants showing their expertise and thus justifying the respect which they enjoy. Nonetheless, some of these problems would be more easily brought to a happy conclusion if parliamentarians with direct popular mandates played a more central role. The acknowledgement of the universality of human rights standards will come easier to parliamentarians than government officials; and elected representatives may be in better positions to indicate which particularities reflect national culture as understood and accepted by the populace.

Certainly, parliamentarians are not perfect creatures, but they must operate under the rule of law, as set forth in constitutions, legislative acts and other sources of national and international law. Originating with elected law-makers, these rules have to meet such minimum standards as equality and non-discrimination for individuals and groups. In the event of disputes, effective remedies must be available under the maxims of equal protection of the law and equality before independent and impartial courts. Issues resting on identical facts, irrespective of which entities are involved, should receive identical treatment and resolution with equal access, equal results and equal treatment for everyone. The links to accountability and transparency must be obvious.

In all instances affecting the legislative and executive branches of government, the voters retain the ultimate control through the option of not reelecting the parliamentarians who fail to take account of the public interest. It is this popular demand and the role of politicians in expressing that demand in line with the rule of law which increasingly must govern national and international relations.

It is with reference to this understanding of democracy, human rights, good governance and the rule of law that I would like to view the current Expert Meeting. The states and intergovernmental organisations were created to serve the people and therefore expectations must be met. In this modern day and age the people want a larger degree of control in their own hands; they want rights for themselves as well as legal and political accountability and openness from the leaders they have chosen; also from those who have been selected to manage international organisations created by democratic states.

In many of these areas, international organisations have made useful recommendations to the member states, but in their work those organisations should also meet the same expectations by observing the same standards of behaviour. The element of consistency is very important. It applies not only to lawyers who are used to working with precedents, but also to the public which is increasingly growing familiar with the work of IGOs and expects nothing less than the universal application of the principles to which I have been referring.

For all of these reasons, the Inspection Panel set up by the World Bank is a significant and praiseworthy step. It contributes to subjecting the Bank to the rule of law by allowing individuals and groups in countries where projects supported by the Bank are underway to test them before a panel of experts with reference to applicable international standards. This step is particularly significant and praiseworthy because it gives a voice to the people corresponding to modern ideas about rights and popular access. Eventually, such a panel should be elevated to a judicial institution delivering binding decisions.

Other intergovernmental organisations with development, economic and political projects in the field should follow the example which the World Bank provides by the creation of the Inspection Panel. National development agencies should also allow challenges to their bilateral projects, either through the courts or, in the beginning, with similar panels of experts. The rule of law and accountability must apply to everyone everywhere.

By instituting an Inspection Panel, the World Bank has taken an important, forward-looking step. By promoting similar review mechanisms within other international organisations, this Expert Meeting is pushing for more steps in the right direction. But let us never forget when discussing developments in other parts of the world that we in Europe have had to learn our democratic lessons the hard way. When the world is clearly changing, the challenge lies in shaping these changes to the benefit of individuals, groups and peoples. The continuing development of democracy, good governance, human rights and the rule of law at the national and international levels foresees a long list of necessary reforms.

The World Bank Inspection Panel – Its Historical, Legal and Operational Aspects*

Ibrahim F.I. Shihata[**]

I. Introduction

The World Bank Inspection Panel, a special, independent mechanism created by the World Bank's Executive Directors in September 1993, has completed at the time of writing (February, 1998) three and a half years of operation. Its experience has just been subjected to a second review by the Bank's Executive Directors. This may therefore be a good time to examine the work of this important mechanism and consider its possible evolution in the future.

This paper describes the most relevant aspects of this mechanism. It traces the developments which led to the establishment of the Panel, analyzes the Resolution by virtue of which it was created, describes how this Resolution has been so far applied in practice, and how some of its provisions have been virtually amended by clarifications issued by the Bank's Executive Directors in the course of the first review of the Panel's experience in 1996. The paper also presents the author's explanation of how the role of the Panel has in many instances turned from the inspection function to the function of triggering remedial action by the Bank or the borrower before or without a full investigation by the Panel of the complaints submitted to it. It concludes with proposals on reconciling these developments with the Panel's original function while preserving its integrity and independence.

* Based on a paper prepared for the Expert Meeting on the Inspection Panel of the World Bank, held at the Raoul Wallenberg Institute of Human Rights and Humanitarian Law in Lund, Sweden, on October 23-25, 1997. This paper has been updated to include developments subsequent to that Meeting.

** Senior Vice President and General Counsel, World Bank; Secretary-General, International Centre for Settlement of Investment Disputes. The views presented in this paper are the personal views of the author and should not be attributed to the institutions he works for.

II. Developments which Led to the Establishment of the Inspection Panel

The creation by the World Bank of an independent mechanism of its own to assess the extent to which it actually lives up to the standards it has set for itself in the design, appraisal and implementation of its operations was unprecedented in the work of international organizations.[1] (The earlier precedent of the jurisdiction of the European Court of Justice over decisions of the European Communities is not counted here. The distinct supranational nature of the latter organization does not provide a comparable precedent.)[2] The circumstances which led to the establishment of the Panel and the factors which influenced its final shape are therefore important both for a general understanding of the inspection function and for the interpretation of the Resolution establishing the Panel.[3]

1.The 1992 Internal Review of Bank Operations

The creation of an operations' inspection function in the Bank emanated from an internal review of its work following the appointment in September 1991 of the late Lewis P. Preston as President of the Bank. This review coincided with, and was influenced by, increasingly strong voices from inside and outside the Bank on what was perceived as the Bank's inadequate attention to the standards reflected in its policies and procedures.

Preston's conviction that the management of the Bank's portfolio of loans required improvement was shared by many Executive Directors, government

---

[1] For a comprehensive legal analysis of the Resolution establishing this unique body, *see* Ibrahim F.I. Shihata, The World Bank Inspection Panel, 35-124 (1994).

[2] The European Community (EC) Treaty, i.e., the former Treaty on the European Economic Community as it has been amended by and incorporated into the Treaty on the European Union, provides for multiple remedies for individuals against acts and omissions of the EC institutions. Any natural or juridical person can challenge the legality of acts of the EC institutions before the European Court of Justice (ECJ), if these acts are addressed to that person or are of "direct and individual concern" to him. (*See* Article 173, Para. 4 of the EC Treaty.) Likewise, individuals can bring an action before the ECJ for failure of EC institutions to act, provided this failure constitutes an infringement of the EC Treaty. (*See* Article 175, Para. 3 of the EC Treaty.) Individuals can also claim compensation before the ECJ for any damage they have suffered, if this damage was caused by EC institutions or by its servants in the performance of their duties. (*See* Article 178 in connection with Article 215, Para. 2 of the EC Treaty.) The existence of such broad remedies for individuals against the EC institutions, while unusual in the context of international organizations, may not, however, be unusual in the context of the EC which, as a supranational organization, is in some respects comparable to a confederation.

[3] For a detailed account of the circumstances which led to the establishment of the Inspection Panel, *see* Shihata, *supra* note 1, at 1-34.

officials, Bank staff and external parties. It led to the establishment of a task force, headed by an experienced senior manager in the Bank, to examine the quality of the Bank's loan portfolio. One of the main findings of the task force's report (which was submitted in November 1992 and came later to be known as the "Wapenhans Report," after the name of its chairman) was that the Bank staff were often concerned about getting as many projects as possible approved under the Bank's lending program.[4] In such an "approval culture", less attention had been given to the commitment of borrowers and their implementing agencies and to the supervision by the Bank of project implementation.[5] The task force recommended a change in the Bank's policies and practices in order to improve performance of its portfolio management. It referred in this context, to the need to enhance the role of the Bank's Operations Evaluation Department (OED.) A subsequent action plan, prepared by Management in July 1993, in response to the task force's recommendations, introduced new business practices and processes.[6] It recommended greater participation in the design and implementation of Bank-financed projects by the people affected by these projects and greater involvement of relevant NGOs in project design and implementation. It emphasized project "ownership" (in the sense of the commitment of the borrower to the project objectives), and better ways of monitoring the performance of Bank operations. In this respect, the plan highlighted the need for the Bank's access, when necessary, "to a reliable source of independent judgment about specific operations that may be facing severe implementation problems."[7] Accordingly, it concluded that "the interests of the Bank would be best served by the establishment of an independent Inspection Panel."[8]

2. External Demands for Greater Accountability

External criticism of the Bank by NGOs and influential circles in certain member countries with large subscriptions in the Bank's capital (and large subscriptions/contributions to the Bank's affiliate, the International Development Association (IDA)) no doubt influenced that conclusion. This external criticism was part of a broader concern expressed in several developed

---

4 *See* Effective Implementation: Key to Development Impact (R92-125), November 3, 1992 (hereinafter Wapenhans Report). The findings of the Wapenhans Report are summarized in Getting Results: The World Bank's Agenda for Improving Development Effectiveness 1-7 (World Bank 1993).

5 *See* Wapenhans Report, *supra* note 4.

6 *See* Portfolio Management: Next Steps, A Program of Action (World Bank, July 22, 1993).

7 *Id.* at para. 60.

8 *Id.*

countries to the effect that international organizations were not adequately accountable for their activities and that they needed to be more open and responsive. The criticism escalated in 1993, in the course of the final negotiations by donor countries on the tenth replenishment of IDA. This was also the time when some UN member states threatened to withhold part of their assessed contributions to the United Nations until that organization set up an independent Inspector General's office.[9]

The Narmada Precedent

The debate on the Bank's accountability had been fueled by the mistakes allegedly made by the Bank regarding two major projects in India: the Narmada River Development Sardar Sarovar Dam and Power Project (in short, the Narmada dam project) and the Narmada River Development Water Delivery and Drainage Project (in short, the Narmada canal project). The first project was partially financed by IDA and the IBRD and the second by IDA alone in the mid-1980s.[10] While the IDA credit for the canal project was fully disbursed and closed on July 1, 1992, the IBRD loan and the IDA credit for the dam project were still under disbursement when the project's implementation became an issue attracting world-wide attention. Under construction since 1987, the projects included a large concrete dam, a 1200-megawatt powerhouse, transmission lines, a canal system and drainage network to serve an irrigation area of about 2 million hectares in Gujarat, India. Besides major environmental impacts, the dam project finally required the resettlement of more than 120,000 people from a submersion area of approximately 370 square kilometers (while the original estimate confirmed in Bank reports had calculated the resettlement of 70,000 persons only). The canal project involved a resettlement of a similar magnitude although that was not foreseen at the time of project appraisal. The Bank funding represented only about 10% of overall costs.

From the beginning of project implementation, the environmental assessment and the resettlement/rehabilitation component of the Narmada projects had been subject to heavy criticism by local and international NGOs. Responding to this criticism, the then President of the World Bank, Barber Conable, decided in March 1991 to commission an independent review, which

---

9 *See* the US proposal for an Office of Inspector General, submitted to the 48th session of the U.N. General Assembly on November 24, 1993; U.N. Document A/C/48/35 (1993). On the role of the inspectorate proposal in the U.S. congressional debate over U.N. appropriations for fiscal year 1994 (H.R. 2519, October 14, 1993), *see* D. Thornburgh, Today's United Nations in a Changing World, 9 American University Journal of International Law and Policy 215, 220 n. 17, and 222 (1993).

10 *See* Loan Agreement No. 2497-IN (1985) and Development Credit Agreement No. 1553-IN (1986).

was chaired by Bradford Morse, a retired Administrator of the United Nations Development Programme who was previously a US Congressman. The objective of that review was to conduct an assessment of the implementation of the projects regarding the resettlement and rehabilitation of the population displaced or affected, and the amelioration of the environmental impact of all aspects of the project, with reference to existing Bank operational directives and guidelines.[11] The independent review team was not meant to be a "commission of inquiry," however, and consultation with various interested groups were not to imply a mediation or adjudication function. The report of Mr. Morse and his team, discussed by the Bank's Executive Directors in June 1992, noted a failure to incorporate Bank policies in the project credit and loan agreements and a subsequent failure to require adherence to enforceable provisions of these agreements.[12] As a consequence of these findings, the Morse report recommended a review of Bank procedures to ensure that the full reach of its policies was implemented in the projects it financed.[13] While Management disputed some of the report's findings and maintained that the loan documents reflected the requirements of applicable policies, it carried out a further internal review of the project and submitted its results to the Board in May 1993.[14] The management review reiterated some of the main findings of the Morse report which, understandably, led external critics to call for general new remedies to avoid similar deficiencies.

---

[11] Terms of Reference dated March 14, 1991 issued by the President of the World Bank following his appointment of Mr. Morse to address this issue on August 30, 1991. It may be noted that the establishment of the "Morse Commission" was not formally discussed by the Bank's Board, even though some Executive Directors took an active role in this matter.

[12] The Report was published by its authors, without prior Bank permission, as B. Morse & T.R. Berger, Sardar Sarovar: The Report of the Independent Review (Ottawa: Resource Futures International 1992) (hereinafter Morse Report); *see also* T.R. Berger, The World Bank's Independent Review of India's Sardar Sarovar Projects, 9 American University Journal of International Law and Policy 33 (1993).

[13] *See* Morse Report, *supra* note 12, at 353-54.

[14] *See* India: The Sardar Sarovar (Narmada) Projects – Management Response (SecM92-849), June 23, 1992. The Bank-wide resettlement review, initiated in 1993, was completed in April 1994; *see* The Bankwide Review of Involuntary Resettlement 1968-1993, Report prepared by the Task Force for the Bankwide Resettlement Review, Environment Department (April 1994). For the details of the further internal review, *see* H. Wyss, Bankwide lessons learned from the experience with the India Sardar Sarovar (Narmada) Project, annexed to SecM93-516, May 24, 1993.

3. *The Bank's Internal Review Mechanisms Prior to the Inspection Panel*

Up to that time (mid 1993), internal mechanisms for quality control in the preparation and implementation of Bank-financed projects operated at three stages of the project cycle: preparation, appraisal, supervision, and evaluation.

While formal responsibility for project preparation rested with the borrower, the Bank assisted the borrower in its preparatory activities in a number of ways.[15] Procedures for project design and appraisal also included numerous safeguards to ensure not only the economic soundness of the project but the assessment as well of its environmental impacts (including prior public consultations by the borrower).[16] Special expert consultations were also required regarding projects on international waterways, and dam and reservoir projects.[17] After a loan was approved by the Bank's Executive Directors, the Bank monitored progress in project implementation and compliance with loan conditions.[18] Supervision concentrated, however, on familiarizing the borrower and the implementing agencies, if any, with the Bank's Procurement Guidelines and the preparation of the progress reports to be reviewed by Bank staff. It included staff visits to the project site. Following project completion, an ex post evaluation of projects was selectively carried out by the Bank's Operations Evaluation Department (OED) to draw lessons from experience, and more generally to enhance the internal and external transparency of Bank operations.[19] OED evaluated each project on the basis of a project implementation report. Each report covered the execution and initial operation of the project, the costs and benefits derived and to be derived from it, the performance by the borrower and the Bank of their respective obligations under the loan agreement and the extent of accomplishment of the project purposes. Furthermore, OED carried out evaluation studies focusing on selected issues and sectors. OED's assessment of the performance of completed operations included an assessment of the technical, financial, economic, social and

---

15 *See* W.C. Baum, The Project Cycle 8-10 (World Bank Publication 1982).

16 *See*, among others, the Bank's Operational Policies on the Economic Evaluation of Investment Operations, OP 10.04 (April 1994), and on draft Environmental Assessment, OP 4.01 (May 1997) (which was first introduced in 1989 under Operational Directive (OD) 4.00 Annex A and formulated in OD 4.01 in 1991 before being converted into an OP). It should be noted that consultations are required to be held with the people potentially affected by the project and local NGOs speaking for these people under the Operational Policies concerning involuntary resettlement and indigenous people. *See* OD 4.20 Indigenous People (September 1991), and OD 4.30, Involuntary Resettlement (June 1990) which has been converted to draft OP/BP 4.12 Involuntary Resettlement (June 1995).

17 *See* OP 7.50 Projects on International Waterways (October 1994) and OD 4.00 Annex on Environmental Policy for Dam and Reservoir Projects (April 1989).

18 For more details, *see* Shihata, *supra* note 1, at 16-18.

19 *Id.* at 19-20.

environmental aspects of the project and provided ratings of overall performance and sustainability.

The Bank had also regular audits by the Internal Auditing Department which periodically audits operational, financial, administrative, personnel and information resource management systems to test their efficiency and compliance with the Bank's internal control systems.[20] On occasion, the Bank also carried out ad hoc independent evaluations such as the one commissioned for the Narmada projects.[21]

The wide attention inside and outside the Bank which both the Wapenhans Report and the Morse Report received triggered a number of proposals in the course of 1993 which contributed to the process of the establishment of the Inspection Panel. Some of these proposals originated within the Bank, others came from external sources.

4. Proposals for an Inspection Function

In February 1993, four Executive Directors (three representing non-borrowing countries and one representing a number of borrowing countries) came forward with a proposal for the establishment of an independent in-house inspection capacity for on-going projects.[22] This proposal, to which a fifth Executive Director later associated himself, was made after submission of the Wapenhans Report but before Management had prepared its full-fledged response to it. The proposal envisaged a small permanent unit staffed with three inspectors selected from among experienced Bank officers, to be part of the Bank structure, possibly under the OED, with sufficient independence of its own. This unit would receive requests for inspection from borrowers or Executive Directors (but not directly from affected parties), undertake the relevant inspection after deciding on the eligibility of the request, and, in addition, carry out random evaluation on a sample of projects in the Bank's loan portfolio. The Bank's Board would take note of the findings of the unit's recommendations but would "ask for an increased role in cases of special importance."

The initial reaction of the Bank's senior staff to this proposal suggested that there was no apparent need for a permanent inspection unit of that type and that an ad hoc inspection capacity would suffice. This position was not, however, adopted. Further developments, culminated meanwhile in several specific proposals made outside the Bank for the establishment of a standing

---

20 *Id.* at 21.

21 *See supra* notes 11-13 and accompanying text.

22 *See* Shihata, *supra* note 1, at 22-23.

inspection function. These included in particular a proposal for the appointment by the Board of a Bank Ombudsman[23] and another for an independent appeals commission with judicial powers, including the power to issue binding decisions on the Bank.[24]

Board Consideration and Adoption of the Resolution Establishing the Panel

Political support for some of these external proposals (including in particular support for the latter proposal in the US House of Representatives in the course of the IDA 10th Replenishment) was widely felt.[25] Bank management moved towards the development of a plan for the establishment of a standing inspection function. A first staff paper contained two proposals, one along the line of the Executive Directors' proposal for an inspection unit within the OED, and one for an independent, in-house inspection panel with three inspectors appointed by the Board upon the President's recommendation.[26] The latter panel was to receive complaints from individual Executive Directors and affected parties, but the complainant party had first to seek an explanation from Management before approaching the Panel. The Panel would, after carrying out an investigation, submit recommendations to the President on projects under preparation and to the Board on projects under implementation.

No consensus on either of these options was reached, however, in informal discussions with the Executive Directors. Concerns were expressed in

---

[23] *See* Daniel D. Bradlow, Why World Bank Needs an Ombudsman, Financial Times, July 14, 1993, at 13.

[24] *See* Statements on behalf of Environmental Defense Fund, National Wildlife Federation and Natural Resources Defense Council before the Sub-Committee on International Development, Finance, Trade and Monetary Policy of the Banking, Finance and Urban Affairs Committee, U.S. House of Representatives (May 5, 1993). *See also* D. Hunter & L. Udall, Proposal for an Independent Appeals Commission (Environmental Defense Fund and Center for International Environmental Law, 1993).

[25] The proposal that an independent appeals commission would be established in the World Bank was incorporated in a U.S. committee draft on conditions for IDA-10. *See* Sub-Committee on International Development, Finance, Trade and Monetary Policy of the Banking, Finance and Urban Affairs Committee, U.S. House of Representatives, Draft "International Development and Debt Relief Act of 1993" (May 26, 1993). While the call for the establishment of an independent appeals commission in the World Bank eventually entered the U.S. appropriation legislation in October 1993 in substantially modified form, the discussion, however, indicated an emerging trend in the U.S. Congress to strongly favor the establishment of a commission or panel of inspectors in the Bank.

[26] For the Executive Directors' proposal, *see supra* note 22 and accompanying text. For the second alternative proposal on an independent, in-house inspection panel, *see* Operations Inspection in the Bank: Issues and Options, Draft Report submitted to the Executive Directors (R93-122), June 10, 1993.

particular over the potential risks such an inspection function could bring to bear on the respective roles of Bank Management and Board. Fears were also expressed regarding the possibility of a large volume of complaints. In an attempt to facilitate agreement, Bank Management prepared a revised paper reconciling the two options, together with a draft resolution.[27] The latter resolution envisaged an independent three-member inspection panel with powers to hear complaints presented either by a group of four or more Executive Directors or by one or more persons directly affected by a failure of the Bank to follow its operating policies, rules and procedures. The revised paper was considered by the Executive Directors at the end of August 1993. While there was still some support for an in-house inspection unit under the OED Director-General, a majority of Executive Directors favored the establishment of an independent panel as a subsidiary body reporting to the Board. However, the discussions on some of the specifics of such a panel revealed that a further revision of the draft resolution was needed. The text of the further revised draft resolution was submitted to the Board on September 21, 1993.[28] During that Board meeting which reconvened on September 22, 1993, the revised draft resolution was further amended before it was finally adopted.[29] The resolution required a Board review of the Inspection function after two years from the date of the appointment of the first members of the Panel.[30] The review was completed in July 1996 and resulted in the issuance by the Board of certain "Clarifications" which in fact introduced some amendments (by addition) to the resolution.[31] Recent discussion in the Board of the Panel's recommendations to investigate two projects resulted in the Board's agreement in September 1997 to carry out a further review which is still being undertaken at the time of writing.

---

27 *See* Functions and Operations of an Inspection Function, Draft Paper (R93-122/1), August 6, 1993 and Draft IBRD/IDA Resolution on The World Bank's Independent Inspection Panel, August 5, 1993.

28 *See* Memorandum from the President, Operations Inspection Function: Objectives, Mandate and Operating Procedures for an Independent Inspection Panel (R93-122/2), September 10, 1993.

29 *See* Resolution No. 93-10 IBRD, Resolution No. 93-6 IDA, The World Bank Inspection Panel, dated September 22, 1993 (hereinafter the Resolution or the Resolution Establishing the Panel), published in Shihata, *supra* note 1, at 127-33.

30 *See* para. 27 of the Resolution Establishing the Panel.

31 *See* Clarifications of Certain Aspects of the Resolution Establishing the Inspection Panel (R96-204), dated September 30, 1996 which were approved by the Board of Executive Directors on October 17, 1996 (hereinafter Clarifications or the 1996 Clarifications).

III. THE RESOLUTION ESTABLISHING THE WORLD BANK INSPECTION PANEL

1. Composition

The Inspection Panel was thus created by a resolution of the Bank's Executive Directors as an independent body within the Bank's structure. The Resolution provides that the Panel is composed of three members of different nationalities of Bank member countries who are nominated by the Bank's President and appointed by its Executive Directors.[32] According to the Resolution, selection criteria for Panel members include their ability, integrity, independence from Bank Management, exposure to developmental issues and living conditions in developing countries.[33] As a desirable, but not a necessary factor, knowledge and experience of the Bank's operations is also mentioned as a relevant criterion.[34] However, in order to serve on the Panel, a member's prior affiliation with the Bank, if any, must date back two years at least.[35] Also, after having served on the Panel, a Panel member is prohibited from returning to or joining the Bank.[36] Panel members may only be removed from office by a decision of the Executive Directors, for cause.[37] Currently, the Chairman of the Panel works full-time on Panel matters, as required by the Resolution.[38] The other two members work on a part-time basis, but the Resolution allows for their full-time engagement "when their work load justifies such an arrangement."[39] The Panel from the beginning has had its own separate Secretariat. The Resolution speaks only of the assignment of a staff member to the Panel as Executive Secretary "who need not act on a full-time basis until the workload so justifies."[40]

2. Objectives

The objectives of the Panel's function are not listed in the Resolution. It is clear, however, from the history detailed above, that the underlying objective is twofold: to enhance quality control in project design, appraisal and

---

32 *See* para. 2 of the Resolution Establishing the Panel.
33 *Id.* at para. 4.
34 *Id.*
35 *Id.* at para. 5.
36 *Id.* at 10.
37 *Id.* at para. 8.
38 *Id.* at para. 9.
39 *Id.*
40 *Id.* at para. 11.

implementation by possibly subjecting staff work to a high level independent inspection when harm appears to have occurred, and to improve transparency in the Bank's work and accountability of the Bank's Management and staff for observance of the Bank's policies and procedures throughout the project cycle.[41] To that end, the Resolution gives the Inspection Panel a mandate to investigate, by authorization of the Bank's Board in each case, complaints by groups of individuals whose rights or interests have been or are likely to be directly and adversely affected by the Bank's failure to abide by its policies and procedures regarding the design, appraisal or implementation of a project financed (or to be financed) by the Bank.[42] One or more Executive Directors may also ask the Panel for an investigation and the Executive Directors acting as a Board may, at any time, take the initiative in instructing the Panel to conduct an investigation.[43]

3. Institutional Coverage

As the Resolution establishing the Panel was issued by the Boards of IBRD and IDA, the institutional coverage of the Panel's mandate extends explicitly to projects financed by these two institutions only. IFC and MIGA activities are not subject to investigation by the Panel, although, as will be mentioned, this has since become a bone of contention.[44] Bank actions as trustee of the Global Environment Facility (GEF) and other trust funds are not explicitly covered. There is, in my view, however, room for including these actions under the Panel's jurisdiction by way of interpretation, subject to the concurrence of the Bank's Executive Directors (and GEF's Council with respect to GEF-financed projects).[45]

---

[41] While the Resolution is silent on the objectives of the inspection function, management papers submitted to the Executive Directors and the discussion of these papers and of the draft resolution prepared by the Office of the Bank's Senior Vice President and General Counsel provide details on these matters. *See* Shihata, *supra* note 1, at 56.

[42] *See* para. 12 of the Resolution Establishing the Panel.

[43] *Id.*

[44] IFC and MIGA are currently considering a system for an inspection function for their respective operations. Such a system might then be extended to all private sector operations of the Bank Group, including those of IBRD and IDA.

[45] *See* Shihata, *supra* note 1, at 39-41.

4. Eligibility of Complaints

Under the Resolution, the Panel's role is to be performed in two stages, except when the request is initiated by the Board where only the latter stage applies. In the first stage, the Panel is to assess whether the request for inspection meets the eligibility requirements of the Resolution. On the basis of this assessment, the Panel recommends to the Executive Directors whether to authorize an investigation. In the second stage, which takes place only after the Board authorizes investigation, the Panel carries out its investigation and reaches its findings on whether the Bank has been in serious violation of its operational policies and procedures, provided, as mentioned, that such violation relates to the design, appraisal and/or implementation of the project involved.

In the exercise of the first stage of its function, the Panel is required by the Resolution to establish four elements of jurisdiction, the first of which does not apply if the request is made by a member or members of the Bank's Board. These eligibility requirements cover (i) the Panel's competence relating to the person of the complainant (jurisdiction ratione personae); (ii) its competence regarding the subject-matter of the complaint (jurisdiction ratione materiae); (iii) its competence relating to the timing of the complaint (jurisdiction ratione temporis); and (iv) the admissibility of the complaint in the absence of other grounds excluding it under the Resolution.[46]

The Panel has competence in respect of the complainant if the latter is an "affected party." An affected party, under the Resolution, must be a "community of persons, such as an organization, association, society or other grouping of individuals," but "not a single individual."[47] While the Panel initially understood this to mean "any two or more persons" and so indicated in the Operational Procedures[48] issued by it, the Board later made it clear (in its 1996 "Clarifications") that it means only "any two or more individuals with common interests or concerns."[49] The affected party must show that its "rights or interests have been or are likely to be directly affected by an action or omission of the Bank," a requirement that effectively excludes complaints on

---

[46] *See* Memorandum of the Senior Vice President and General Counsel, Role of the Inspection Panel in the Preliminary Assessment of Whether to Recommend Inspection (SecM95-11), January 3, 1995. This memorandum was made publicly available by decision of the Board of Executive Directors. It is available at the Bank's Public Information Center and is also published in 34 ILM 525 (1995).

[47] *See* Resolution Establishing the Panel, at para. 12.

[48] *See* Operating Procedures, adopted by the Panel on August 19, 1994, at para. 4(a).

[49] *See* Clarifications, *supra* note 30, on the term "affected party" in the section on eligibility and access.

behalf of the public at large (actio popularis).[50] Finally, the affected party must be "in the territory of the borrower."[51] Such a party can act in its name or through a local representative.[52] In exceptional cases, the Resolution authorizes the affected party to employ a foreign representative such as an international NGO, when local representation is not available and foreign representation is approved by the Bank's Board at the time it authorizes inspection.[53]

To ascertain its subject-matter jurisdiction, the Panel must, according to the Resolution, make sure that (a) the request is based on an alleged "failure of the Bank to follow its operational policies and procedures with respect to the design, appraisal and/or implementation of a project financed by the Bank (including situations where the Bank is alleged to have failed in its follow-up on the borrower's obligations under loan agreements with respect to such policies and procedures);"[54] (b) such alleged violation of the Bank's policies and procedures is of a serious character; (c) the alleged violation relates to the Bank's own policies and procedures, within the limits of flexibility provided therein (the latter phrase, "policies and procedures," means, according to the Resolution, the Bank's Operational Policies, Procedures and Operational Directives and similar documents (previously called "Operational Manual Statements" and "Operational Notes"), but not "Guidelines" and "Best Practices and the like");[55] and (d) the alleged violation, if established, would have "a material adverse effect" on the affected party, i.e., a harm which, in the judgment of the Panel, seems to be material enough as to warrant investigation of the complaint.[56]

A request would be excluded under the Resolution for reasons of its timing, if it were filed "after the Closing Date of the loan financing the project" or "after the loan financing the project has been substantially disbursed."[57] The Resolution left no doubt as to the meaning of "substantial" disbursement by defining it, in an accompanying note, to mean disbursement of at least 95 percent of the loan amount," regardless of the stage of project completion.[58] This mathematical specificity was meant to leave no doubt as to the intended meaning. It did, however, give rise to a different interpretation in an actual case, where, at the time of the request for inspection, a supplemental loan was 94.2 percent disbursed after an initial loan financing the same project was

---

[50] *See* Resolution Establishing the Panel, at para. 12.

[51] *Id.*

[52] *Id.*

[53] *Id.*

[54] *Id.* at para. 13.

[55] *Id.* at para. 12.

[56] *Id.*

[57] *Id.* at para. 14(c).

[58] *See* footnote accompanying para. 14(c) of the Resolution Establishing the Panel.

fully disbursed. (As the Bank's General Counsel, I took the view that that in itself did not disqualify from inspection the project's design or appraisal as well as measures taken under the supplemental loan.)[59]

Finally, a request may be barred for the following other reasons: First, if the subject matter of the complaint had not been first dealt with by the Bank Management, because the complainant had failed to submit its complaints to Management before resorting to the Panel.[60] Second, if after the complaint was submitted to Management, the Panel is satisfied that Management has complied, or intends to comply with the Bank's relevant policies and procedures.[61] Third, the Panel is barred from investigation of a complaint that is based on actions which are the responsibility of parties other than the Bank, such as the borrower.[62] Fourth, the Panel is further barred from accepting complaints from suppliers, contractors or losing bidders against procurement decisions under Bank-financed projects.[63] (This was later "clarified" to include Bank procurement decisions, and not only those of the borrower.)[64] Finally, requests related to a particular matter or matters on which the Panel has already made its recommendation are excluded from being entertained again.

5. The Inspection Function

Once the Panel finds the request eligible, it would, according to the Resolution, recommend to the Board that it authorizes an investigation.[65] After the Board decides that the matter is to be investigated, the Panel conducts the investigation by checking the pertinent Bank records, interviewing Bank staff and other persons, consulting as needed with the Director-General of the Bank's OED and the internal Auditor-General, as well as with the borrower itself and the Executive Director representing the borrowing (or guaranteeing) country.[66] The Panel may also carry out the investigation in the territory of the borrowing country after obtaining the borrowing country's prior consent.[67] The Panel considers all relevant facts and then submits its findings on whether the Bank has complied with its policies and procedures in a report to the

[59] *See* Legal Opinion of the Senior Vice President and General Counsel, Time-Limits on the Eligibility of Complaints Submitted to the Inspection Panel (SecM97-693), July 28, 1997.
[60] *See* Resolution Establishing the Panel, at para. 13.
[61] *Id.*
[62] *Id.* at para. 14(a).
[63] *Id.* at para. 14(b).
[64] *See* Clarifications, *supra* note 30, emphasizing that "no procurement action" is subject to inspection by the Panel in the section on eligibility and access.
[65] *See* Resolution Establishing the Panel at para. 19.
[66] *Id.* at para. 21.
[67] *Id.*

Board.[68] At this stage, Management is given the opportunity to comment on the Panel's findings; it is expected to submit a report to the Board including its recommendations on remedial actions. The Board, based on all information before it, will then decide on any actions to be taken in this respect.[69]

6. Disclosure Requirements

All information regarding the request, including the text of the request, the Panel's recommendation on the eligibility of the request, the Board's decision to authorize or deny investigation, the Panel's findings, Management's comments and the final Board decision are made publicly available after Board consideration of each document.[70] Management's initial response to the request submitted to the Panel is not mentioned among the documents for which the Resolution requires public disclosure. It was, however, included by virtue of the 1996 Board "Clarifications."[71]

IV. Application of the Resolution by the Panel, Management and the Board

1. Overview

As of September 1997, the Panel has received ten requests for inspection and registered eight of them. Of the two requests which were not registered, the first was submitted on behalf of foreign persons whose property in a borrowing member country was allegedly confiscated many years earlier. The request suggested that by continuing to lend to the country involved, IDA had violated a long standing policy which requires the Bank "not to lend for projects in a country if it considers that the position taken by it with respect to alien owners of expropriated property is substantially affecting its international credit standing."[72] It also suggested that IDA had violated the policy on disclosure of information and requested investigation of these matters. The Panel refused to register the request on the basis that "the requesters failed to complete the

68 *Id.* at para. 22.
69 *Id.* at para. 23.
70 *Id.* at para. 25.
71 *See* Clarifications, *supra* note 30, under the section on outreach noting that Management will make its response to requests for inspection available to the public within three days after the Board has decided on whether to authorize an inspection.
72 *See* OMS 1.28 on Disputes over Defaults on External Debt, Expropriation, and Breach of Contract.

filing of a request for compensation in accordance with the laws of [the country] and therefore failed to establish that the lack of compensation was the direct consequence of any alleged acts or omissions of IDA as required by the Resolution."[73] In effect, that request was inadmissible for the obvious reason that it did not relate to alleged failure by the IDA relating to the design, appraisal or implementation of any specific project. The second unregistered request related to an IFC investment in the construction of a hydroelectric project. It was not registered because of its obvious inadmissibility as it concerned an IFC rather than an IBRD or IDA operation.[74]

2. Registered Requests – The Panel's Case-Load

Out of the other eight requests, four related to IBRD and four to IDA projects. Seven of these requests concerned large infrastructure projects such as hydroelectric dams, power stations, natural resources management projects, bridges, and an irrigation area and water reservoir. In all the requests concerning infrastructure projects, non-compliance with primarily environmental policies and procedures was alleged by the complainants. Only one of the eight requests related to a sector adjustment operation. The Panel recommended investigation for five of the registered requests.

Arun III Dam Project – Nepal

In the first request (registered in October 1994), a group of Nepalese citizens claimed non-compliance by the Bank with, among other things, its policies on disclosure of information, environmental assessment, involuntary resettlement and indigenous people in connection with a proposed hydroelectric project in Nepal (Arun III) which was then under consideration but not yet financed by the Bank.[75] On the basis of the Panel's recommendation, the Board authorized an investigation with respect to the issues of environmental assessment, involuntary resettlement and indigenous people. A report was sent to the Board by the Panel, including its findings which confirmed that remedial actions proposed by Management (after the investigation had started but before its completion) would satisfactorily meet the Bank's requirements if

---

[73] *See* First Annual Report of the Inspection Panel covering the period of August 1, 1994 to July 31, 1996 reproducing the Panel's decision at 56.

[74] *See* Request for Inspection – IFC Financing of Hydroelectric Dams in the Biobío River in Chile (INSP/SecM95-8), December 1, 1995.

[75] *See* Request for Inspection: Panel Report – Nepal Arun III Proposed Hydroelectric Project (IDA/SecM94-378), December 16, 1994 (including in Attachment (1) the text of the request itself). For Management's response, *see* Attachment (2) of the Panel's Report.

diligently followed.[76] However, the matter became moot after the Bank's new President, James D. Wolfensohn, informed the Board that, based on a comprehensive internal review, he had decided not to proceed with the project.[77]

Power Project – Tanzania

Environmental policies were also mentioned in a request, registered in March 1995, of a group of US and Tanzanian citizens (as, respectively, owners and employees of a corporation) regarding an IDA-financed power project in Tanzania.[78] In this case, the Panel did not recommend an investigation, because of the complainants' failure to show a violation of IDA policies or the project's adverse environmental effect.[79]

Natural Resources Management Project – Rondonia, Brazil

In a request registered in June 1995, a group of NGOs from the state of Rondonia in Brazil acting as agents of Rondonia residents regarding the Bank-financed Rondonia Natural Resources Management Project claimed non-compliance with a number of Bank policies, including the environmentally relevant policies on forestry, wildlands, indigenous people and NGO participation.[80] This request became an important precedent for the Bank in that its handling by the Panel, Management and the Board contributed to the above-mentioned clarifications on the Resolution of the Inspection Panel. After receiving the Panel's recommendation to authorize investigation for reasons of non-compliance, in particular with environmental policies,[81] the Board asked the Panel to conduct an additional review to further substantiate the materiality of damages and to establish whether such damages were caused by deviation from Bank policies and procedures. Based on the Panel's additional report[82] and on a comprehensive Management report on the status of the

---

76 *See* Request for Inspection: Panel Investigation Report – Nepal Arun III Proposed Hydroelectric Project (INSP/SecM95-3), June 22, 1995.

77 *See* Arun III Hydroelectric Project – Management Response to the Inspection Panel's Investigation Report (INSP/SecM95-5), August 2, 1995.

78 *See* Request for Inspection – Tanzania: Power VI Project, Panel Recommendation (INSP/SecM95-6), August 16, 1995 (including in Annex 1 the text of the request itself).

79 *Id.* at para. 15. The Board agreed with that approach.

80 *See* Request for Inspection – Brazil: Rondonia Natural Resources Management Project, Panel Recommendation (INSP/R95-2), August 18, 1995 (including in Annex 1 the text of the request itself). For Management's initial response to the request, *see* Annex 2 of the Panel's Recommendation.

81 *See* Request for Inspection – Brazil: Rondonia Natural Resources Management Project, Panel Recommendation (INSP/R95-2), August 18, 1995, at para. 14.

82 *See* Request for Inspection – Brazil: Rondonia Natural Resources Management Project, Panel Report on Additional Review (INSP/R95-4), December 12, 1995.

project's implementation (which included a remedial action plan that Management had prepared in the meantime),[83] the Board decided not to authorize an investigation but to review the execution of the action plan after 6 to 9 months with the assistance of the Panel. That review took place in the projected time to the satisfaction of the Board.

Bridge Project – Bangladesh

In a request registered in August 1996, failure of the Bank to comply with the policies on environmental assessment, resettlement and participation of NGOs was alleged by a Bangladeshi NGO, representing people living on mid-channel islands that emerge periodically from the Jamuna River bed as a result of accretion, in the context of the construction of a multipurpose bridge over the Jamuna River.[84] In particular, non-compensation for the damages that the allegedly affected people incurred as a result of their resettlement was claimed. The Panel visited the project site and gathered information from Management on the general resettlement action plan and on the erosion and flood policy (which included a system of compensation for affected people) that was adopted by the Government shortly after the request was registered. Based on the information it gathered, the Panel found that an investigation was not warranted at that stage.[85] The Board approved the Panel's recommendation, but asked Management to provide a progress report on the project's implementation for its review, to which it would invite the Panel to participate.

Yacyreta Hydro Electric Project – Argentina/Paraguay

In a request registered in October 1996, a Paraguayan NGO claimed on its own behalf and on behalf of people living in the project area that the Bank had, among other things, failed to follow its policies on resettlement, indigenous people, wildlands, and environmental assessment in the design and implementation of the Yacyreta Hydroelectric Power Plant financed by a Bank loan to Argentina.[86] While the Panel recommended that the Board authorize

---

[83] *See* Brazil: Rondonia Natural Resources Management Project, Management Report on the Status of Implementation (SecM95-1271), December 20, 1995.

[84] *See* Request for Inspection – Bangladesh: Jamuna Bridge Project, Panel Report and Recommendation (INSP/SecM96-14), December 2, 1996 (including in Annex 1 the text of the request itself). For Management's initial response, *see* Annex 2 of the Panel's Report and Recommendation.

[85] *Id.* at para. 56.

[86] *See* Request for Inspection – Argentina/Paraguay: Yacyretá Hydroelectric Project, Panel Report and Recommendation (INSP/R96-2), December 26, 1996 (including in Annex 1 the text of the request itself). For the Management response, *see* Annex 2 of the Panel's Report and Recommendation.

an inspection,[87] the Board, which received objections related to the eligibility of the complaint from Bank Management and the Government of Argentina, and received from Management a remedial action plan agreed with the governments of Argentina and Paraguay, invited the Panel to undertake a "review of the existing problems of the Yacyreta project regarding environmental and resettlement issues" in order to provide an assessment of the adequacy of measures agreed between the Bank and the countries concerned (Argentina and Paraguay) within the next four months. It also stated that the Panel could "review consistency of the Bank's actions with its procedures."[88] A controversy later arose as to whether the latter review should be confined to the Bank's "procedures" (as stated in the decision), or should also include its policies (as is normally the case in the inspection envisaged under the Resolution). The Panel's report, submitted in September, 1997, in fact covered issues of compliance with applicable Bank policies and procedures in detail.[89] The report was discussed in the Board in December 1997. The Board noted that the implementation of the action plan had made significant progress towards resolving the environmental and resettlement problems of the project. It requested Management to continue its follow-up on the implementation of the action plan and to report to it on the further progress in the matter within six months. The Board also noted that it would determine later whether to give the Panel a further role in this follow-up.

Sector Adjustment Loan – Bangladesh

Owners of private jute mills in Bangladesh requested the Panel in November 1996 to investigate the economic losses they suffered as a result of IDA's failure in the design and implementation of a jute sector adjustment program, which was subject to delay and failure by the borrower to meet agreed conditions.[90] This is the only request so far which is related to an adjustment (rather than a specific investment) loan. While the Panel considered the request eligible under the Resolution for a number of reasons, it did not find an investigation useful in that particular case, given that a new government was negotiating with the Bank a revised time-table for the implementation of

---

87 *Id.* at para. 43.

88 *Id.* at para. 3.

89 *See* Request for Inspection – Argentina/Paraguay: Yacyretá Hydroelectric Project – Panel Review and Assessment (INSP/R97-10), September 18, 1997.

90 *See* Request for Inspection – Bangladesh: Jute Sector Adjustment Credit, Panel Report and Recommendation (INSP/R97-3), March 20, 1997 (including in Annex 1 the text of the request itself). For Management's initial response to the request, *see* Annex 2 of the Panel's Report and Recommendation.

the program to rectify the problems caused by the government's delay.[91] The Board readily agreed with the Panel's recommendation.

Resettlement and Irrigation Project – Itaparica, Brazil

Non-compliance with environmental policies has been alleged in a recent request concerning a resettlement and irrigation project in Itaparica, Brazil.[92] A local union of rural workers representing people living in the project area alleged the Bank's violation of its policies for dam and reservoir projects, on environmental assessment, involuntary resettlement, and indigenous people. The Bank did not finance the dam and reservoir project but only provided a loan to help mitigate their environmental and resettlement effects. The Panel recommended investigation of the complaint but sought the Board's confirmation that it was not time-barred.[93] (This was the case of the project initially financed by a Bank loan, which was fully disbursed, then financed by a supplemental loan – introduced through an amendment of the original loan agreement – which was almost, but not quite, 95 percent disbursed.)[94] In September 1997, the Board decided not to authorize an investigation but concluded that the Bank should help supervise the implementation of the Brazilian Government Action Plan which required the disbursement by Brazil of an additional $290 million for the purpose of the project to ensure completion of works providing productive infrastructure and technical assistance to resettlers. Both the Action Plan and the request for Bank supervision of its implementation were initiated by the Brazilian Government. The Board decided further that it would review the progress of the project in a year and invite the Panel to assist in that review.

Power Project – India

The last case submitted to the Panel concerned the NTPC Power Project in India which was meant to strengthen the borrower's capacity to implement new investment policies and upgrade environmental performance and

---

91 *Id.* at para. 89. The fact that the loans involved did not finance any specific project did not deter the Panel from considering it eligible in principle for inspection; nor did it invite Board objections to the Panel's position.

92 This request was received in March 1997. It is attached to Request for Inspection – Brazil: Itaparica Resettlement and Irrigation Project, Panel Report and Recommendation (INSP/R97-7), June 27, 1997 in Annex 1. For Management's initial response to the request, *see* Annex 2 to the Panel's Report and Recommendation.

93 *Id.* at para. 46.

94 For an analysis of the situation where the same project is financed by more than one loan in different disbursement statuses, *see* Legal Opinion of the Senior Vice President and General Counsel, Time-Limits on the Eligibility of Complaints Submitted to the Inspection Panel (SecM97-693), July 28, 1997.

management as well as to increase its power generation capacity.[95] The residents in the project area who filed the request claimed non-compliance by the Bank with its policies on environmental assessment, involuntary resettlement and indigenous people. Management recognized its partial failure to observe some of the policies involved and submitted a detailed remedial action plan.[96] The Board, which had just declined to authorize investigation of the Bank's role in the Itaparica project in Brazil after a divisive discussion, approved the Panel's recommendation for an investigation of the Bank's role in the NTPC project in India. But bearing in mind that the Panel had already undertaken a preliminary review at the project site, the Board decided that the investigation should be conducted at the Bank's headquarters in Washington. The Panel was asked to report its findings to the Board within three months. At that point, the Board would decide whether any further action would be deemed appropriate. The Board took also notice of the action program of corrective measures agreed between the borrower and Bank Management after the request was submitted to the Panel and requested Management to submit periodic progress reports on the implementation of that program. The Panel presented its report on the investigation it conducted in the NTPC case in December 1997.[97] The Panel's desk study confirmed violations of Bank policies and procedures regarding the involuntary resettlement and associated aspects of the project which had been referred to in the Panel's earlier recommendation. Management agreed in substance with the Panel's main conclusions but disputed some of the facts on which these conclusions were based.

3. Analysis of the Experience

It is interesting to note from the cases submitted to the Panel that investigation was authorized by the Board explicitly in only two cases, the first and the latest, i.e., the Arun III project in Nepal, which had not been financed by the Bank at the time of inspection (and where Bank financing was eventually withdrawn), and the NTPC Power project in India, where inspection took place only at the Bank's headquarters. The Board virtually authorized

---

95 *See* Request for Inspection – India: NTPC Power Generation Project, Panel Report and Recommendation (INSP/R97-9), July 25, 1997 (including in Annex 1 the text of the request itself).

96 *See* India: NTPC Power Generation Project, Management Response to Request for Inspection, June 3, 1997, reprinted in Annex 3 of the Panel's Report and Recommendation regarding this request, *see supra* note 94.

97 *See* Request for Inspection – India: NTPC Power Generation Project, Panel Report on the Investigation (INSP/R97-15), December 24, 1997.

inspection in a third case, the Yacyreta dam project, but stood short of stating so. The reason for the evolution of a practice that seems different from that suggested by the wording of the Resolution may be twofold. The straightforward approach provided for in the Resolution requires the Panel to limit its role at the initial stage to ascertaining on a prima facie basis whether eligibility criteria are met. However, this was complemented from the beginning by a procedure which the Panel introduced on its own initiative. On August 19, 1994, the Panel introduced its "Operating Procedures" for the purpose of facilitating its work and providing practical guidance to those who may submit requests for inspection to it. In these Procedures, the Panel provided for its power to carry out, after receiving the Management response and any clarifications provided, "a preliminary review" in order to "determine whether conditions required by provisions of the Resolution exist."[98] The review at this initial stage, i.e. before Board authorization of a full investigation, was introduced by the Panel to be undertaken if it is "satisfied [on the basis of the information available at this stage] that Management has failed to demonstrate that it has followed, or is taking adequate steps to follow the Bank's policies and procedures."[99] (Under the Resolution, this language appears in paragraph 13 which speaks of the preliminary condition that the Panel, *before hearing a complaint*, should be satisfied that its subject-matter had been submitted first to Management and that Management had failed to adequately address it.) In this "preliminary review," according to the Operating Procedures, the Panel "may not investigate Management actions in depth."[100] However, the purpose of this review, according to the text, is "to determine whether Management's failure to comply with the Bank's policies and procedures meets the following three conditions: (a) whether such failure has had, or threatens to have, a material adverse effect; (b) whether the alleged violation of the Bank's policies and procedures are, in the judgment of the Panel, of a serious character; and (c) whether remedial actions proposed by Management do not appear adequate to meet the concerns of the Requester as to the application of the Bank's policies and procedures."[101] (Under the Resolution, determining such conditions in any definitive manner would constitute the subject matter of the investigation which has yet to be authorized.) The Panel's objective in introducing this procedure seems to have been its concern to base its recommendation (on whether to carry out a full investigation) on firm grounds and, if possible, to see if Management could propose remedial action to obviate the need for that full investigation.

---

98 *See* Operating Procedures of the Inspection Panel, at para. 34.
99 *Id.*
100 *Id.* at para. 35.
101 *Id.* at para. 35(a) – (c).

In a "working paper" prepared by the Panel on the occasion of the first review of its experience, the Panel explained that the Board, by asking the Panel to take further time to produce additional reports during the preliminary review stage, had practically modified the Resolution's requirements.[102] The Panel described that "modification" as "a pragmatic approach, developed by the Board in response to very real problems."[103] It also noted on that occasion that "the extent of information expected by the Board at the preliminary stage is sometimes equivalent to the content of an investigation."[104] For that reason, the Panel argued for an extension of the period of the preliminary assessment it had introduced in its Procedures, indicating that such an assessment "reduces the need for a formal investigation/inspection which can still be authorized by the Board as a last resort."[105] After the Rondonia case, the Bank's Board in effect agreed with that approach. It therefore accordingly allowed the Panel in the 1996 "Clarifications" to extend the period of this preliminary assessment, as may be needed, within certain limits.[106] Board majority seemed to have found in this approach a convenient method to redress the situation, without having to authorize the full "investigation" which the Resolution envisaged in each case where it is warranted. Although the purpose of the Panel's investigation is to ascertain Bank compliance with its own policies and procedures, the borrowing countries involved have typically seen it as an embarrassment to the government. Opposition groups within these countries also used it to press the government to make new concessions. An attitude against full investigation whenever it could be avoided thus evolved among borrowing member countries and created a divisive climate every time the Board had to discuss a Panel recommendation to investigate. The preparation of a remedial action plan mitigated these negative effects but also focused attention on measures to be taken by the borrower, rather than on the subject-matter of inspection according to the Resolution which is the Bank's own failures.

The above procedure, first adopted by the Panel and later endorsed by the Board, was probably based on a certain understanding of paragraph 13 of the Resolution which may differ from its literal meaning. This paragraph reads as follows:

---

102 *See* Review of the Inspection Function – Practical Suggestions Based on Experience to Date, Working Paper for the World Bank Executive Directors prepared by the Inspection Panel in November 1995.

103 *Id.*

104 *Id.*

105 *Id.*

106 *See* Clarifications, *supra* note 30, on the extension of the period allowed for the understanding of a preliminary assessment under the section on the Panel's function.

> The Panel shall satisfy itself before a request for inspection is heard that the subject matter of the request has been dealt with by the Management of the Bank and Management has failed to demonstrate that it has followed, or is taking adequate steps to follow the Bank's policies and procedures. The Panel shall also satisfy itself that the alleged violation of the Bank's policies and procedures is of a serious character.

As the above language speaks of a condition that has to be fulfilled before a request for inspection is "heard," it clearly makes the prior submission of the subject matter of the request to Management and the lack or inadequacy of response by Management conditions for the admissibility of the request by the Panel. It also envisages that Management's adoption at this early stage of what the Panel would see as adequate steps (i.e. adequate remedial action) to follow the Bank's policies and procedures would obviate the need for investigation and cause the Panel not to recommend it. However, in every case where a remedial action plan was prepared by Management this was done *after* the request for inspection was submitted to the Panel and (in all but one case – Arun III) before the Board was to discuss the Panel's recommendation to investigate. The submission of such a plan could not therefore bar the request from being "heard" by the Panel. Yet, it created a dilemma for the Board which saw in the plan a satisfactory solution that addressed the underlying complaints and spared all parties the embarrassment of an investigation. The result, however, was seen by many to short-cut the process envisaged in the Resolution to let the Panel proceed with investigation when the eligibility conditions are met. Under a literal reading of the Resolution, remedial action may be adopted by Management before the matter reaches the Panel. It may also be adopted after the Panel undertakes its investigation and reaches its findings. In the latter case, Management is required to submit to the Board its recommendations in response to such findings (pursuant to paragraph 22 of the Resolution). The Resolution does not require the adoption by Management of an action plan in the intermediate stage between the registration of a request for inspection and the submission of the Panel's findings. Although it does not exclude this possibility, the Resolution simply envisages that Management would provide the Panel with a response within 21 days to enable the Panel to decide whether the request was eligible for investigation and that the Panel would make a recommendation to the Board only on this question within a similar period.

As already mentioned, an action plan on remedial measures to be taken by the borrower alone is likely to divert attention from the main issue of whether the Bank has followed its policies or procedures. Yet, it could, as a practical matter, make a full investigation superfluous from the viewpoint of many Board members. This has in fact contributed to the above-mentioned practice of the Board declining to authorize the investigation and requesting instead progress reports on the implementation of the plan. The occurrence of this possibility was not unforseen, however, at the time of the adoption of the Resolution and its possible preemption of the Panel's role was in fact among the criticisms levelled against the Resolution at the time. However, this criticism would not be justified if the action plan addresses also the measures to be taken by the Bank to remedy any failures that may be attributed to it. As I had the occasion to explain in my book on the Inspection Panel, the "obviation of the need for inspection in such cases should be seen as a positive development to the extent that it allows for correcting Bank failures in a speedy manner."[107] It may thus be surmised that the preparation of the remedial action plans which obviated the need for inspection has practically served the purpose of the affected parties but not always that of the inspection function itself. It has also caused much frustration and misunderstanding, especially for those watching the process from the outside. This matter was discussed at length in the second review of the Panel's experience. As will be shown, its candid discussion by the Executive Directors in February 1998 may help develop a solution which serves both the purposes of affected parties and the inspection function.

V. First Review of the Inspection Panel Experience

As already mentioned, the Resolution establishing the Panel provides for a review by the Executive Directors of the experience "after two years from the date of the appointment of the first members of the Panel."[108] This review started in February 1996, when the Executive Directors held a preliminary discussion of the matter in light of four papers prepared by Management which covered (i) a non-exhaustive list of issues for discussion; (ii) a table summarizing the manner in which requests before the Panel were handled; (iii) a list summarizing comments received from the Panel and the NGOs which had communicated their views to Bank Management; and (iv) a note and a table comparing the Bank's Inspection Panel with the inspection panels established by IDB in 1994 and ADB in 1995.[109]

In this informal meeting, the Executive Directors agreed that the Board's Committee on Development Effectiveness (CODE) would first review the matter in depth in light of Management's recommendations before final recommendations were made to the Board. A number of papers received from

---

107 *See* Shihata, *supra* note 1, at 100. (Emphasis added.)

108 *Id.* at para. 27.

109 *See* Review of the Inspection Panel Function – Background Documents; February 23, 1996, discussed in an informal Board meeting on February 27, 1996.

several NGOs[110] on the subject were circulated to the Committee before it received in May 1996 a paper from Management[111] outlining different issues which arose in the implementation of the Resolution and summarizing the positions of the Panel and outside sources with respect to such issues. The Panel also submitted a report to CODE commenting on Management's paper.[112] One of the major issues highlighted in the Management paper was whether the inspection function was to be extended to the activities of the IFC and the MIGA, and, if so, whether inspection of private sector operations across the World Bank Group (i.e. including those of the Bank itself) should have a different Panel or the same Panel operating under different procedures which take account of the special circumstances of the private sector.

Discussion in CODE revealed a broad preference among its members to keep the original Resolution establishing the Panel intact while providing for measures of flexibility in its implementation. Rather than introducing amendments to the Resolution, it was felt that the Board should consider the issuance of directives to guide its application in practice. Such directives, being issued by the Board, would have the same force as the Resolution and would in fact complement its text. On the possible application of the inspection function to IFC and MIGA operations, a separate paper prepared by the IFC Management was subsequently discussed in CODE. It was agreed that IFC and MIGA would consult with the business community, co-financiers and Executive Directors representing borrowing countries and report back to CODE. Once CODE had completed its consideration of the inspection mechanism for IFC and MIGA projects, it was Management's intention to propose a common approach to inspection for all Bank Group private sector projects. In October 1997, CODE discussed an IFC report on "Consultations with Private Sector Clients and Co-financiers on the Possible Establishment of an Inspection Mechanism for IFC and MIGA." The report showed that a majority of those consulted were not in favor of an inspection function and would not, at any rate, welcome inspection under the established procedures of the existing Panel. Discussion in CODE was not conclusive and Management was asked to present different options to a subsequent meeting which has yet to be held. The matter might become part of the discussion in the projected second review of the Bank's Panel.

In its first review in 1996, after considering the proposals submitted by Management and the Panel on all other matters, and aware of the views submitted by NGOs on the issues involved, CODE, then the full Bank Board

---

[110] *See* Letters from Oxfam International and International Rivers Network, March 26, 1996.
[111] *See* Review of the Resolution Establishing the World Bank Inspection Panel, May 7, 1996.
[112] *See* Memorandum from the Chairman of the Inspection Panel, Review of the Resolution Establishing the World Bank Inspection Panel, May 14, 1996.

reached certain conclusions which were conveniently termed "clarifications" of the Resolution.[113]

On the Panel's function and procedures, suggestions were made by some NGOs to do away with the first phase of the process (where the Panel recommends and the Board approves whether to investigate). Other suggestions were made by the Panel and accepted by Management to extend the 21-day period given by the Resolution for the Panel to make its recommendation on this matter (after receiving Management's response to the complaint, which response has to be submitted within 21 days from notification of the request to Management). The Board decided that the Panel's recommendation should normally be completed within 21 days as originally envisaged.[114] However, it gave the Panel the requested discretion when it found it appropriate to carry out a preliminary assessment of the alleged damage (in particular when this could lead to a resolution of the matter without the need for a full investigation).[115] The Board asked that the Panel, in undertaking such a preliminary assessment, indicate to the Board the date on which it would present its findings and recommendation as to whether a full investigation was still required.[116] If such a date was expected by the Panel to exceed eight weeks from the date of receipt of Management's response, the Panel would seek Board approval for the extension, possibly on a "no-objection" basis.[117] The Board also made it clear in that respect that what was needed at this preliminary stage was not to establish that a serious violation of the Bank's policy had actually resulted in damages suffered by the affected party.[118] Rather, it was to establish whether the complaint was prima facie justified and warranted a full investigation because it was eligible under the Resolution.[119] The Board also agreed that the Panel's investigations should continue to result in "findings" (not in recommendations to the Board on the substance of the project subject to the complaint or on the Bank's overall policies and procedures, as suggested by some NGOs).[120] The Board would continue to act on the basis of recommendations of Management with respect to such remedial action as may be needed, in light of the Panel's findings.[121]

---

[113] *See* Review of the Resolution Establishing the Inspection Panel – Clarification of Certain Aspects of the Resolution, September 30, 1996, discussed and approved in the Board on October 17, 1996. For a reference to the text of the Clarifications, *see supra* note 30.

[114] *See* Clarifications, *supra* note 30, under the section on the Panel's function.

[115] *Id.*

[116] *Id.*

[117] *Id.*

[118] *Id.*

[119] *Id.*

[120] *Id.*

[121] *Id.*

On the issues of access to the Panel and eligibility of requests for inspection, Management had no objection to extending such access to all affected parties, including a single individual, as suggested by NGOs (and as was originally mentioned in the first draft Resolution). The Board, however, favored maintaining the present language of the Resolution with the understanding that the affected party, which the Resolution describes as "a community of persons such as an organization, association, society or other grouping of individuals," includes "any two or more persons who share some common interests or concerns."[122] This confirmed an interpretation given on an earlier occasion by the Bank's General Counsel.[123] The Board did not support extending the inspection function as requested by some NGOs to requests submitted by foreign NGOs, local NGOs whose rights or interests were not affected by the project or, more generally, to claims submitted in the public interest. The Board also declined the Panel's request to authorize inspection upon the request of the Bank's President, noting that the Panel was established by the Board to perform an independent function for the Board.

The Board also clarified that the request for inspection may relate either to a project under consideration by Bank Management, i.e. a project in the design, preparation, preappraisal or appraisal stage, or to a project already approved by the Board and financed by the Bank.[124] It also reconfirmed an earlier Board understanding (in July 1995) to the effect that the term "project" as used in the Resolution had the same meaning as generally used in the Bank's practice.[125] As also agreed in July 1995, it was clarified that the Panel's mandate did not extend to reviewing the consistency of the Bank practice with all of its policies and procedures but, as stated in the Resolution, was limited to cases of alleged failure by the Bank to follow its operational policies and procedures with respect to the design, appraisal and/or implementation of projects, including cases of alleged failure by the Bank to follow-up on the borrowers' obligations under loan agreements, with respect to such policies and procedures.[126]

On the question of disclosure of information, the Board agreed to make Management's response to the request for inspection as well as the opinions of the General Counsel of the Bank on matters related to the Panel available

---

[122] *Id.* under the section on eligibility and access.

[123] *See* Memorandum of the Senior Vice President and General Counsel, Role of the Inspection Panel in the Preliminary Assessment of Whether to Recommend Inspection, *supra* note 46.

[124] *See* Clarifications, *supra* note 30, under the section on eligibility and access.

[125] *Id.* For details on the discussion regarding the meaning of the term "project" under the Resolution Establishing the Panel, *see also* First Annual Report of the Inspection Panel, *supra* note 72, at 57-58.

[126] *See* Clarifications, *supra* note 30, under the section on eligibility and access.

to the public promptly after the Board had discussed these documents.[127] It also shortened the period of disclosure of all documents to three days from the date of Board decision.[128]

No change in the composition of the Panel was proposed but it was agreed that once a decision was made on inspection of private sector operations the question of the composition of the Panel might be revisited unless a separate panel were to be established for that purpose (perhaps to be served by the same secretariat).[129]

The Board also clarified that the authority to interpret the Resolution was vested in the Board.[130] The Panel would apply the Resolution in specific cases as it understood it subject to the Board's review when the matter was submitted for its consideration.[131] The Board also reconfirmed the Resolution's requirement that the advice of the Bank's Legal Department be sought by the Panel "on matters related to the Bank's rights and obligations with respect to the request under consideration."[132] The request of some NGOs that the Board should have a legal counsel to advise on Panel matters, separate from the Bank's General Counsel, was not granted. It was recalled that the General Counsel provided independent legal advice to both the President and the Board on all matters and was not, in any event, involved in the preparation of Management's response to the requests for inspection. (The recent case of the Itaparica project in Brazil proved the point; the General Counsel's legal opinion to the Board differed in its conclusions from Management's response on the eligibility question.)

Also the Board agreed that significant efforts be made to make the Inspection Panel better known in borrowing countries, but stated that the Bank should not provide technical assistance or funding to potential requesters.[133]

Finally, the Board clarified that the exclusion of procurement decisions from the Panel's jurisdiction was not limited to decisions taken by the borrower (as the letter of the Resolution suggests) but extends to all procurement decisions, including those taken by Bank Management.[134] It was noted in this respect that a separate mechanism existed for addressing procurement-related complaints.

---

[127] *Id.* under the section on outreach.
[128] *Id.*
[129] *Id.* under the section on the composition of the Panel.
[130] *Id.* under the section on the role of the Board.
[131] *Id.*
[132] *Id.*
[133] *Id.* under the section on outreach.
[134] *Id.* under the section on the eligibility and access.

VI. Second Review of the Inspection Panel Experience

The clarifications of 1996 did not reduce the divisiveness in the Bank's Board when it addressed Panel recommendations with respect to subsequent complaints in the following year. The decisions on the courses of action to be followed regarding the complaints concerning the Yacyretá and NTPC projects led the Executive Directors to agree on the need for a second review of the whole experience.

The first informal Board meeting on that review took place on November 13, 1997 on the basis of a management paper[135] which, after referring to the Panel's experience explained above (as presented in a paper by this author), suggested that the Board had two options. The first option would be to literally follow the original text of the Resolution, limiting remedial plans submitted by Management to the very initial stage (before the complaint is submitted to the Panel) and the latest stage (after the investigation is completed). The second option, which is closer to the Board's practice codified in the 1996 Clarifications, would allow remedial plans in the intermediate stage (between the date of registration of the complaint and the Board's consideration of the Panel's recommendations) but with certain refinements. The plan would in this case be submitted first by Management to the Panel which would comment on its adequacy in its report to the Board. The Panel might then agree that the Plan obviated the need for inspection or might still recommend a full investigation. The informal Board discussion showed a broad preference for the second option. It also revealed a great mesure of dissatisfaction on the part of Executive Directors representing borrowing countries who saw that the remedial plans were always concerned with measures to be taken by the borrowers at the borrowers' own expense and thus departed from the purpose of the inspection function which was meant to address the failures of the Bank and no other party.

This led to an approach proposed by this author as a commentary on the going debate.[136] The purpose of this approach is to ensure full respect for the scope established in the Resolution for the inspection function while benefiting from the practical position preferred by the Board under the 1996 Clarifications. The proposed approach consists mainly in tailoring the procedure to be followed to the nature of each response made by Management to the request for inspection, while paying full regard to two important points: (i) The Resolution's requirement (Paragraph 14 (a)) that complaints with respect to actions which are the responsibility of parties other than the Bank are excluded from the Panel's mandate, and (ii) the need to address any harm

[135] *See* Second Review of the Inspection Panel Experience, November 6, 1997.

[136] *See* Second Review of the Inspection Panel Experience – A Commentary, January 7, 1998.

resulting from Bank financed projects regardless of whether this harm results from Bank failures or other factors. The following scenarios had thus to be dealt with separately:

A first possible scenario envisages that Management's response would be that there is no serious violation of any Bank policy or procedure applicable to the operation involved. Such a response should normally be made within the 21-day period provided for in the Resolution. Depending on whether or not it agrees with Management's position, the Panel will in such a case formulate its recommendation to the Board on whether an investigation is needed. The Panel will follow in this process the requirements of the Resolution, limiting itself to alleged actions or omissions attributed to the Bank and to no other party.

A second possible scenario envisages response by Management to the Panel to the effect that the request does not meet the Resolution's requirements for reasons other than the absence of any serious violations, such as that the complainant was not an affected party or that the loan was more than 95 percent disbursed. Again in this case, the 21-day period provided by the Resolution should normally be adequate for providing such a response. The Panel would assess the eligibility of the complaint and formulate its recommendation on whether an investigation is needed. The Panel's assessment may agree or disagree with Management's response but would exclusively address actions or omissions attributed to the Bank. Under the Resolution as clarified in 1996, the Panel would normally make its recommendation within a 21-day period but has the possibility of extending this period up to eight weeks and may even seek a longer extension from the Board.

A third possible Management response is that failures do exist but they are exclusively attributable to the borrower or to other factors external to the Bank. If the Panel agrees that there was no prima facie evidence that any failure was attributed to the Bank, it would not recommend an investigation. But it would recommend it if it feels that the alleged harm could be attributed to the Bank in whole or in part, or, which is likely, if it is unable to make a determination on this matter at this early stage. However, Management would be expected under this scenario to present to the Board a remedial action plan on the measures the borrower agreed to take to remedy the situation. The 21-day period provided for in the Resolution may not suffice for the preparation of Management's response. Management would need to discuss the remedial plan with the borrower and the affected parties and reach agreement on it with the borrower before presenting it to the Board. In such a case, Management may be allowed an extension, up to eight weeks, from the day it received the complaint, for the preparation of the response including the action plan, if any. The Panel does not have a role under the Resolution with respect to an action plan that exclusively addresses measures to be taken by the borrower, not the Bank. Nothing, however, would prevent the Board from asking the Panel to assist in the review of the implementation of such a plan, if the Board so wished. This would be an ad hoc assignment outside the scope of the Panel's Resolution. In any event, the Board would consider the remedial plan only after it receives the Panel's view on whether it agrees that there is no scope for inspection due to absence of any failure on the part of the Bank.

A fourth possible response by Management is that failures do exist which are exclusively attributable to the Bank. In this case, the Bank's response should indicate the measures the Bank intends to take to rectify such failures. Management may need the above-mentioned extension of the 21-day period to prepare this response and consult with the borrower and the affected party on the corrective actions. The Panel, on its part, will assess the situation in light of Management's response and any consultation it may wish to make. It will have the extended period approved in the 1996 "Clarifications" (eight weeks subject to possible further extension) for this purpose. Clearly, the Panel would in this case consider whether the Bank's response satisfactorily disposed of the matter and therefore obviated the need for inspection. Should this not be the case, the Panel would recommend a full investigation of the Bank's alleged failures.

A fifth possible answer is that Management agrees that certain failures have occurred, some of which are attributable to the borrower and some to the Bank. Typical of such situations are those where the borrower has not honored its obligations under the loan agreement but poor supervision on the part of the Bank has resulted in the continuation of such a failure on the part of the borrower with resulting harm to affected parties. As the Panel's mandate under the Resolution is related to the failures attributable to the Bank and not to "actions which are the responsibility of other parties such as a borrower," a distinction has to be made between the action required in each case and the role of the Panel would be defined accordingly. Management would, in such situations, prepare, within the extended period, two separate sets of corrective measures: those related to the Bank itself and meant to correct any failure on its part, and those agreed with the borrower and addressing what the borrower should do to correct its failures (and, failing this, what remedies are or will be taken by the Bank under the loan agreement as a result of continued violations). While the first set of proposed corrective measures relating to the Bank's own failures will be addressed in the first instance to the Panel, the second set of measures are to be addressed directly to the Board and would be dealt with by the Board as in the case when Management takes the position that failures are exclusively attributed to the borrower or other external factors. Upon receipt of the remedial plan proposed by the Bank to correct its own failures, the Panel will determine, in the extended period already granted to it, whether an investigation is needed and, therefore, should be recommended to the Board. It may do so if it believes that the measures proposed by the Bank are not adequate to rectify all the Bank's failures or that the Bank's failures in fact exceed those characterized in Management response as Bank failures. In deciding whether to authorize the investigation, the Board will review the assessment made by the Panel, taking into account the views expressed by Management. Clearly, if such investigation is approved by the Board on the recommendation of the Panel, it will be limited to the Bank's actions and omissions alleged in the request for inspection and to the adequacy of the Bank's plan to address them.

The above scenarios attempt to capture different possibilities and tailor a practical procedure for each one, within the framework of the Resolution and its 1996 "Clarifications." The only addition to pre-existing procedures is the possibility of extending the 21-day period provided for in the Resolution for Management response. If additional scenarios arise in practice they could be dealt with under the same understanding: the Panel will independently determine whether investigation is needed in each case, but such investigation, if authorized by the Board, will be limited to the Bank's behavior and the adequacy of the Bank's response with respect to that behavior. Meanwhile, any borrower's failure discovered in the process would be remedied under an agreed plan between the Bank and the borrower, following appropriate consultation with the affected parties, and would be directly submitted to the Board for approval.

The approach elaborated above was endorsed by the Bank's President. A Board committee consisting of six Executive Directors was later formed in March 1998 to consider and recommend a solution to the full Board.

VII. Issues of Bank Liability and Accountability

As mentioned earlier, the main function of the Panel under the Resolution is to ascertain, upon receipt of an eligible request and authorization from the Board to investigate it, whether the Bank has failed to observe its policies and procedures regarding the design, appraisal and/or implementation of the project to which the request is related, including situations where the Bank is alleged to have failed in its follow-up on the borrower's obligations under the loan agreement with respect to such policies and procedures. Unfortunately, for a variety of reasons, much confusion has arisen as to what is expected from the Panel in its preliminary assessment at the early stage, what is the scope of its investigation after the Board authorization and what is expected from

Management so that it may be found in compliance with the Bank's policies and procedures. If the steps explained above have clarified the Panel's role which it exercises with full independence from the Bank's Management, the meaning and extent of the Bank's obligations for the actions and omissions to be investigated remain to be explained.

1. Scope of the Bank's Failure

The Bank has over the years adopted many policies and procedures which are meant to be observed by Bank staff in Bank operations within the limits of flexibility provided therein. Some of these policies and procedures originated in Board-approved policy papers and some are scattered in different instructions issued by Management to staff under varied titles over the years. In addition, many "guidelines" and "best practices" have been issued by Management to staff which are not meant to be strictly followed in each case but represent what Management considers as good standards which guide the work of the staff but may be adapted to the circumstances of each borrower and each project. The Resolution establishing the Panel makes a clear distinction between the Bank's policies and procedures which are meant to be strictly followed by staff subject only to the exceptions provided for therein and the non-binding guidelines and practices. According to the Resolution (Paragraph 12), the Panel's mandate is limited to the inspection of alleged Bank failure to follow "the Bank's 'Operational Policies,' 'Bank Procedures,' 'Operational Directives' and similar documents" and does not extend to "'Guidelines,' 'Best Practices' and similar documents or Statements."

Some of the Bank's policies and especially its procedures are addressed only to the Bank staff. Most Bank operational policies, however, describe the manner in which Bank-financed projects are to be prepared and implemented and thus pertain mainly to actions the Bank should seek from its borrowers. Some such actions may be required before negotiation of the legal documents or before their presentation to the Board. Policies related to project implementation are normally reflected in covenants which appear in the loan agreement or in a project agreement attached to it. In some cases, detailed action plans are attached to these agreements where the borrower's obligations are provided in detail. Since the borrower, and not the Bank, implements the project, the Bank's failure would occur in such cases when it fails to reflect its operational policies in the actions required from the borrower or when, after having reflected them as required, it fails to properly supervise project implementation to ensure that the borrower does abide by its contractual obligations. The harm to affected parties resulting from project implementation would in the first instance be attributed to those who implement the project, even though there could be instances where the Bank would have contributed to the harm by not strictly following its policies in the design or appraisal of the project, in the actions it requires from the borrower or in the supervision of their implementation.

In all the above respects, if the Bank's binding policies or procedures relate exclusively to measures to be taken by the Bank staff, a failure would take place if the staff fail to take such measures as envisaged, unless of course there were exceptions allowed under the policies and procedures which were properly followed. If, on the other hand, the policies related to potential measures to be taken by the borrower, as is often the case under Bank operational policies, e.g. the preparation and implementation of environmental assessment reports or resettlement plans, the staff responsibility would clearly be limited to seeing to it that the borrower's obligations were clearly provided for, the plans expected from the borrower were drawn up in the appropriate time and such obligations and plans were then carried out by the borrower as agreed. Clearly, the obligation of the staff with respect to actions to be taken by the borrower is not to guarantee that the intended outcome will materialize in each case, but to make their best effort, with the due diligence required under the Staff Rules, to ensure that the borrower will indeed carry out its obligations. To quote a French legal expression, this is an "obligation de moyens" and not an "obligation de résultat."

In order, therefore, to attribute to the Bank an existing or potential harm associated with a project, it is not enough to prove that the project is being or will be financed by the Bank. The harm must result, in whole or in part, from the Bank's own failure either in accepting the project design, in appraising the project or in the supervision of its implementation. Without this clear distinction and the causality related to it, the confusion between the Bank's failure and the borrower's failure would continue to prevail.

2. Bank Liability and Accountability for Alleged Failures

Many questions have also been raised concerning the Bank's possible legal liability for its failures and the scope of its accountability for such failures. A distinction is called for between the two concepts.

Liability

The question of the Bank's liability in cases where a harm is clearly attributed in whole or in part to the Bank's failure to observe its policies and procedures was raised by some Executive Directors who suggested that the Bank should bear the cost of remedial actions. One has to distinguish here between the Bank's liability to its borrowers and its liability to third parties, such as the parties affected by the projects it finances. By virtue of provisions in the General Conditions applicable to Bank loan agreements, the rights and obligations of the Bank, the borrower and the guarantor are enforceable in accordance with their terms notwithstanding any conflicting law in the borrowing country, and disputes between the Bank and the borrower may be resolved by negotiations and, failing this, through international arbitration.[137] (In practice, such disputes have always been resolved amicably by negotiations.) The inspection function does not interfere with this process; it relates exclusively to the inspection of the harm caused to affected parties in the territories of the borrower and not to the borrower itself.

As for the Bank's possible legal liability to affected parties in the territory of the borrower, it has to be noted first that the Inspection Panel is not a court of law that bases its findings on strict judicial procedures and rules of evidence and second that, as a public international organization, the Bank and its staff have immunity in their operations from legal action before national courts, except when this immunity has been waived.[138] Assuming for the sake of discussion that such immunity is not recognized, the question of legal liability must then be discussed in light of applicable law in each case. In principle, such liability will be based on fault (intended harmful action or omission, or negligence) under applicable law, unless that law imposes strict or absolute liability (regardless of fault) in certain situations. The mere failure by the Bank to observe its policies would rarely amount to a fault under applicable law; these policies typically require high standards beyond what borrowers or their foreign financiers otherwise need to observe under national or international law. In any event, the obligations the Bank would have to meet under such laws, if they were applicable to it, would be different from the obligations of the party which actually implemented the project. They would be limited to the exceptional cases of lender liability where this was recognized and established through a judicial or arbitral process. This point was clear in the intervention of those Executive Directors who, in the context of the inspection function, spoke of a moral or ethical obligation, rather than a legal one, to assist the borrower in alleviating the harm.

The remedial action plans to be agreed upon with borrowers and any complementary financing such plans may entail would normally represent the action expected from the Bank in such circumstances, in addition, of course,

---

[137] *See* Article X, Sections 10.01 and 10.04 of the General Conditions Applicable to Loan and Guarantee Agreements, dated January 1, 1985.

[138] For details of the immunity in this context (which does not apply to suits initiated by Bank creditors against the Bank), *see* Shihata, *supra* note 1 at 105-113.

to any internal measures the Bank may take with respect to the staff responsible. To the extent that the Bank's own legal liability is established in a specific case, as a result of its violation of a legal obligation applicable to it, the Bank would of course be expected in such rare circumstances to take appropriate measures as a responsible international organization. This should not, however, be confused with the failure of the Bank to observe any of its policies or procedures which do not amount to a legal obligation vis-à-vis the affected party with whom the Bank has no contractual relationship. The Bank's attempt to protect the interests of such an affected party, even if it proved unsuccessful, should not be taken as a valid basis for holding the Bank legally liable for the harm caused by other parties. The Bank's liability for harm to affected parties must be based on a legal cause of action which such parties can take up against the Bank either on the basis of a contractual relationship with them or a tort under applicable law. It cannot, therefore, arise in the absence of either of these bases. A failure by a borrower to comply with the requirements of a loan or guarantee agreement with the Bank would, on the other hand, constitute a violation of a legal obligation vis-à-vis the Bank for which the borrower is accountable to the Bank pursuant to the provisions of the loan agreement.

Accountability

Accountability is a broader concept than legal liability. The Bank as an international organization is accountable to its members. Under the Bank's Articles of Agreement, any dispute between the Bank and a member on the interpretation of the Bank's Articles is to be resolved by the Board of Executive Directors, subject to possible appeal by a member before the Board of Governors (Article IV). Bank staff have immunity from legal process before national courts with respect to acts performed by them in their official capacity, unless of course the Bank waives such immunity (Article VII, Section 8(a)). These staff are nevertheless subject to disciplinary action for any misconduct as well as for negligence in the performance of their duties under the Bank Staff Rules. The Bank's internal system of accountability requires that staff be accountable to the President, the President to the Executive Directors and the Executive Directors to the Board of Governors.

The creation of the Inspection Panel has complemented this internal system of accountability by giving a direct access to affected parties before the Panel (which is a facility of the Bank) and by requiring Management to present to the Board recommendations for corrective action in case the Panel finds a serious violation of Bank policies and procedures resulting in harm to such affected parties in the situations described above. The Board's decision on the actions to be taken by the Bank demonstrates the Bank's accountability for its actions or omissions, regardless of the question of liability.

VIII. Conclusion

The World Bank Inspection Panel is an innovative mechanism which is meant to enhance the Bank's accountability for its role in the projects it finances and, more generally, to strengthen the quality of the Bank's work through an independent inspection function readily accessible to affected parties.

The Panel was originally intended to carry out its investigative function as a routine matter whenever the eligibility of the request for inspection was established. In practice, the Panel, Management and the Board of the World Bank have contributed to a somewhat different approach which seemed from a practical viewpoint to address the harm while reducing the possible embarrassment of an actual investigation. In this practice, Management, after receiving the request from the Panel for inspection, tended to agree with the borrower on a remedial action plan whenever this was needed. The Panel also seemed to be inclined towards carrying out preliminary assessments which might invite remedial action and obviate the need for inspection. A Board majority has often found in such action plans a useful answer which would render the inspection unnecessary but give the Panel the opportunity to participate in the review of the plan's implementation. This orientation of the Panel's practice has taken place for practical reasons but seems to have been widely misunderstood. When it was recently questioned, the Bank's President made it clear that he supports the role of the Panel and welcomes its inspection of any eligible request. He also pointed out that remedial action taken by Management "should not stop the inspection." In its second review of the Panel's experience, the Bank's Board discussed whether an approach based on a literal reading of the Resolution establishing the Panel should be strictly followed or whether the approach which has been followed in many cases in practice should be formally adopted. An agreement has yet to be reached on procedures tailored to each Management response which would confine the inspection function to the Bank's alleged failures, as envisaged from the outset, but allow for remedying other failures attributable to other factors, for the benefit of the project and those affected by it.

The creation of the Panel has provided private parties with a direct legal access to an international forum where they can submit their complaints and see them addressed in a process previously known to them, with prompt disclosure of information upon the Board's consideration of each action. This is a progressive step in the development of both the law of international organizations and the international law of human rights. Prior to the establishment of the Panel, review mechanisms of international organizations were limited to the internal activities of these institutions. The Panel is the first mechanism introducing a non-judicial process to assist in ensuring compliance with the policies and procedures of a global international organization's operational activities, i.e. its activities with direct effects on other parties. This mechanism has primarily been used by groups of individuals whose rights or interests have been allegedly affected by the Bank's operations. Similar mechanisms have since been followed in two other international financial institutions, the Inter-American Development Bank in 1994 and the Asian Development Bank in 1995. This may mark a new trend in international organizations' law. The World Bank, which was a pioneer in introducing participation of affected parties in the design and implementation of projects, has thus pioneered also in giving them direct access to an independent grievance mechanism. It is in the common interest that this process be seen in this light and not be mistaken as a process to pressure borrowing governments into taking measures not required under loan agreements.

Introduction – Broadening the Scope of the Applicable Standards

*Gudmundur Alfredsson**

The Lund Workshop on the Inspection Panel of the World Bank was intended to serve several purposes. One of them was to promote a relatively unknown Panel[1] and similar mechanisms available at other international financial institutions.[2] The history of the Panel, composition, applicable standards and policies, procedures, access and affected parties, case-law, remedies, the place of the Panel in the Bank's hierarchy of institutions, the weight and fate of its recommendations, and the interaction with project-based States were discussed openly and at length.[3]

Some of the participants at the Workshop wanted international standards not adopted under the World Bank's auspices to be applied by the Panel. This position explains the title of the present introductory article. In this respect, references were made to human rights standards agreed upon under the auspices of the United Nations and its specialized agencies, not least when they are contained in the UN Charter, anchored in international customary law or set forth in treaties ratified by the States where the Bank is engaged.

Other related questions discussed at the Workshop concerned the mainstreaming of human rights in the UN system, objectivity and consistency in the work of international organizations and their duty not to contradict the

* Cand. jur (University of Iceland 1975), Mc.J. (New York University Law School 1976) and S.J.D. (Harvard Law School 1982). The author was a staff member with the UN Secretariat in New York and Geneva 1983-95. He is now Director of the Raoul Wallenberg Institute of Human Rights and Humanitarian Law and Professor at the University of Lund in Sweden.

1 Up-to-date informative and promotional material on the mandate, the procedures and the case-law of the Inspection Panel are available in its newsletters and annual reports and on the home page of the World Bank at "www.worldbank.org/ins-panel". See also Alvaro Umaña (ed.), *The World Bank Inspection Panel. The First Four Years (1994-1998)*, Washington, D.C.: Published for the Inspection Panel by the World Bank, 1998, 327 pages.

2 For inspection activities at the Asian Development Bank and the Inter-American Development Bank, see separate articles in this book.

3 Statements at the Workshop were delivered in private capacities, not necessarily reflecting the positions of organizations or institutions by which the authors are employed.

standards or operational activities of sister organizations. Certainly, the international law commitments of States should not be undermined.

This line of argumentation was supported by the proposition that respect for human rights is not only an issue of law but also a matter of good economic sense and an incentive for sustainable development. The multiple links and possible bridge-building between good governance and human rights were used to underline the argument. Similar comments were made in favour of environmental standards.

Still another purpose of the Workshop was to promote the Inspection Panel as a pioneering body for measuring the conduct of an international organization against its own standards. In this respect, the Panel was seen as a model for the type of scrutiny which the operational activities of other organizations should undergo. As to possible changes in current arrangements for the Panel, several participants wanted to see it further strengthened in terms of independence, applicable standards, available expertise and the weight of its recommendations. Such bodies would not only enhance the rule of law within States and in international relations but also generate worthwhile debate and contribute to respect for human rights, transparency and accountability in the work of international organizations.

II. Outline of the Book's Contents

Two prominent authors set the parameters for the entire book. The President of the Republic of Iceland, H. E. Ólafur Ragnar Grímsson, emphasizes democracy and democratization on the world scene and the role which a broad range of human rights can play in that process. In so doing, he draws on his experience as scholar of political science and former President of Parliamentarians for World Action. In his article, the then Senior Vice President and General Counsel of the World Bank, Ibrahim Shihata, outlines in an authoritative manner and considerable detail the historical, legal and operational aspects of the Inspection Panel.[4]

In a second cluster of articles, Laurence Boisson de Chazournes, Sabine Schlemmer-Schulte, Richard E. Bissell, Alvaro Umaña, Michelo Hansungule, Dana Clark and David Hunter deal with the standards applicable before the Inspection Panel, its existing case law, procedural aspects such as access to the Panel and the notion of affected party, lessons drawn from experience already acquired, and the role of individuals in sustainable development. Eugenia McGill and Gay Davis Miller describe the inspection and investigation

[4] See also Ibrahim Shihata, *The World Bank Inspection Panel*, Oxford: Published for the World Bank by Oxford University Press, 1994.

mechanisms of the Asian Development Bank and the Inter-American Development Bank.

A third cluster of articles looks at other intergovernmental organizations. Jakob Th. Möller and Lee Swepston analyze complaints procedures and supervision methods for human rights and labour standards as employed by the United Nations and the International Labour Organisation. Furthermore, Patricia Feeney elaborates on the need for a dedicated complaints mechanism for non-Europeans as to the protection of rights under the aid programs of the European Union. These articles address a core question: how to examine the performance of international organizations as compared with the relatively advanced evolution of independent and impartial scrutiny of the human rights conduct of States as available under treaties and declarations.

Finally, written submissions by non-governmental organizations, that is the Bank Information Center and OXFAM,[5] were distributed at the Workshop. Constructively critical of the World Bank and its Inspection Panel and their records, these contributions were frequently referred to at the meetings and there is no doubt that they influenced and enriched the deliberations.

The present article draws on an introductory statement to the Workshop. It seeks to show that respect for human rights is good for the economic development of States, to highlight the relevance of human rights and rule of law considerations for the World Bank and the Inspection Panel, to identify links and encourage bridge-building between good governance and human rights, to promote independent expert bodies as models for placing stronger emphasis on legal considerations and objectivity in the activities of development agencies and financial institutions, and to underline the good reasons for mainstreaming human rights in the work of the UN family of organizations.

III. Economic Benefits of Human Rights and Good Governance

The World Bank is primarily a lending institution for development purposes. It is not an international policeman, as Senior Vice-President Shihata said at the Workshop. The Bank's Articles do not carry a direct mandate for adopting, promoting or protecting human rights. It is the role of the Bank to render financial assistance to programs and projects which make sense for improved

[5] Lori Udall, *The World Bank Inspection Panel: A Three Year Review*, Washington D.C.: The Bank Information Center, October 1997, 113 pages plus useful annexes; and *The World Bank Inspection Panel: Analysis and Recommendations for Review, Extended Paper*, Oxford: OXFAM Policy Department, February 1996, 44 pages and annexes; and *Safeguarding Standards in Resettlement: OXFAM's Recommendations on the Proposed Revision to the World Bank's Policy on Involuntary Resettlement*, Oxford: OXFAM Policy Department, March 1997, 22 pages and annexes.

economic performance and sustainable development in the countries concerned.

Notwithstanding this approach, in the process of regulating the use of funds and maximizing benefits, albeit more as a sideline rather than a priority effort, the World Bank in many ways and increasingly touches upon human rights and the rule of law as part of an overall approach to successful development. Work programs and/or policy directives thus address the status of women, good governance, legal reform, the independence of the judiciary, involuntary resettlements, indigenous and tribal peoples, the environment, child labour, the role of non-governmental organizations, the social consequences of lending advice or instructions, and other issues.

Direct quotations to the international human rights instruments may be missing in the World Bank's policy directives and other human rights issues have not yet been addressed, but the trend is certainly welcome from a human rights perspective given the Bank's influence. For an ever more active World Bank involvement in human rights and rule of law issues, it is therefore necessary to show that such engagement will positively contribute to the Bank's development efforts on its own economic terms.

To this end, a series of convincing arguments can be and have been presented. This type of reasoning seeks, *inter alia*, to demonstrate:

(a) that the Bank's investment is more likely to reap long-term benefits when its programs and projects are truely in the interest of the whole people as administered by a representative government,

(b) that good governance and law reform as pursued by the Bank will often have human rights angles from which the governance approaches stand to benefit,

(c) that adverse social consequences that may result from the Bank's economic and financial policies could, at least in part, be mitigated or even avoided through greater attention to civil, cultural, economic, political and social rights as set forth in international human rights instruments, and

(d) that attention to the above-mentioned factors will often reduce the risk of social upheaval and/or violent ethnic conflicts which can so easily result in the undoing of the Bank's contributions. Additional lines of reasoning for mainstreaming human rights, such as IGO-coordination and the backing of several donour States, may be pursuasive vis-a-vis the World Bank in a political sense, even as a matter of law.

Not everybody agrees to the economic benefits of respect for human rights, in neither the short nor the long term. Some persons in governments which say they prioritize development over human rights will maintain that line, meaning that human rights will follow in the wake of prosperity. The argument is a convenient one, if suspicious and not always convincing, as the power and privileges of these same persons are likely to be maintained as a result. Similar arguments rely on different cultures, values, duties and other particularities as justifications for departures from the universality of human rights, but the cultures must be those of the people as a whole, not only the leadership and elites.

Furthermore, the World Bank is not the only source of money on the market. Attempts to lengthen the list of Bank requirements for loans, some would say, may have to be balanced against the conditions prevailing for its competitors so as not to make the Bank unwieldy and unattractive as a lender. Better still, efforts should be undertaken to make Bank assistance more attractive as befitting an international lender and/or to convince the competition of the same considerations in the name of economic sense, such as access to markets, attractiveness to qualified staff, avoidance of law suits and profitabilty.

IV. Building Bridges between Human Rights and Good Governance

An attempt will now be made to show where bridges between good governance guidelines and human rights standards should be built. As the two have indeed many things in common, a few words on the characteristics of good governance and of human rights precede the attempts at bridge-building. The challenge is not to merge them or to set one above the other, but to look for ways of mutual strengthening and benefit, notwithstanding differences that may exist between them. If good governance and law reform are good for economic development, the same is quite likely to be true for the substantive and procedural backup available for human rights on the basis of legal commitments.

A. The Characteristics of Good Governance

Good governance is technically formulated as guidelines for States. Primarily characterized by an approach of economic nature, the guidelines aim for enhanced development and growth as a result of better governments which are accountable for their actions. Unlike human rights, these guidelines are drafted by economists and political scientists, not by lawyers. Even contents and wording may differ from one adopting institution to another, adding another challenge to the bridge-building between the disciplines of good governance and human rights.

As to substantive issues, the good governance guidelines have much in common with democracy and a wide range of international human rights standards. Below, after outlining the main characteristics of human rights, a few links between transparency and the freedom of information, between accountability and media checks on officialdom, between equal rights and non-corruption and so on will be identified with mutual benefits of the two approaches in mind.

As an integral part of development work, the good governance guidelines carry significant weight because of the major influence exercised by the adopting and oversight institutions, like the World Bank, the OECD and UNDP. Human rights are drafted for universal consumption, but good governance is aimed at developing countries. This limitation is mistaken; the so-called developed world as demonstrated, for example, by repeated corruption scandals is also in need of good governance instructions.[6]

The good governance guidelines to States are not legally binding, with the exception of anti-corruption treaties now being adopted. While human rights are for the most part based on individual rights and corresponding State obligations, it is not foreseen that the good governance guidelines establish such rights, although it is possible to imagine that the introduction of appeals avenues for individuals, groups and NGOs at the World Bank and some of the regional banks will lead in that direction.

Not only civil and political rights but also cultural, economic and social rights are important for good governance, including standards on work conditions, labour unions, education, cultures, health and social security. The same is true for the rights of minorities and indigenous peoples, as set forth in article 27 of the International Covenant on Civil and Political Rights, ILO Convention No. 169 and other instruments, with emphasis on the protection of identities, languages, cultures, land rights and self-management. It is in the interest of good governance to respect the rights of the said groups, as their denial clearly has a negative impact on society, as evidenced by violent ethnic conflicts.

B. The Characteristics of Human Rights

The human rights of individuals and obligations of States are set forth in law instruments. At the national level, most constitutions carry bills of rights, and

---

[6] As far as international organizations are concerned, see also below under Internal or In-House Aspects.

legislative acts provide for additional rights. Remedies for addressing grievances and providing relief are generally available through the courts and ombudsmen institutions.

At the international level, human rights law is a sub-category of public international law. Several hundred multilateral treaties and declarations establish minimum human rights standards with corresponding obligations of the States in which the beneficaries live. The treaties are technically binding only for the States which have formally consented to them, but many treaties enjoy wide or almost universal ratification.

In addition, many human rights standards, such as the prohibition of discrimination on the basis of race and sex and the prohibition of torture, have undoubtedly become rules of international customary law which is binding on all States. The United Nations, in line with articles 1 and 55 of its Charter, also monitors the compliance of all States with the standards contained in the Universal Declaration of Human Rights and other declaratory texts. While these standards are adopted by vote and are not subject to ratification, the UN expectation contributes to their emergence under customary law.

Individuals are the main holders and beneficiaries of human rights. As exceptions to the individualistic approach, the international standards acknowledge group rights (f.ex. the rights of minorities and indigenous peoples) and peoples (f.ex. the right of self-determination), also with certain international petition options. States continue to be the primary subjects of international law, but individuals and occasionally collectivities are secondary subjects, to the degree they have limited legal personality with rights, the corresponding duties and procedural standing to pursue their causes with international organizations.

A dominant feature of international human rights law is equality in dignity and rights and the prohibition of discrimination, in line with articles 1 and 55 of the UN Charter, articles 1 and 2 of the Universal Declaration of Human Rights and plentiful of other human rights provisions. Specifically, the instruments spell out equal protection of the law, equality before the courts and equal access to public service.

The obligations of the State can be about refraining from action, that is not interfering with the freedom of individuals to act. The obligations can also involve the legal duty of States to take action in order to make sure that rights are implemented. In response to patterns of discrimination, the instruments insist on affirmative action/positive measures for eliminating discrimination, as demonstrated by calls in the instruments for action on the human rights of women and on minority rights.

Civil and political rights are the frontrunners among human rights, intended for absolute and immediate implementation and based on unambigous legal formulations with few exceptions allowed. They are thus readily available for judicial decisions. Many cultural, economic and social rights still aim merely at progressive or step-by-step realization, but UN official policy considers all human rights of equal value and efforts are underway to upgrade these standards and the relevant monitoring procedures.

As to the distinctions between civil and political rights and economic, social and cultural rights, it is sometimes said that the implementation of civil and political rights is free of charge for the State while the realization of economic, social and cultural rights is a costly one. This is not always true; holding elections and the administration of justice costs money just as running schools and health systems. If the realization of all human rights and labour standards is helpful and even necessary for sustainable development, the financial institutions should support activities requiring expenditures.

As to the adopting institutions, the human rights standards originate from the highest organs of organizations with broad political/ legislative agendas, like the UN General Assembly or the ILO Labour Conference. In adopting human rights standards, the Organization for Security and Co-Operation in Europe (OSCE) and lately the United Nations take peace and security considerations into account.

International organizations actively and increasingly monitor the compliance of States with their human rights standards. As mentioned above, individuals, and even groups, are allowed to file complaints against States. The monitoring procedures are more elaborate and effective for treaty commitments, with regional courts and quasi-judicial expert procedures in place at international organizations.

Under the UN and ILO petition procedures, individuals, groups and/or unions can file complaints against States for alleged violations of human rights and labour standards. The more impressive of these petition procedures are based on treaty commitments, rely for decisions on independent expert bodies set up under the treaties and require exhaustion of national remedies. These bodies address the performance of States under human rights and labour standards but not the conduct of the organizations themselves; in that way they are quite different from the Bank's Inspection Panel.

The International Labour Office regularly examines field projects with regard to human rights standards, while the UN Secretariat does so sporadically at best, but appeals procedures against UN and ILO decisions and projects are not available to individuals and groups. In this context, the Inspection Panel is a major innovation and very much a worthwhile model.

Human rights are a matter of law. Individuals and sometimes collectivities have rights, and States must respect the rights in law and in fact. The rights also come with duties towards the society in which the holders/beneficaries live and their fellow human beings. Under international human rights law, human rights are universal, but sovereign States have narrow margins of appreciation in the application of the law and may take into account domestic circumstances or particularities which form part of the national culture provided they meet with popular acceptance.

With legal standards and legal avenues available for redress, it is not surprising that the law profession dominates human rights. The lawyers will continue to play a crucial role, but at the same time it is very important for spreading the message and gaining popular support that other professions and disciplines study and work with human rights while making sure, in education and otherwise, that the contents and interpretation of human rights are uniform.

C. The Bridge-Building

The characteristics, the emphasis and the motivations behind human rights and good governance may differ, but they share the overall aim of improving national societies and the quality of life for the inhabitants. Different terms and methods may be used, but the same concerns are being addressed. Different forces are at work, but the common elements, on a two-way street, could and should be exploited.

The building of bridges between human rights and good governance could be helpful in may ways. Combining forces should help narrow the gaps, conceptually and otherwise, between different organizations and for the members of various theoretical disciplines and academic professions which now engage in similar work but on two or more separate tracks. The benefits are not only academic, but also practical inasmuch as human rights and good governance stand to gain from mutual reliance and coordinated approaches of additional actors.

It is thus argued that, on a number of issues, the good governance guidelines could be strengthened by drawing on the legal and political experience acquired in human rights work. Backup justification for the guidelines could be sought in human rights standards with regard to democracy, transparency, accountability and non-corruption. Likewise, the human rights community would benefit from economic reasoning and democratic governance ideas which the good governance guidelines stand for. The connections are plentiful, and some of them will now be identified.

1. Democracy, Accountability and Transparency

For the first time in history, the majority of States are democratic or on the move in that direction. This allowed Secretary-General Boutros Boutros Ghali to say straightforward in his 1995 UN Agenda for Development that democracy is a fundamental human right. Democracy has not yet been defined for the purposes of human rights law, but the acceptance and growth of international and other multilateral programs for electoral assistance and monitoring of elections as well as the democratic content of good governance indicate a trend in this direction.[7] It is argued that sustainable development is dependent upon both human rights standards and the good governance guidelines on political participation. One author, in this context, has pointedly referred to governance and constitutionalism as Siamese twins.[8]

Article 21 of the Universal Declaration, article 25 of the Covenant on Civil and Political Rights and other human rights texts prescribe the right to stand for office and to vote in elections. Other provisions in multiple human rights instruments, for example on the freedoms of opinion, expression, information, association and assembly, the right to education and the contributions of NGOs/civil society, all stand for processes which are essential to democracy. In his eloquent statement to the Workshop, the President of Iceland addresses democracy and the input and role of elected representatives.[9]

Free and periodic elections are a crucial tool for an informed public to hold politicians accountable for their conduct and performance in office. The freedom of expression allows for free and public debate about that performance, not least independent media outlets, the freedom of assembly allows for political meetings and street protests, and the freedom of association foresees trade unions and political parties so that the like-minded can submit their demands and other messages in an organized and effective manner. The independence and impartiality of the judiciary and of other national institutions are also essential for accountability and transparency in government, requiring legal reform as frequently called for under the good governance banner.

---

[7] David Gillies, "Human Rights, Governance and Democracy: The World Bank's Problem Frontiers" in *Netherlands Quarterly of Human Rights*, vol. 11 (1993), no. 1, pp. 3-24; and *Participatory Development and Good Governance*, in Development Co-Operation Guidelines Series of the OECD, Paris, 1995.

[8] J. Oloka-Onyango, "The Dynamics of Corruption Control and Human Rights Enforcement in Uganda: The Case of the Inspector General of Government" in *East African Journal of Peace and Human Rights*, vol. 1 (1993), no. 1, pp. 23-51.

[9] On this topic, see also Edwin Rekosh (ed.), *In the Public Eye. Parliamentary Democracy in Europe and North America*, Washington, D.C.: International Human Rights Law Group, 1995.

2. Non-Corruption

As with accountability and transparency, the good governance-oriented fight against corruption has an obvious relationship to human rights.[10] The roles of police and prosecutors in fighting corruption are acknowledged in the 1979 UN Code of Conduct for Law Enforcement Officials, in article 7 and the attached commentary, and the 1990 UN Guidelines on the Role of Prosecutors, in paragraph 15.

Equal rights are denied and discrimination often results from cases of corruption, as for example with equal access to public service, equality before the courts and equal protection of the law. The negative impact of corruption on the equal enjoyment of all rights as well as positive results of anti-corruption efforts further fill in this picture. Human rights standards requiring the independence and impartiality of the judiciary, fair trial, other aspects of criminal justice, and independent national human rights institutions are clearly relevant to the anti-corruption efforts.[11]

It is argued that non-corruption regulations and enforcement, extending to both the public and private sectors, are necessary for sustainable development.[12] An accountable government and an independent judiciary are necessary not only for reasons of safeguarding the business sector and facilitating investment but also for regulating such activities and ensuring their honesty.[13] Increasingly being adopted by business enterprises, voluntary codes of conduct and guidelines relating to ethics and human rights are good, but maybe not good enough. Economic gains without public participation and public contentment will not last.

3. Law Reform

When financial institutions and development agencies support law reform, they do not always make use of human rights standards for improving national laws and implementation avenues. Logically, considering the legal commitments involved, law reform based on good governance, ought to draw on the relevant human rights standards. This would be one example of the benefits of enhanced bridge-building between human rights and good governance.

---

[10] For an explanation of how human rights figure in the work of a leading non-governmental organization, see Jeremy Pope (ed.), *The TI Source Book*, Berlin: Transparency International, 1996.

[11] See again the above-mentioned article by Oloka-Onyango.

[12] *Helping Countries Combat Corruption. The Role of the World Bank*, The Poverty Reduction and Economic Management Network, the World Bank, Washington, D.C., 1997.

[13] See a number of articles in Michael K. Addo (ed.), *Human Rights Standards and the Responsibility of Transnational Corporations*, The Hague/London/Boston; Kluwer Law International, 1999.

The incorporation of international human rights standards could, inter alia, support democratic practices and institutions, an independent judiciary and law-abiding law enforcement. Similarly, the good governance guidelines ought to be among the reference points of technical co-operation in the field of human rights, including human and institutional capacity building through human rights training and education, reaching out to both public and private targets through bilateral, regional and international channels.

4. Adverse Social Consequences

Structural adjustment policies are often mentioned as a source of possible conflicts with human rights standards. Reductions in public spending on health, social security and education services, as a result of adjustment policies, will negatively affect human rights, at least in the short term and especially social and cultural rights. Even if the relevant human rights instruments call for progressive achievement which may depend on available resources,[14] the economists are well advised to formulate their adjustment policies so that the human rights consequences are taken into account. The public and the human rights community should be convinced and reassured, which may be more easily said than done, that the adjustment policies will eventually lead to the realization of the prescribed economic, social and cultural rights.

Social deficits and the welfare aspects of development ought to be of concern to the good governance people. Attention to economic, social and cultural rights could mitigate the adverse social consequences of lending policies, thus making the World Bank's contributions not only more acceptable but also more effective. Human rights will much of the time correspond to human needs, and the will of the people is after all the foundation of the authority of government, as stated in article 21 of the Universal Declaration of Human Rights.

Partly in response to negative reaction to adjustment policies, the UN debate on the right to development has not been helpful in establishing and elaborating on the relationship between human rights and good governance. Debates in the working groups on the right to development of the UN Commission on Human Rights and the non-adoption of a Polish draft resolution against corruption at the 1998 session of the Commission are evidence of the same. Such unfortunate responses should not discourage a continued examination and analysis of the issues, as this is one instance where the human rights community can learn from a wide range of good governance guidelines.

---

[14] Such as article 2, paragraph 1, of the International Covenant on Economic, Social and Cultural Rights.

5. Prevention of Violent Conflicts

Thousands of minorities and indigenous peoples around the world suffer from discrimination in their enjoyment of civil, cultural, economic, political and social rights. There is plentiful of evidence to support that observation in UN and NGO reports. It is acknowledged that respect for human rights, in particular minority and indigenous rights, will reduce the risk of violent conflicts.

The cost argument is obvious. Discrimination against groups denies them dignity and identity, excludes them from political participation and deprives them of economic and social benefits. Violent ethnic conflicts are more often than not rooted in such discrimination, and they can majorly interrupt the economic performance of the State as a whole. The argument also holds true for the maintenance of international peace and security as ethnic conflicts have a tendency to spill across borders. Prevention of these conflicts removes tremendous expenses, for both the State concerned and the international community, in terms of peace-making, peace-enforcement and peace-restoration.

Human rights and good governance can and should be empoyed to pave the way for securing internal stability. The growing interest of international and regional organizations in preventing conflicts by way of respect for minority and indigenous rights has undoubtedly much to do with human rights, with hundreds of millions of individuals and thousands of groups suffering, but also with the realization that ecouragement of and active support of respect for group rights is an inexpensive method of avoiding violent conflicts and the much more costly ways of resolving them and restoring the peace.

It would be a good and wise use of funding if financial institutions and development agencies were to pay much greater attention to their possible contributions in this respect. Respect for minority and indigenous rights should be part and parcel of the good governence guidelines. Beyond seeking to protect the distinctiveness of indigenous and tribal peoples and guarding against their vulnerability, the World Bank should also consider adopting a policy directive on national or ethnic, religious and linguistic minorities in order to allow for their dignities, identities and cultures and to make sure that they are equal recipients and active participants in national development, with affirmative action if necessary for overcoming discrimination.[15]

---

15 Article 4, paragraph 5, of the UN Declaration on the Rights of Persons belonging to National or Ethnic, Religious and Linguistic Minorities reads: "States should consider appropriate measures so that persons belonging to minorities may participate fully in the economic progress and development in their country." Article 9 reads: "The specialized agencies and other organizations of the United Nations system shall contribute to the full realization of the rights and principles set forth in this Declaration, within their respective fields of competence." The text was adopted by consensus at the General Assembly in 1992.

After all, unlike the right of peoples to self-determination, one of the very aims of minority and indigenous rights is to keep the groups content within a country, and a stable State is a much better place for development and investment. It is likely that the World Bank's pursuasive powers would in this respect complement and sometimes have greater impact on governments than do the UN human rights monitoring bodies.

6. Monitoring Institutions and Procedures

Good governance considerations may also benefit from human rights with regard to not only the applicable standards but also the methods used for monitoring State respect for the human rights standards, with States as parties, as outlined by Jakob Th. Möller in his article in the present book. Human rights monitoring institutions and procedures could provide useful precedents for techniques and tools in following up on the good governance guidelines and other World Bank policies. As borrowing countries have agreed to Bank projects, one idea could be to give the borrowers a formal role in proceedings before the Inspection Panel, as parties or co-parties.

In the soft version, in technical co-operation activities, the development agencies and financial institutions can bolster their good governance arguments by reference to human rights standards accepted by or applicable to States with which they are working. Needs and impact assessments are no less necessary for human rights than, for example, the environment.

It may even be argued that human rights technical assistance should increasingly be left in the hands of development agencies and financial institutions, usually with field presence, which could thus assume the role of the good cops. At the United Nations, UNDP has been assuming this role. The headquarters-based human rights monitoring bodies should continue to primarily focus on State compliance, with the more unpopular role of the bad cops. In this way, human rights field workers could avoid difficult and unnecessary confrontations with governments when trying to carry out the widely different, difficult and conflict-prone tasks of simultaneously reporting on rights violations and providing expert advice.

V. The Rule of Law and the World Bank

As mentioned above by way of introduction, one may ask whether international standards not adopted under the Bank's auspices should be applied by the Inspection Panel. In this respect, one can refer to human rights instruments as agreed upon by the international community, not least treaties ratified by States. This argument comes back to the proposition that respect for human rights standards is not only a matter of law but also a matter of good economic sense and an incentive for sustainable development, as evidenced by the multiple links between good governance and human rights.

Other questions concerning the international rule of law relate to co-operation and coordination within the UN system of organizations, the mainstreaming of human rights, implementation, and the internal or in-house aspects.

1. Commitments of States

The primary responsibility for respecting and implementing the international human rights instruments rests on States. But it can also be argued that financial institutions and development agencies as part and parcel of the UN system have a duty, also under general international law, to support and certainly not to contradict international law commitments which States have entered into. The World Bank and other institutions should never find themselves in the position of undermining respect for or causing States to violate international law commitments made under the auspices of sister organizations, like the UN, the ILO and UNESCO, commitments which have been achieved by ratifications of or accessions to human rights treaties.[16]

Likewise, the financial institutions and development agencies should respect international customary law, like equal rights and non-discrimination, which may be relevant in the absence of treaty commitments.

It goes without saying that these international rule of law considerations should also apply to bilateral development agencies.[17] National actors, like ministries and development agencies, should be accountable for their field or operational activities which directly touch or impact upon actual people. They should have to respond to complaints in the courts or be answerable under comparable mechanisms.

---

16 See, for example, Clarence J. Dias, "Influencing the Policies of the World Bank and the International Monetary Fund" in Lars Adam Rehof and Claus Gulman (editors), *Human Rights in Domestic Law and Development Assistance Policies of the Nordic Countries*, Dordrecht/Boston/London: Martinus Nijhoff Publishers, 1989, pp. 53-67.

17 As to bilateral development agencies and the rule of law, including the question of access to national courts, see my article entitled "A Few Practical Suggestions on Development Co-Operation and Human Rights" in Per Sevastik (editor), *Legal Assistance to Developing Countries. Swedish Perspectives on the Rule of Law*, Stockholm: Norstedts Juridic & Kluwer Law International, 1997, pp. 81-105.

2. Sister Organizations

A powerful argument in favour of the World Bank and similar institutions to heed human rights is not only the legal character and universality of the international standards, but also the consistency and predictability in their application. Similarly, the human rights community should draw on the bridges to the good governance lessons. Such consistency would certainly enhance both the effectiveness and credibility of the UN family of organizations.

As mentioned above, the sister organizations have many things to learn from each other. Human rights and labour standards complaints procedures of the United Nations and the International Labour Organisation, which are directed against States and accepted in law and politics, are working and bringing significant results. Likewise, all the intergovernmental organizations should themselves live up to the same recommendations which they are making to States and expecting States to follow in terms of the good governance guidelines.

3. The Mainstreaming of Human Rights

In the last few years it has become fashionable at the United Nations to call for the mainstreaming of human rights, that is their integration into all activities of the UN system, away from the relative isolation of politicized meetings at the Geneva-headquarters. The World Conference on Human Rights in the 1993 Vienna Declaration and Programme of Action called for the system-wide integration of human rights,[18] and the UN High Commissioner on Human Rights likes to emphasize mainstreaming in her statements.[19]

This approach makes good operational sense, also seen in light of article 1 of the UN Charter about the purposes of the Organization, but it is yet to be fully appreciated and implemented by many entities in the UN family. There are, however, welcome signs of change. In addition to the more traditional human rights contributions of the ILO and UNESCO, several country programs of the UNDP now include support for human rights, like the setting up of independent national institutions. UNICEF has played a major role in

---

[18] The Vienna Declaration and Programme of Action, in UN document A/CONF.157/23, in particular paragraphs 1-4 of the Programme.

[19] For one of her many statements on the topic, see Mary Robinson, "Human Rights: Challenges for the 21st Century" in *Development Dialogue*, Uppsala: The Dag Hammerskjöld Foundation, 1998:1, pp. 5-16.

obtaining State acceptance of and promoting the implementation of the Convention on the Rights of the Child.

The United Nations University (UNU) and the UN Research Institute for Social Development (UNRISD) are engaged in research which has bearings on human rights, like the roots of ethnic conflicts and the relationship of economic and social rights to development. The FAO has shown interest in the right to food, and the WHO is paying attention to the right to health and discrimination against Aids-victims. As mentioned before, encouragingly, the World Bank in its policy directives and Operations Manual has adopted many human rights-oriented points of view.

Still, there is resistance. Many governments fear conditionalities and prefer weak and isolated human rights sectors at international headquarters far away from home. Partly, the reasons are to be sought in ineffective coordination mechanisms of the intergovernmental organizations themselves and in their constant internal struggle for jurisdiction and limited funds. We are also talking about the education and training of international civil servants on a cross-organizational basis, something which is sorely lacking. The human rights and good governance people, on a two-way street, need to learn about human rights, labour standards, good governance and other applicable rules, guidelines and procedures.

4. Implementation

Ultimately, the international rule of law requires an independent and impartial judiciary or, as a minimum, quasi-judicial independent expert bodies. Expectations of voluntary compliance are insufficient. Human rights monitoring procedures are by their nature confrontational inasmuch as they may lead to criticism and even condemnation of non- performing governments, something they do not like and will resist, by denial, diversion or other means. This is a frequent problem encountered by the United Nations in its monitoring efforts. Still, it is the only way forward with the rule of law.

In seeking alternatives to the confrontational dilemma, the United Nations has been offering governments softer human rights options in the form of technical co-operation. There is nothing but good to say about these efforts, except that the Office of the High Commissioner for Human Rights and before that the Centre for Human Rights have been largely ineffective in their advisory services; also there is the persistent possibility of conflict of interest by way of trade-offs between confrontation and co-operation.

For these reasons, attention is drawn to the suggestion made above that development agencies and financial institutions, as well as non-governmental organizations and academic institutions, might be more suitable and effective actors in the technical assistance and advisory services arena, leaving the traditional UN human rights forums with the monitoring job which they are mandated and best-suited to execute.

As to the universality of human rights, part of the approach must be the equal and objective treatment of all States, both the so-called developed and developing countries. For the former, some of the heat is absorbed in regional organizations like the Council of Europe and its European Court of Human Rights, with cases lost and the results generally respected by the governments concerned. Unfortunately, the same developed countries do not always display the desired maturity when their alleged human rights violations are deservedly brought up in international forums, leaving the impression of bias and unequal attention.

The monitoring of State compliance with human rights standards should be based on objective criteria, with sole reference to international instruments. The law should prevail over politics and foreign policy considerations. That is why judicial avenues or treaty-based or other independent expert bodies are more desirable, for all parties, than the politicized debates and selective criticism in the UN Commission on Human Rights. The same universality and monitoring observations are true for the good governance guidelines; they should be applied to all countries in both the north and the south.

It is more difficult to accept the strong objections by developing countries to conditionality of development assistance or strings attached to human rights assistance, based on human rights and good governance performance.[20] It is hard for donour countries to accept that international organizations or bilateral agencies foot the bill for governments which do not employ the funding for the public good, whether as a result of human rights violations, non-accountability or corruption. Eventually, the tax-payers in the donour countries will rebel against such use of their money. It is also understandable that like-minded governments, like for example democracies, choose to work together for development.

5. Internal or In-House Aspects

This article has so far focused on the external aspects of the rule of law in the work of intergovernmental organizations. For a more complete picture of legal considerations in the work of international organizations, however, reference

[20] For other points of view, see two books by Katarina Tomaševski, *Development Aid and Human Rights Revisited*, London/New York: Pinter, 1993, and *Between Sanctions and Elections. Aid Donors and their Human Rights Performance*, London/Washington: Pinter, 1997.

must also be made to the internal aspects of their work which may have a significant bearing on lawfulness and accountability in their activities. Written regulations and internal review, oversight, auditing and inspection mechanisms, as well as grievance panels, joint appeals boards, joint disciplinary boards and administrative tribunals or similar bodies are supposed to uphold the law in internal settings.

Adherence to the law, the outlawing of nepotism and other forms of in-house corruption, access to justice and the availability of remedies should, as a matter of course, apply at the international organizations. For reasons of mainstreaming and credibility, the good governance guidelines and the human rights standards, when applicable, should systematically exend to the international organizations themselves.[21] Furthermore, the activities of these organizations should be subject to judicial examination or, as a minimum, quasi-judicial scrutiny. The Inspection Panel of the World Bank constitutes a significant step in that direction. Mainstreaming also calls for the Panel's ability to apply international human rights standards in its work.

Based on this author's experience as a pro bono lawyer in internal UN appeals proceedings, the institutions concerned are less than independent and impartial in terms of their capacity to rule against management. The internal appeals bodies are woefully inadequate to the degree they are institutionally and intentionally subservient to the managers, rely in part on unpublished rules of the game, are often non-transparent in their work and otherwise fall below the standards which the same international organizations promote vis-a-vis national justice systems. These internal aspects have an inevitable impact on the rule of law in and hence ethe credibility of the international organizations.

Some of the same objections can be directed against the World Bank's Inspection Panel. The experts are selected and appointed by management. The Panel can only issue recommendations, with the final say belonging to the managers. The applicable standards are limited to the Bank's own production line of regulations and policies rather than the whole set of relevant international standards. The Panel members have so far been drawn from the financial and development fields, without much input yet from international law and human rights experts.

---

[21] In this light, it is praiseworthy when the World Bank investigates in-house corruption and when the United Nations examines its possible responsibility for genocide in Rwanda and Bosnia-Herzegovina.

VI. Concluding Observations

It is suggested that there ought to be no serious conflict between the substance of the human rights standards and the good governance guidelines. Perceptions or occurrences of the same can be put aside by training and knowledge about the two disciplines, combined with mutual efforts to build bridges between them and learn lessons from their respective successes and failures. This requires education, dialogue and understanding between the human rights and good governance communities.

As to the future evolution of the Inspection Panel, the general mood at the Lund Workshop was in favour of its further strengthening in terms of independence, the range of applicable standards and the weight of its recommendations. The Panel was also seen and appreciated as a worthwhile model for other intergovernmental organizations.

Many of the issues identified above, from all points of view, were addressed at the Workshop and again in the present book. In addition to the multiple purposes listed at the outset of this article, the Lund exercise has been worthwhile if it serves to consolidate the place and role of the Inspection Panel and to narrow the gaps or build bridges between the good governance guidelines and the human rights standards. The Raoul Wallenberg Institute looks forward to continued co-operation with the World Bank in pursuing these goals.

Compliance with Operational Standards: The Contribution of the World Bank Inspection Panel

Laurence Boisson de Chazournes[*]

The establishment of the Inspection Panel broke new ground in the international legal order. As a pioneering endeavor in the international organizations field, individuals were granted the right to bring complaints in an international forum for alleged failures of an international organization: under the procedure put in place, private persons are given direct access to the World Bank (hereinafter the "Bank") if they believe they are directly and adversely affected by a Bank-financed project due to the bank's failure to observe its policies and procedures regarding the design, appraisal and implementation of the projects it finances.[1] Not only is the Inspection Panel innovative from an institutional viewpoint, but it also provides a mechanism by which to increase scrutiny over the Bank's activities in sheding light on a feature of great interest, i.e. the standards governing the operational activities of an international organization – in the present case, the World Bank – and the extent to which the organization ensures its respect in its lending activities.

The creation of the Inspection Panel was triggered by the goal of improving quality control in the Bank's operations during project preparation and in the supervision of the implementation of projects financed by the Bank.[2] In this context, the Inspection Panel was established as an independent and permanent organ within the Bank's structure. It was granted the competence to receive and, subject to the approval of the Bank's Board, to investigate complaints from groups of individuals whose rights or interests have been or are likely to be directly and adversely affected by the Bank's failure described above. An individual Executive Director in the Bank and the Bank's Board may also instruct the Panel to conduct an investigation.

---

* Senior Counsel, Environment and International Law Unit, Legal Department, World Bank

1 The mandate of the Inspection Panel covers projects financed by the International Bank for Reconstruction and Development (IBRD) and the International Development Association (IDA).

2 On the motives for the establishment of the Inspection Panel, see I.F.I. Shihata, The World Bank Inspection Panel, IBRD – Oxford University Press, 1994, pp.5-13.

The present contribution will focus on the applicable standards for review of complaints by the Inspection Panel. They constitute the normative instruments against which the quality of the Bank's activities is assessed by the Panel when exercising its investigatory powers. First, the notion of applicable standards and the related eligibility criteria to be met will be introduced so as to evaluate the competence ratione materiae of the Inspection Panel. Second, the policies and procedures which have been the most often referred to in complaints brought before the Inspection Panel, i.e., the environmental and social policies and procedures will be presented. This will include the relationship of the Bank's operational policies and procedures with international law standards. Third, this article will highlight the contribution of the Inspection Panel for promoting compliance with the Bank's policies and procedures. Lastly, it will discuss the Inspection Panel and sustainable development.

1. APPLICABLE STANDARDS AND RELATED ELIGIBILITY CRITERIA FOR REVIEW OF COMPLAINTS

The Resolution establishing the Inspection Panel (hereinafter, the "Resolution") refers to the applicable standards for review of complaints under the notion of "operational policies and procedures". It indicates that this notion of a generic nature, although of a specific meaning, consists "of the Bank's Operational Policies, Bank Procedures and Operational Directives, and similar documents issued before these series were stated, and does not include Guidelines and Best Practices and similar documents or statements".[3]

Notion of operational policies and procedures and their mode of adoption

The notion of operational policies and procedures, as referred to by the Resolution, consists of instructions from the Bank Management to its staff. These instructions are numerous, deal with a wide array of topics and are designed to assist the staff of the Bank in their operational work. Some have been more particularly designed to avoid or mitigate detrimental impacts on certain groups of people and on the environment in the conduct of operational activities. They encompass documents entitled "Operational Policies", "Bank Procedures", and "Operational Directives", as well as various other documents including operational statements and ad hoc circulars embodying the Bank

[3] Resolution No.IBRD 93-10, Resolution No.IDA 93-6, "The World Bank Inspection Panel", paragraph 12.

policies and procedures. These headings are those of the various generations of documents reflecting the Bank's policies which have successively been adopted.[4]

Operational policies and procedures are issued by the Management through a specific process within the Bank, including in some occasions a consultation process with external partners. Some of these instructions originate in policy papers which are documents approved by the Board of the Bank. In certain cases, the policy papers submitted to the Board which address sensitive or complex questions have the draft operational policy attached to them so that the Board can discuss them. The operational policy is then issued after Board approval of the policy paper and it reflects the policy as agreed to by the Board.[5] As a general requirement, all policies and procedures, be they originating from a policy paper or not, have to be consistent with the Bank's constituent agreement, i.e. the Articles of Agreement, as interpreted by the Board.

The topic-approach on which operational policies and procedures are based is in great part due to their mode of adoption. Their issuance is part of an ad hoc process, a matter considered, at one point, to be important and relevant enough for the organization to adopt an operational policy or procedure on it.[6] This mode of adoption differs from one relying on a systematic internal legislative process. It may also be noted that operational policies and procedures were not originally accessible to the public at large, their purpose being to guide Bank staff in the conduct of their operational activities. The decision to make them public and accessible began at the end of the 1980s and was reinforced subsequently.[7]

Binding nature of operational policies and procedures

In discussing operational policies and procedures, one issue is to identify the applicable standards, the other one is to assess the degree of their binding

---

4 For most of the Bank's history, operational policies and procedures have been codified in a reference document called, the Operational Manual. A system of Operational Manual Statements (OMS) and Operational Policy Notes (OPN) was used in the 1970s and 1980s. After 1987, they were consolidated into Operational Directives (OD); see World Bank Operational Policies: Lessons of Experience and Future Directions, CODE97-73, November 20, 1997.

5 I.F.I. Shihata, The World Bank Inspection Panel, op.cit., p.43.

6 For example, the Bank issued in 1982 an Operational Manual Statement on "Tribal People in Bank-financed Projects" (OMS 2.34) whose objective was to protect the interests of relatively isolated and unacculturated tribal groups.

7 A policy on disclosure of operational information was formally adopted in 1993. See I.F.I. Shihata, The World Bank and Non-Governmental Organizations, The World Bank in a Changing World, Volume II, Martinus Nijhoff Publishers, 1995, pp.265-266.

nature, some being mandatory requirements for Bank staff. With respect to the Inspection Panel, alleged policies' mandatory character is a condition of eligibility of complaints. The question of the binding nature of the standards as contained in these series of documents was, in great part, resolved with a decision of the Management of the Bank adopted in 1992 in order to ensure greater clarity of, and compliance with, the standards. This decision was the result of discussions about the need to clarify the limits of flexibility in the application of the Operational Directives, as well as the need to simplify the Bank's business practices.[8] In this context, it was decided to gradually replace the documents called "Operational Directives" (ODs) with statements termed "Operational Policies" (OPs), "Bank Procedures" (BPs) and "Good Practices" (GPs).

While OPs and BPs are binding on the staff of the Bank within the limits of flexibility provided therein,[9] GPs are not. The latter are intended to disseminate knowledge and indicate successful examples. The consequences of this decision for the Inspection Panel's competence is that requests alleging failure of the Bank to follow requirements as spelled out in the recent series of documents entitled OPs and BPs, meet one of the eligibility requirements with respect to the ratione materiae competence of the Panel as they are binding on the staff of the Bank.[10]

At present, however, not all ODs and other documents issued before the ODs series was launched, have been converted to OPs, BPs and GPs. In addition, requests brought to the Inspection Panel may originate in "pre-conversion" situations in which the relevant instruments for appreciation of an alleged Bank's failure are ODs and other series of documents.[11] These situations may be sources of legal controversies. Such controversies could

---

[8] I.F.I. Shihata, The World Bank Inspection Panel, op.cit., pp.44-45.

[9] With regard to the content of OPs and BPs, the World Bank Policy on Disclosure of Information states that "'Operational Policies' as short statements (usually one or two pages) of policy. 'Bank Procedures' spell out the required documentation and common set of procedures needed to ensure operational consistency and quality." (Washington, DC: March 1994)

[10] As provided by the Resolution, the Panel's *ratione materiae* competence is ascertained in the light of four requirements: 1) an alleged failure of the Bank to follow its operational policies and procedures in the design, appraisal and/or implementation of a project financed by the Bank, 2) the alleged failure must be of a certain gravity, 3) the alleged failure must relate to the Bank's own policies and procedures and 4) the alleged failure must be such as to have or to be likely to have an adverse material effect on the complainant, see Role of the Inspection Panel in the Preliminary Assessment of Whether to Recommend Inspection – A Memorandum of the Senior Vice President and General Counsel, January 3, 1995, 34 International Legal Materials 503 (1995), pp.525-534.

[11] See, for example, Inspection Panel Report on Review of Present Project Problems and Assessment of Action Plans (Argentina/Paraguay: Yacetà Hydroelectric Project), in which the Inspection Panel listed a series of Operational Directives and other documents applicable to the request, INSP/R97-10, p.56.

arise due to the fact that ODs may contain standards which are not binding on the staff of the Bank. An assessment of the binding nature of their provisions on the staff depends on the wording of each standard.[12]

Having stated the principle that operational policies and procedures as defined in the Resolution are applicable standards, the violation of which may give rise to complaints before the Inspection Panel, the Resolution also indicates that the notion of operational policies and procedures "does not include Guidelines and Best Practices and similar documents or statements". This sentence makes clear that non-binding operational statements do not pertain to the competence of the Panel.

Procurement Guidelines

Special mention should be made of the "Procurement Guidelines" as the title may be misleading. While they are called "guidelines", they become in fact mandatory requirements once referenced to in loan agreements. The Resolution itself makes clear that complaints against procurement decisions reached by the Bank borrowers in connection with supplies of goods and services financed by Bank loans are beyond the scope of an investigation by the Panel.[13] This should, in fact, be viewed as a reiteration of the principle according to which complaints brought for borrowing countries' violations do not fall within the mandate of the Inspection Panel.[14] In the course of the Panel's activities, a problem, however, arose as to procurement action taken by the Bank. Following a request brought before the Inspection Panel, the Executive Directors adopted a decision,[15] reiterated in the Clarifications endorsed by the Executive Directors on October 17, 1996, (hereinafter the Clarifications)[16]. It made clear that "No procurement action is subject to inspection by the Panel, whether taken by the Bank or a borrower" and that "A

---

[12] I.F.I. Shihata, The World Bank Inspection Panel, op.cit., p.45.

[13] Paragraph 14 (b) of the Resolution reads as follows: "*Complaints against procurement decisions by Bank borrowers from suppliers of goods and services financed or expected to be financed by the Bank under a loan agreement, or from losing tenderers for the supply of any goods or services, which will continue to be addressed by staff under existing procedures*"

[14] L.Forget, Le "Panel d'inspection" de la Banque mondiale, Annuaire français de droit international, 1996, p.656.

[15] See Decision Number 1: Inspection Panel's Mandate on Procurement Matters, The Inspection Panel, Report, August 1, 1994 to July 31, 1996, pp.55-56.

[16] Under the basis of paragraph 27 of the Resolution, a Board review of the Inspection was conducted and completed in July 1996. It resulted in the issuance by the Board of Clarifications "which in fact introduced some amendments (by addition) to the resolution", I.F.I. Shihata, The World Bank Inspection Panel – A Background Paper on its Historical, Legal and operational Aspects, this volume.

separate mechanism is available for addressing procurement-related complaints".[17]

Related eligibility criteria

Together with their alleging of a violation of operational policies and procedures, the complainants must demonstrate that the violation is due to an omission or action of the Bank with respect to the design, appraisal, and implementation phases of a project financed by the Bank.[18] The Clarifications have made clear that "the word 'project' as used in the Resolution has the same meaning as in the Bank's practice, and includes projects under consideration by Bank management as well as projects already approved by the Executive Directors." As defined, the notion of "project" is wide and encompasses all developmental activities eligible to be financed by the Bank[19]. As to the notions of design, appraisal and implementation, they should be understood in light of the concept of project cycle in Bank operations encompassing various phases, the Bank having a certain role, and therefore different responsibilities, in each of them.[20]

The request for inspection may relate either to a project under consideration by Bank Management, i.e. a project in the design, preparation, pre-appraisal or appraisal stage, or to a project already approved by the Board and financed by the Bank. More particularly, with respect to the implementation phase, the Resolution specifies that a complaint can be lodged for "situations where the Bank is alleged to have failed in its follow-up on the borrower's obligations

---

[17] See para 1.15, Guidelines on Procurement under IBRD Loans and IDA Credits (Washington, DC: January 1995, revised January and August 1996 and September 1997).

[18] The Resolution refers to the "*(...) failure of the Bank to follow its operational policies and procedures with respect to the design, appraisal and/or implementation of a project financed by the Bank (including situations where the Bank is alleged to have failed in its follow-up on the borrower's obligations under loan agreements with respect to such policies and procedures)(...)*"

[19] The notion of project is not limited to specific investments. It includes projects consisting of programs or activities other than specific physical works, see Decision No.2 of the Executive Directors: Scope of the Panel's Mandate – Compensation for Expropriation and Extension of IDA Credits to Ethiopia under OMS 1.28, The Inspection Panel, Report, August 1, 1994 to July 31, 1996, p.57. More generally, see "Project and Non-Project Financing under the IBRD Articles", Legal Opinion of the Senior Vice-President and General Counsel, December 21, 1984.

[20] The Bank's project cycle covers the life of a project from identification of needs and priorities until the final completion of work and evaluation of results; see W. C. Braum, The Project Cycle, IBRD, 1982; The World Bank's Partnership with Nongovernmental Organizations, The World Bank, May 1996, p.7.

under loan agreements" with respect to operational policies and procedures[21]. The Panel has the mandate to investigate whether the Bank has properly followed up on the carrying out by the borrower of its obligations under a loan agreement. The latter include the notion of green conditionality. As a matter of fact, a number of legal techniques have been developed for ensuring that policy requirements are reflected in loan agreements. Specific loan covenants as well as other techniques, such as the attachment of an implementation program or plan of action as a schedule to the loan agreement, are used for specifying the actions to be taken by the borrower.[22] Within the framework of its responsibilities, the Bank should exercise all due diligence required to make sure that the borrower's obligations are fully complied with in a timely fashion, i.e. that the borrowing country does abide with all its contractual obligations.

2. ENVIRONMENTAL AND SOCIAL STANDARDS AND THEIR RELATIONSHIP WITH INTERNATIONAL LAW

The Bank's operational policies and procedures integrate a number of social and environmental issues and considerations, ranging from the protection of specific vulnerable groups of people to water resources management issues. Some of these instruments are of a general application, others more specific. They provide for guidelines and requirements to be followed by Bank staff in Bank financed projects. They also indicate the borrower country's responsibilities in taking into account the environmental and social issues.

Most of the requests so far made to the Inspection Panel allege that the Bank has not followed its environmental and social policies and procedures.[23] Among the most quoted, are the Environment Assessment policy, the Indigenous Peoples policy and the Involuntary Resettlement policy, as well as the policies dealing with the Involvement of Nongovernmental Organiza-

---

21 The Resolution states as a principle that no requests will be declared eligible regarding a project after the project's loan "closing date" or after 95 percent or more of the loan proceeds have been disbursed. For an interpretation of this requirement, see "Time-Limits on the Eligibility of Complaints Submitted to the Inspection Panel", Legal Opinion of the Senior Vice President and General Counsel, July 28, 1997.

22 On the use of such techniques for environmental protection purposes, see I.F.I. Shihata, The World Bank And the Environment : Legal Instruments for Achieving Environmental Objectives, The World Bank in a Changing World, op.cit., 1995, pp.199-208.

23 See R. E. Bissel, An Environmental Inspection Mechanism for World Bank Projects, Ecodecision, Spring 1997, pp.47-50. For an analysis of the Planned Arun III Hydroelectric Project in Nepal (1994); D. D. Bradlow, A Test Case for the World Bank, American University Journal of International Law & Policy, 1996, Vol. 11, pp. 247-294.

tions (NGOs) in Bank-supported Activities and Disclosure of Operational Information.[24]

Environmental assessment policy

The Bank's operational policy on environment assessment (EA) constitutes a cornerstone for project activities with potential environmental consequences. It lays down standards and procedures for the conduct of environment assessment. Its purpose is to ensure that the project options are environmentally sound and sustainable, and thus to improve decision making. All Bank projects are screened in reference to three categories (categories A, B and C) to determine the appropriate level of environment assessment.[25] Such an assessment will be conducted to ensure that development options under consideration are environmentally sound and sustainable and that any environmental consequences are recognized early in the project cycle and taken into account in the project design. Environmental assessments identify ways for improving projects environmentally, and minimizing, mitigating or compensating for adverse impacts. Among other issues to be taken into account, the environment assessment should also make sure that the project is in full compliance with domestic law requirments as well as with the international treaties to which the borrowing country is a party.

The most rigorous assessment process is required for a project which is likely to have significant adverse environmental impacts (i.e category A projects), such as impacts that are sensitive, diverse or unprecedented or that affect an area broader than the sites or facilities subject to physical works. If the environmental impacts are less adverse (category B projects), a less exhaustive form of environmental assessment is required. In the case where the project has no, or minimal, adverse environmental impacts (category C projects), no environmental assessment is required. Meaningful consultations with project-affected groups and local NGOs are required during the environment assessment process. Consultations should be initiated as early as

[24] The operational policies and procedures are available on the Bank's web site (www.worldbank.org). As of February 20, 1998, the Environment Assessment policy, the Indigenous Peoples policy and the Involuntary Resettlement policy are still in the OD format. GP 14.70 on Involvement of Nongovernment Organizations in Bank-supported Activities was issued in March 1997 and BP 17.50 on Disclosure of Operational Information was issued in September 1993.

[25] OP 4.01 on Environmental Assessment (forthcoming) includes a fourth category, i.e: "Category FI: A proposed project is classified as Category FI if it involves investment of Bank funds through a financial intermediary, in subprojects that may result in environmental impacts". It also specifies that in the context of a proposed project, the analysis of alternatives to environmental implications should include a "without project" situation.

possible. For Category A projects, the projects with the most potential significant environmental impacts, public participation is required at least at two stages, i.e. shortly after environmental screening and before the terms of reference for the EA are finalized, and once a draft EA is prepared, as well as throughout project implementation.

Dam and reservoir projects receive a special treatment in the Bank's EA procedures. The purpose is to avoid, minimize, or compensate for adverse environmental impacts wherever possible, using design features and measures implemented as part of the project. The potential project impact is determined at an early stage with the advice of environmental specialists. At the earliest stage, during project identification and before assigning an environmental category to the project, the Bank must ensure that the borrower selects independent, recognized experts to carry out environmental reconnaissance that includes identification of the project impacts, ascertainement of the scope of the EA, assessment of the borrower's capacity to manage an EA process and advising on the need for an independent advisory panel which would normally be set up for large dam projects.

Indigenous peoples

The Bank has a specific policy which addresses the concerns of indigenous peoples. The notion of indigenous peoples covers groups including "indigenous ethnic groups", "tribal groups" and "scheduled tribes", but is not restricted to these groups. They are defined as social groups whose social and cultural identity is distinct from that of the dominant society and makes them vulnerable to being disadvantaged in the development process. The definitional criteria focused on the issue of vulnerability and distinctiveness, although other criteria have a role to play: close attachment to ancestral territories, indigenous language, self identification, presence of customary social and political institutions and primarily subsistence-oriented production. The purpose of the policy is that these social groups benefit from development projects and that potentially adverse effects of Bank projects on indigenous people are avoided or mitigated. The Bank calls for their "informed participation" in projects and programs that affect them. To this effect, an indigenous peoples development plan is prepared by the borrowing country to provide the framework for indigenous peoples' participation in project activities and to ensure that these peoples receive socially and culturally appropriate benefits. From a legal viewpoint, the policy requires that the development plan assesses: (i) the legal status of groups covered by the policy, as reflected in the country's constitution and legislation; and (ii) the ability of such groups to obtain access to and effectively use the legal system to defend their rights.

Involuntary resettlement

As a basic policy objective, involuntary resettlement should be avoided or minimized where feasible and all viable alternative project designs should be reviewed. Any operation that involves involuntary land acquisition is reviewed for potential resettlement requirements early in the project cycle. The objective of the policy is to assist displaced people who have lost their land, houses, or both, or their means of livelihood, in their efforts to restore or improve former living standards and earning capacity.

Where displacement is unavoidable, the borrower country is required to prepare and carry out resettlement plans or development programs indicating the compensatory measures to be carried out, an implementation scheme, including a reference to a grievance mechanism permitting affected peoples to bring complaints, as well as a time-table and a budget. The policy defines the reference standards for determining the compensatory measures. Displaced people should be (i) compensated for their losses (land-for-land/market value/mixture of land-based and non-land-based strategies), (ii) assisted with the move and supported during the transition to the resettlement site, and (iii) assisted in efforts to improve their former living standards and income earning capacity. Particular attention should be paid to the needs of the poorest.

Informed participation and consultations with the affected people is required during the preparation of the resettlement plan. Community participation in planning and implementing resettlement should also be encouraged. Appropriate attention should be given to indigenous peoples, ethnic minorities and "pastoralists" who may have customary rights to the land or other resources taken for the project.

NGOs and disclosure of information

Bearing in mind the potential contribution of NGOs, among others, in areas concerning environmental degradation, involuntary resettlement and indigenous peoples, a Bank policy – at present, a "Good Practices" policy – sets out a framework for involving these organizations in Bank-supported activities and provides staff with guidance for working with them. The policies and procedures on environment impact assessment, indigenous peoples and unvoluntary resettlement also contain specific provisions requiring the involvement of NGOs.

The policy on disclosure of operational information sets out the procedures with respect to Bank documents.[26] In particular, it states the procedures to be followed for making accessible to affected groups and local NGOs in borrowing countries copies of environmental assessments and of environmental action plans. This policy, as well as the one on the involvement of NGOs, complement in many respects the other above-mentioned policies. All together, the policy requirements "operationalize" important international standards, such as access to information, public awareness and participation in decision-making through Bank's projects.

Relationship with international law standards

As can be seen, the World Bank does not operate in a closed world. The environmental and social operational policies and procedures reflect concerns related to the promotion of sustainable development as expressed in many other fora. Operational policies and procedures are in fact vehicles for achieving this objective, although they are not necessarily exhaustive in covering all issues which pertain to their scope of application.[27] The relationship between these policies and international law standards contributes to promoting sustainable development. In particular, the policies' references to international law promote respect for good practices as endorsed in international instruments of a binding character as well as of a non-binding character.

Before presenting the relationship of the operational policies and procedures with international law standards, it should be remembered that operational policies and procedures are not by themselves binding under international law. Policy requirements related to the implementation of projects only become binding when they are reflected in loan agreements. By entering into an agreement, the borrowing state is under the obligation to take necessary measures to comply with its contractual obligations which may include policy issues. Within the framework of its responsibilities, the Bank should exercise all due diligence required to make sure that all borrower's obligations are fully complied with.

---

26 The Bank has established a Public Information Center, presently called "Infoshop", through which much of the material covered by the policy is available. It is located at the Bank Headquarters and serves the public in member countries through the Internet and through Bank field offices.

27 As a note of caution, on each operational policy figures a standard notice which states that the policy is "not necessarily a complete treatment of the subject".

At the outset, it is to be noted that the policies on environment assessment, indigenous populations and involuntary resettlement require that the projects financed by the Bank are in compliance with the domestic legal order of a borrowing country. Various means allow for countries to integrate their international commitments in their legal order. As such, they become part of the domestic legal order of the borrower and should be taken into consideration when implementing the relevant policies and procedures. Moreover, as a general requirement, first stated through a policy adopted in 1984,[28] the Bank has committed itself not to finance projects that contravene any international environmental agreements to which a member country concerned is a party. This principle was reiterated in the OP on forestry[29] and in the OP on environment assessment.[30] This commitment, which shapes the conduct of the Bank with respect to international environmental agreements, also increases the awareness of borrowing countries with respect to the significance of international environmental law requirements and the importance of their being implemented.

Operational policies and procedures may also expressly refer to international standards as a means for identifying the good and best practices to be followed. As an example, the OP on management of cultural property in Bank-financed projects makes explicit reference to country obligations under international treaties for defining cultural property under the policy.[31] The OP on pest management also refers to international law instruments as an indication of good practices to be followed in the area covered by the policy.[32] Other international instruments, even though not referred to explicitly, may play a similar role, at least for interpretation purposes. This may, for example, be the case when the UN convention on biological diversity[33] is considered in the context of the application of the policy on indigenous peoples. These various interactions between international law and operational standards underline, if needed, the pragmatic nature of the latter aimed at identifying best practices for sustainable development purposes.

---

[28] See OMS 2.36 on Environmental Aspects of Bank Work (1984).

[29] Operational Policy (OP) 4.36 on Forestry.

[30] Operational Policy (OP) 4.01 on Environment Assessment (forthcoming)

[31] The Convention Concerning the Protection of the World Cultural and Natural Heritage (1972) is given as a reference, see OP 4.11, par.2 (a) (forthcoming).

[32] For the purpose of the policy (OP 4.09), minimum standards are defined with reference to the FAO's Guidelines for Packaging and Storage of Pesticides (Rome, 1985), Guidelines on Good Labeling Practice for Pesticides (Rome, 1985) and Guidelines for the Disposal of Waste Pesticide and Pesticide Containers on the Farm (Rome, 1985). See also, the forthcoming policy on application of EA to projects involving pest management (BP 4.01-Annex C).

[33] Ph.Sands, R. Tarasofsky and M.Weiss, Documents in international environmental law, Manchester, Manchester University Press, 1994 p.845.

The fact of taking into consideration the international instruments to which a borrowing country has committed itself or which are considered as reflecting agreed international good practices, shows the close relationship of the operational policies and procedures with international law principles and standards in areas which fall within the scope of application of the policies. In addition, operational policies and procedures constitute means which generate new practices and standards in borrowing countries and as such favor the emergence or consolidation of international practices.[34] The highlighting of this "model" role reveals in some respects the difficulties surrounding the application of operational policies and procedures. As a matter of fact, they promote respect for progressive and process-oriented standards whose application on the ground may face resistance or uncertainty as to how to implement them in a sound manner.

The required public participation policy and/or meaningful consultations provides a good example of how challengeable and difficult it may be to meet these standards from one region to another or from one country to another. It is one thing to establish the sequencing of actions to be conducted and the timing for certain procedural requirements in terms of public participation, but quite another to put in place a real and meaningful participation process. Factors such as cultural traditions, the notion of public space for debate, the existence of an institutional framework or the rate of literacy, all play a significant role towards implementing these principles and should be taken into account in the context of the flexibility provided by the relevant operational policies and procedures. In this context, the borrowing country should do its best efforts to take the most appropriate measures for implementing the policy requirements in light of the aim of meaningful public participation for ensuring the protection of the environment and of the affected people.[35] The Bank, on its side, should exercise due diligence for making sure that the

---

34 The Bank's operational policies and procedures may also serve as a model for other multilateral and bilateral donors. In this context, co-financing of investment operations is one way to promote such practices. See S. Mahony, World Bank's Policies and Practice in Environmental Impact Assessment, Environmental and Planning Law Journal, 1995, Vol.12, pp. 97-115; S. Guyett, Environmental & Lending, Lessons of the World Bank, Hope for the European Bank for Reconstruction and Development, New York University Journal of International Law and Politics, 1992, Vol.24, p.896.

35 Parallels can be drawn with international law notions for interpreting the notion of best efforts. Such can be the case with the obligation to undertake to take steps with a view to achieving progressively the full realization of economic, social and cultural rights, as spelled out in Article 2, para.1 of the International Covenant on Economic, Social and Cultural Rights. On this matter, see the General Comment of the UN Committee on Economic, Social and Cultural Rights, Compilation of General Comments and General Recommendations adopted by Human Rights Treaty Bodies, HRI/GEN/1/Rev.3, para.1-14.

borrower complies with the policy requirements dealing with public participation.

3. The Inspection Panel and the promotion of compliance with operational policies and procedures

Compliance with environmental and social operational policies and procedures is undoubtedly an important tool for ensuring quality in the Bank's activities. Although the creation of the Inspection Panel is an important achievement in this respect, various other means contribute to compliance with operational policies and procedures. Besides checks and balances, mechanisms and procedures such as internal review processes during the preparation of a project and the imposition eventually of measures of a disciplinary nature, there are rule-oriented mechanisms which promote respect with policy requirements. This is the case, for example, with the legal techniques mentioned earlier which have been developed for ensuring that policy requirements are reflected in loan agreements, the borrower thereby being legally committed to implement them. On its side, the Bank exercises with due diligence its supervisory functions to ensure that the borrower comply with its contractual commitments. As a final resort, the Bank may take more extreme measures, such as the suspension of disbursement or the cancellation of a loan if the borrower does not carry out its contractual obligations.[36]

The establishment of the Inspection Panel complements the above-mentioned series of means because it allows individuals to put under scrutiny the Bank's compliance with its operational standards. The Bank has institutionalized the compliance concern in establishing a specific organ to conduct investigation and by providing for the possibility of remedial action taken by the Bank in the case of a violation of operational policies and procedures which has impaired the rights or interests of a group of people. Moreover, besides allowing for remedies to individuals, the establishment of the Inspection Panel has encouraged a process on a Bank-wide level which demonstrates its potentialities for clarifying the content of operational policies and procedures and to increasing awareness of the need to comply with these policies and procedures.

---

[36] See I.F.I. Shihata, The World Bank and the Environment: Legal Instruments for Achieving Environmental Objectives, op.cit., pp.199-208.

Powers of the Inspection Panel

Before looking at this two-fold contribution, it should be noted that the Inspection Panel is not vested with normative powers of a general nature. Its rule-making powers are strictly limited to the adoption of rules for "procedural matters relating to the work of the Panel".[37] The Panel adopted such rules on August 19, 1994 (hereinafter the "Operational Procedures"). These rules are based on the Resolution establishing the Inspection Panel and are aimed at providing detail on its operational aspects.[38] The Inspection Panel therefore does not have the competence to legislate or enact new standards, nor does it have the competence to amend existing operational policies and procedures.

Vested with investigatory powers, the latter are however of a limited scope. They can only be exercised with respect to requests alleging a failure by the Bank to follow its policies and procedures in specific operational activities. This entails that the Panel is not entitled to review "the consistency of the Bank's practice with *any* of its policies and procedures"[39] regardless of its content, nor is the Panel entitled to decide on a general basis the adequacy of a particular policy or procedure.[40] Within the limits of its mandate, however, the Panel plays an important role for promoting compliance with operational standards.

Clarification and awareness as means to promote compliance with operational standards

The Panel exercises its investigatory and quasi-investigatory powers[41] on a case-by-case basis, not to say on a project-by project basis. In so doing, the Panel must decide on the applicability of relevant policies and procedures. The Panel must then interpret their content with regard to the possible failure of the Bank in complying with them. Through its interpretative function,[42] it may

---

37 See paragraph 24 of the Resolution establishing the Inspection Panel

38 See introduction to the Operating Procedures.

39 See Clarifications (Eligibility and Access)

40 See L. Forget, Le "Panel d'inspection" de la Banque mondiale, Annuaire français de droit international, op.cit., pp.654-655.

41 In reference to the practice developed so far and described by I.F.I. Shihata, The World Bank Inspection Panel – A Background Paper on its Historical, Legal and Operational Aspects, op.cit. The Clarifications issued by the Bank's Executive Directors state, in fact, the practice which has been followed by the Panel by providing that "*where the Inspection Panel believes that it would be appropriate to undertake a "preliminary assessment" of the damages alleged by the requester (in particular when such preliminary assessment could lead to a resolution of the matter without the need for a full investigation), the Panel may undertake the preliminary assessment and indicate to the Board the date on which it would present its findings and recommendations as to the need, if any, for a full investigation*".

42 This interpretative function is limited to operational policies and procedures and is exercised under the overall review of the Bank's Board, and to the extent that they do not involve the Bank's

contribute to the promotion of compliance with operational policies and procedures. This process allows, in fact, for clarification of the content of operational policies and procedures. It also gives the Inspection Panel the opportunity to highlight best practices in applying these instruments, but most importantly, it allows the Inspection Panel to publicize bad practices which have given rise to complaints before the Inspection Panel, and as such reveal possible failures and inconsistencies in complying with operational policies and procedures.

The dynamics attached to such interpretative function should also be seen in a broader institutional context. As provided for by the Resolution, the Panel is engaged in a dialogue with the Management when discussing an alleged failure of the Bank to follow its operational policies and procedures. The Executive Directors also play a pivotal role when exercising their powers as prescribed by the Resolution. A process is stirred, the end result of which may also contribute to clarifying the content of policies and procedures, as well as remedying the problems through the adoption of action plans. In addition, the Executive Directors may also adopt decisions on general matters relating to the Inspection Panel. They have done so for defining the scope of the Panel's mandate in light of the Resolution. Incidentally, such exchanges of views may contribute to clarifying some operational policies and procedures' requirements.[43]

Another contribution of the Inspection Panel relates to the enhancement in general of the quality of Bank operations. The conclusions and recommendations of the Inspection Panel may signal possible failures of the Bank in following operational policies and procedures and may increase the awareness of the Bank's staff in the importance of implementing operational policies and procedures. Most of the requests brought so far to the attention of the Panel have dealt with environmental and social policies and procedures. The ensuing recommendations and findings of the Inspection Panel have stressed the need for giving greater attention to compliance with these instruments. Such a contribution is reinforced when the Executive Directors authorize fullfledged

legal rights and obligations. For matters related to the Bank's rights and obligations with respect to a request under consideration, the Panel shall seek the advice of the Bank's Legal Department, see Resolution, paragraph 15.

[43] The Decision of the Executive Directors on the Scope of the Inspection Panel's Mandate – Compensation for Expropriation and Extension of IDA Credits to Ethiopia under OMS 1.28 may provide an example of nurturing process or "constructive dialogue". Although the main issue was the scope of the Inspection Panel's mandate, the exchange of views which took place provided some guidance as to the interpretation of OMS 1.28 (now OP 7.40 on Disputes over Defaults on External Debt, Expropriation, and Breach of Contract). See The Inspection Panel, Report, August 1, 1994 to July 31, 1996, pp.56-58.

investigations to be conducted under the basis of paragraph 20 of the Resolution.

Compliance and access to information

Making public all the documents related to the Inspection Panel's activities, as provided for in the Resolution and the Clarifications (i.e. the request itself, the Management's response to it, the Panel's recommendation on the eligibility of the request, the Board's decision to authorize or deny an investigation, the Panel's findings, the Management's comments and the final Board decision),[44] enhances the twofold contributions of the Panel with respect to compliance with operational policies and procedures. These clarifying and awareness contributions could in the future also be supported by a decision to publish in a more systematic way the sets of documents issued at the different stages of the procedure. This could, for example, be done through the setting up of an official Bank collection or series. Such a decision would simplify access to and dissemination of information, as well as help "make the Inspection Panel better known in borrowing countries".[45] In addition, while this information is publicly available it is not easily accessible for all interested people. In this context, more extensive use should be made of the existing electronic technologies.

Moreover, making public all documents contributes to "objectivizing" the issues at stake in making them known to the public at large. In so doing, it contributes to fairness and accountability at all stages. These aspects would in fact be strengthened with an increased formalization of the process driven by the Resolution establishing the Inspection Panel. Resort to comparative jurisprudence and to legal interpretative methods have a role to play for deciding on the eligibility of a complaint brought to the Panel, for interpreting the operational policies and procedures and for drafting the recommendations to the Executive Directors. Such processes would also facilitate the building-up of the decision-making process onto decisions and recommendations of the various organs as well as favour consistency and predictability. The Inspection Panel, the Management of the Bank and the Executive Directors may want to

---

44 See paragraph 25 and paragraph 26 of the Resolution and paragraph 41, paragraph 56 and paragraph 65 of the Operating Rules. In addition, see the Clarifications (Outreach) which state that: "*Management will make its response to requests for inspection available to the public within three days after the Board has decided on whether to authorize the inspection. Management will also make available to the public opinions of the General Counsel related to the Inspection Panel matters promptly after the Executive Directors have dealt with the issues involved, unless the Board decides otherwise in a specific case*".

45 See Clarifications (Outreach)

take this plea into consideration when exercising their respective powers within the framework of the Resolution establishing the Inspection Panel,[46] bearing in mind, at the same time, the mere purpose of this innovative procedure which is to provide effective access to affected private parties in an international forum of a non-judicial character.

4. Concluding remarks: the Inspection Panel, public participation and sustainable development

Different concepts and notions gained legitimacy in the course of the preparation of the 1992 Rio Conference on Environment and Development. They contributed to substantiating the concept of sustainable development and revealing the possible integrative nature of development efforts. Such was the case with the notions of good governance, public participation and access to justice, the Rio instruments stressing the fact that representatives of the civil society were important actors who should be part of the decision-making process and should be granted the right to exercise remedies for ensuring sustainable management of resources.[47]

With the adoption of its various social and environmental operational policies and procedures, the Bank had already ackowledged the fact that public participation is a core principle for development assistance activities. Moreover, in establishing the Inspection Panel in 1993, the Bank created a new path for public participation: it allowed individuals to bring complaints before a newly established organ against its failures if they believe that their interests have been impaired. More generally, in promoting such access, the Panel mechanism demonstrates the growing importance of the individual as an emerging rights holder in areas of development and environment. The Inspection Panel, in fact, is at the crossroads of the fields of development, environment and human rights, highlighting their close interrelationships for promoting sustainable development and providing a new venue for a dialogue

---

[46] It has been suggested that at least one of the members of the Inspection Panel should have legal expertise, see D. Bradlow, International Organizations and Private Complaints: The Case of the World Bank Inspection Panel, Virginia Journal of International Law, 1994, Vol.34, p.573.

[47] See Principle 10 of the Rio Declaration on Environment and Development, Ph. Sands, R. Tarasofsky and M. Weiss, op.cit., p.52. See also, Programme for the Further Implementation of Agenda 21, adopted by the Special Session of the General Assembly, 23-27 June 1997 (A/S-19/33), Environmental Policy and Law, Vol.27, No5, 1997, p.428. On the notion of sustainable development, its content and the challenges for implementing it, see K. Ginther, E. Denters & P. J.I.M. de Waart (eds), Sustainable Development and Good Governance, Dordrecht/Boston/London, Martinus Nijhoff Publishers, 1995, 483p.

between a lending institution and the direct beneficiaries of its developmental activities.

The Inspection Panel's Case Law*

*Sabine Schlemmer-Schulte***

I. Introduction

The Inspection Panel has been in operation for slightly more than three years.[1] It has, however, already built up an impressive record of work on cases that were brought before it.[2]

As of October 1997, the Panel has received ten requests and registered eight of them. The two requests which were not registered fell clearly outside the Panel's mandate as described in the Resolution establishing it. The first request which was not registered concerned the Bank's lending to a country involved in a dispute on an expropriation matter. This request was not related to the Bank's operational activities (i.e. a Bank-financed project), which a Panel investigation is meant to cover. The other request which was not

---

* Paper presented at the Expert Meeting on the Inspection Panel of the World Bank, held at the Raoul Wallenberg Institute of Human Rights and Humanitarian Law in Lund, Sweden, on October 23-25, 1997. This paper has been updated to include developments until the end of 1997.

** Counsel, Office of the Senior Vice President and General Counsel, World Bank.

1 For a detailed account on the developments which led to the establishment of the Inspection Panel and a legal analysis of this unprecedented mechanism under international law, *see* Ibrahim F.I. Shihata, the World Bank Inspection Panel (1994). *See also* Ibrahim F.I. Shihata, The World Bank in a Changing World, Vol. III (1998), Chapter on The World Bank Inspection Panel – Its Historical, Legal and Operational Aspects (discussing the application of the Resolution Establishing the Inspection Panel by the Panel, Management and the Board after the Panel's creation as well as issues of the first and second review of the Inspection Panel's experience). *See further* Daniel D. Bradlow & Sabine Schlemmer-Schulte, The World Bank's New Inspection Panel: A Constructive Step in the Transformation of the International Legal Order, 54 Zeitschrift für ausländisches öffentliches Recht und Völkerrecht (ZaöRV) – Heidelberg Journal of International Law 392 (1994) (discussing the impact of the Panel's creation on the individual's standing, and the international organizations' and the States' status under international law).

2 For a summary of the Panel's case work from the Panel's perspective, *see* the First and Second Annual Report of the Inspection Panel, the former covering the period from August 1, 1994 to July 31, 1996, and the latter from August 1, 1996 to July 31, 1997. *See also* Richard E. Bissell, Recent Practice of the Inspection Panel of the World Bank, 91 American Journal of International Law 741 (1997).

registered concerned an IFC investment in the construction of a hydroelectric project rather than an IBRD or IDA operation, the latter being so far the only institutions among the affiliates of the World Bank Group[3] into whose activities the Panel is mandated to look.

Out of the other eight requests, four related to IBRD and four to IDA projects. Seven of the requests concerned large infrastructure projects such as hydroelectric dams, power stations, natural resources management projects, bridges, and an irrigation area and water reservoir. One request related to a sector adjustment operation. In all the requests concerning infrastructure projects, non-compliance with primarily environmental policies and procedures and those on social rights of people was alleged by the complainants.

The concrete cases have contributed to two features: One may be referred to as "case law" or "jurisprudence" under the Resolution Establishing the Inspection Panel;[4] the other could be called a "commentary" on the Resolution.

The outcome of Panel assessments and investigations may be called "case law,"[5] although not in the narrow sense given to it in the common law context where precedents, i.e. court decisions on cases, traditionally constitute the sole source of law. It is, however, legitimate to speak of a case law of the requests before the Panel in the broader sense, i.e. in the meaning of an aggregate of reported cases that interpret codes, statutes, and regulations similar to the courts' jurisprudence complementing the written law in civil law systems. The jurisprudence resulting from cases brought before the Panel consists of

---

3 The World Bank Group consists of the International Bank for Reconstruction and Development (IBRD) and the International Development Agency (IDA), both lending and making guarantees to developing countries but with IDA lending to the poorest of them; the International Finance Corporation (IFC), making loans and equity investments in private enterprises in developing countries; the Multilateral Investment Guarantee Agency (MIGA), providing guarantees to foreign investors in developing countries against losses caused by non-commercial risks; and the International Centre for Settlement of Investment Disputes (ICSID) providing facilities and procedures for arbitration and conciliation of disputes between private investors and host country governments.

4 For the Board document embodying the Board's decision to create an inspection function, *see* Resolution No. 93-10 IBRD, Resolution No. 93-6 IDA, The World Bank Inspection Panel, dated September 22, 1993 (hereinafter the Resolution or the Resolution Establishing the Panel). The Resolution requires that the requests, the Panel's recommendations on the eligibility of requests, the Board's decisions to authorize or deny investigation, the Panel's findings, Management's comments and the Board's decisions on the Panel's findings are made publicly available. Management's initial response to the request submitted to the Panel is not mentioned among the documents for which the Resolution requires public disclosure. Disclosure of that document was, however, expressly provided for in the 1996 Clarifications, *see infra* note 7. All disclosed documents are available at the Bank's Public Information Center.

5 The term "case law" is used here to mean the aggregate of reported cases that interpret the Resolution Establishing the Inspection Panel as the "statute" or "legislative basis" for the work of the Panel, Management and the Board in connection with cases brought before the Panel.

interpretations of, and practices developed under the Resolution. This jurisprudence is contained in decisions of the Board which, under the Resolution is the organ making the two decisions that can be taken in the course of an inspection (i.e. the decision on the authorization of an investigation and the decision on remedial actions etc. after an investigation was carried out). While it is the Board making these decisions, the body of case law includes the bases for the Board's decisions in the concrete cases, i.e. the Panel recommendations, Management responses, legal opinions issued by the General Counsel, as well as debates in the Board itself, provided the Board's decisions allow for the latter to be truly identified as express or implicit bases for the Board's decisions.

In this context, it should be noted that, on a number of legal issues, while raised in the context of the cases, the Board did not take a final position. This happened in the cases in which the Board denied the Panel recommendations in favor of an investigation its support without, however, siding with Management's view on the issue. It also happened in the cases in which the Board agreed with the Panel's general recommendation not to carry out an investigation without, however, expressly endorsing specific arguments made by the Panel in furtherance of the recommendation.

In an indirect way, i.e. outside the discussions on a concrete case, the cases have also contributed to the development of an authoritative "commentary"[6] on the Resolution. This commentary is contained in the Clarifications of Certain Legal Aspects of the Resolution.[7] The Clarifications include general interpretations of, and flexible practices developed under the Resolution which the Board agreed upon in the course of the first general review of the Resolution in 1996 and which took place outside the context of a concrete case.

II. The Actual Cases Before the Panel

The following summarizes the factual background of the cases brought before the Panel in chronological order, i.e. in the order the requests were received. It includes references to both the interpretations of, and practices developed under the Resolution endorsed by the Board and the issues which remain unsolved.

---

6 The term "commentary" is used here to denote a remark or note on some statutory provision intended to illustrate or explain its meaning. Analogies in domestic legal systems include the US Code Annotated or the classical commentaries on the civil codes of France and Germany.

7 *See* Clarifications of Certain Aspects of the Resolution Establishing the Inspection Panel (R96-204), dated September 30, 1996 which were approved by the Board of Executive Directors on October 17, 1996 (hereinafter Clarifications or 1996 Clarifications). The Clarifications have also been made publicly available.

1. Planned Arun III Hydroelectric Project – Nepal

In the first request (registered in October 1994), a group of Nepalese citizens claimed non-compliance by the Bank (IDA) with, among other things, its policies on disclosure of information, environmental assessment, involuntary resettlement and indigenous people in connection with a proposed hydroelectric project in Nepal (Arun III) which was under consideration but not yet financed by the Bank.[8]

After the Panel had recommended to the Board that an investigation be authorized but before the Board decided on that recommendation, the General Counsel issued a legal opinion responding to questions from several Executive Directors.[9] While there is no need to go into the details of this legal opinion in which the General Counsel comprehensively discussed the scope of the role of the Panel in the preliminary stage of whether to recommend an inspection in general (without however commenting on the Panel's report and recommendations on the actual request), there is one point in the General Counsel's legal opinion that is worth mentioning here. That point concerns the interpretation of the meaning of the term affected party which had been subject to some debates. The Resolution defines an affected party as being not a single individual but a community of persons.[10] By contrast, the Panel's Operating Procedures state that an affected party, could be "any group of two or more people."[11] Some writings had also found that an affected party could be "any two or more persons."[12] In his legal opinion, the General Counsel pointed out

---

8 *See* Request for Inspection: Panel Recommendation – Nepal Arun III Proposed Hydroelectric Project (IDA/SecM94-378), December 16, 1994 (including in Attachment (1) the text of the request itself). For Management's initial response, *see* Attachment (2) of the Panel's Recommendation.

9 *See* Ibrahim F.I. Shihata, Memorandum of the Senior Vice President and General Counsel, Role of the Inspection Panel in the Preliminary Assessment of Whether to Recommend Inspection (SecM95-11), January 3, 1995. This memorandum, which is not among the documents that are automatically made publicly available under the Resolution, was disclosed to the public by decision of the Board of Executive Directors. The memorandum is available at the Bank's Public Information Center and is also published in Ibrahim F.I. Shihata, The World Bank in a Changing World, Vol. II (1995), Annex III(D), and in 34 ILM 525 (1995).

10 *See* Resolution Establishing the Panel, *supra* note 4, at para. 12.

11 *See* Operating Procedures, adopted by the Panel on August 19, 1994, at para. 4(a).

12 *See* Daniel D. Bradlow, International Organizations and Private Complaints: The Case of the World Bank Inspection Panel, 34 Virginia Journal of International Law 553, 583 (1994) (stating implicitly that any two or more persons may lodge a request with the Panel by noting that "any 'affected party' except a single individual" is allowed to bring a complaint under the Resolution and omitting a reference to any interests that complainants must share); Kathigamar V.S.K. Nathan, The World Bank Inspection Panel – Court or Quango, 12 Journal of International Arbitration 135, 141 (1995) (stating that "[t]he 'jurisdiction' of the Panel extends to an affected party which should consist of at least two persons in the territory of the borrower country," but also not referring to any common interest that the requesters must share); and

that these interpretations would not be consistent with the Resolution which explicitly explains the notion of an affected party as "a community of persons such as an organization, association, society or other grouping of individuals." According to the General Counsel's opinion, this explicit language of the Resolution suggests that complaints submitted individually by a number of persons, each acting in his own single capacity, without any common bond between them, will not meet the requirement of a community of persons. While the group of individuals need not have the juridical personality of an association, corporation etc., it has to be a group which represents a commonality of interests. The Board endorsed the General Counsel's legal opinion, including the point on the affected party. The understanding of this term was further confirmed on the occasion of the review of the Resolution Establishing the Inspection Panel. The 1996 Clarifications of Certain Aspects of the Resolution emphasize that an affected party means "any two or more persons who share some common interests or concerns."[13]

Apart from the issue of a requester's standing before the Panel, the Board authorized an investigation in the case at hand with respect to the issues of environmental assessment, involuntary resettlement and indigenous people on the basis of the Panel's recommendation. Later, a report was sent to the Board by the Panel, including its findings which confirmed that remedial actions proposed by Management after the Board had approved of an investigation by the Panel would satisfactorily meet the Bank's requirements if diligently followed.[14] The Panel's report also expressed some concerns about inadequate economic analysis of the project. However, the matter became moot after the Bank's President commissioned a comprehensive internal review, on the basis of which he decided later not to proceed with the project.[15]

Daniel D. Bradlow, A Test Case for the World Bank, 11 American University Journal of International Law and Policy 247, 261 (1996) (arguing against an interpretation of the term "affected party" as requiring a commonality of interests from complainants by making the case that such a requirement would unduly restrict access to the Panel and, for example, exclude individuals who are affected by the same Bank-financed project, but on different grounds).

13 *See* Clarifications, *supra* note 7, on the term "affected party" in the section on eligibility and access.

14 *See* Request for Inspection: Panel Investigation Report – Nepal Arun III Proposed Hydroelectric Project (INSP/SecM95-3), June 22, 1995.

15 *See* Nepal Arun III Proposed Hydroelectric Project – Management Response to the Inspection Panel's Investigation Report (INSP/SecM95-5), August 2, 1995.

2. *Compensation for Expropriated Assets – Papassinos/Ethiopia*

In March 1995, the Panel received its second complaint on behalf of two Greek citizens.[16] In their complaint the requesters alleged that the Bank (IDA) had failed to comply with a specific Bank policy by continuing to lend to Ethiopia, although the latter country had not compensated them for the expropriation of their assets. According to the policy referred to by the complainants, the Bank has to take a borrowing country's position with respect to an alien's expropriated property into account in its lending if this position is substantially affecting the country's international credit standing.[17] In May 1995, the Panel decided that it would not register the request because the requesters had failed to exhaust local remedies for their compensation claim and consequently had not shown that the failure of the government to compensate them was caused by the Bank's continued lending to Ethiopia.[18]

Management also concluded that the request should not be registered but for different reasons than the Panel had put forward. In the view of Management, the request was outside the scope of the Panel's mandate because neither the requester's claim nor the allegedly violated policy did relate to the design, appraisal or implementation of a project.[19]

Before the divergent views were taken up in the Board, a discussion between Management and the Panel took place on the issues of which policies and procedures and which projects would be covered by the Panel's mandate under the Resolution. As a result of that discussion, Management and the Panel stated their common understanding that (i) the Panel's mandate is limited to reviewing compliance with Bank policies and procedures with respect to the design, appraisal and/or implementation of projects as provided for in the Resolution; and (ii) the term "project" as used in the Resolution and the above mentioned memoranda has the same meaning as used in Bank

---

[16] *See* First Annual Report of the Inspection Panel, *supra* note 2, at 56 (summarizing the details of the Request for Inspection: Compensation for Expropriation and Extension of IDA Credits to Ethiopia).

[17] *See* OMS 1.28 on Disputes over Defaults on External Debt, Expropriation, and Breach of Contract requiring the Bank "not to lend for projects in a country if it considers that the position taken by it with respect to alien owners of expropriated property is substantially affecting its international credit standing."

[18] *Id.*

[19] *See* Memorandum from the President ad interim to the Executive Directors, Request for Inspection: Compensation for Expropriation and Extension of IDA credits to Ethiopia (IDA/R95-83), dated May 30, 1995.

practice, i.e. including in principle programs and activities other than specific physical works.[20]

In July 1995, the Board decided to approve the decision not to register the request expressly following Management's arguments in its decision. The 1996 Clarifications confirmed this approach.[21] They state that the Panel's mandate does not extend to reviewing the consistency of the Bank's practice with any of its policies and procedures without qualification, but, as stated in the Resolution, is limited to cases of alleged failure by the Bank to follow its operational policies and procedures with respect to the design, appraisal and/or implementation of projects, including cases of alleged failure by the Bank to follow-up on the borrower's obligations under loan agreements, with respect to such policies and procedures. The Clarifications also provide that the word "project" as used in the Resolution has the same meaning as it generally has in the Bank's practice, and includes both projects under consideration by Bank Management as well as projects already approved by the Executive Directors.

3. Emergency Power Project – Tanzania

Failure to follow provisions in IDA's Articles of Agreement on the consideration of alternative private sector financing before approving IDA financing and failure to follow environmental policies were mentioned in the third request.[22] This request was submitted in March 1995 by a group of US and Tanzanian citizens (as, respectively, owners and employees of a corporation) and concerned an IDA-financed power project in Tanzania. In this case, the Panel did not recommend an investigation, because of the complainants' failure to show non-consideration of alternative financing, a violation of environmental policies, or the project's adverse environmental effect.[23] The Board took notice of, and approved the Panel's recommendation not to investigate on a no-objection basis in September 1995.

---

20 *See* Memorandum to the Executive Directors and Alternates, Scope of the Mandate of the Inspection Panel: Compensation for Expropriation and Extension of IDA Credits to Ethiopia, dated June 16, 1995.

21 *See* Clarifications, *supra* note 7, on the meaning of the terms "project" and "policies and procedures" in the section on eligibility and access.

22 *See* Request for Inspection – Tanzania: Power VI Project, Panel Recommendation (INSP/SecM95-6), August 16, 1995 (including in Annex 1 the text of the request itself).

23 *Id.* at para. 15. (Panel Recommendation.)

4. Rondonia Natural Resources Management Project – Brazil

In the fourth request registered in June 1995, a group of NGO's from the state of Rondonia in Brazil acting as agents of Rondonia residents regarding the Bank-financed Rondonia Natural Resources Management Project (PLANAFLORO) claimed non-compliance with a number of Bank (IBRD) policies, including the environmentally relevant policies on forestry, wildlands, indigenous people and NGO participation.[24] Alleged non-compliance with other policies concerned those on investment lending, accounting, financial reporting and auditing, project monitoring and evaluation, procurement, use of consultants, project supervision, and borrower compliance with audit covenants, suspension of disbursements.

On the basis of an initial field study, the Panel recommended to the Board that an investigation into a potential violation of policies related to the design, appraisal, and execution (i.e. supervision and monitoring of the execution of PLANAFLORO) was warranted.[25]

The Panel did not recommend an investigation of the Bank's compliance with its procurement and use of consultants guidelines because of an earlier decision that such matters would not be within its mandate. In the course of a query from a Bangladeshi NGO, the Panel, after having received the Board's approval of its approach, had clarified in its response to the NGO in April 1995 that the provision of the Resolution excluding complaints against procurement decisions of borrowers from the scope of the Panel's mandate would extend to procurement decisions by the Bank.[26] Quoting from the General Counsel's book on the Inspection Panel[27] and noting that there was a separate procedure for addressing complaints related to procurement, the Panel stated that procurement decisions by the Bank, while not expressly mentioned in the Resolution, were meant to be excluded from the Panel's jurisdiction. The 1996 Clarifications later confirmed that no procurement action is subject to inspection by the Panel, whether taken by the Bank or by the borrower.[28]

After receipt of the Panel's recommendation, the Board asked the Panel to conduct an additional review to further substantiate the materiality of damages

---

[24] *See* Request for Inspection – Brazil: Rondonia Natural Resources Management Project, Panel Recommendation (INSP/R95-2), August 18, 1995 (including in Annex 1 the text of the request itself). For Management's initial response to the request, *see* Annex 2 of the Panel's Recommendation.

[25] *Id.* at para. 14. (Panel Recommendation.)

[26] *See* First Annual Report of the Inspection Panel, *supra* note 2, at 55-56.

[27] *See* Shihata, The World Bank Inspection Panel, *supra* note 1, at 51-52.

[28] *See* Clarifications, *supra* note 7, on the issue of procurement decisions in the section on eligibility and access.

and to establish whether such damages were caused by deviation from Bank policies and procedures. This step was not based on an explicit provision in the Resolution. The Resolution limits the first phase of the inspection process to ascertaining the eligibility of the request, normally completed within the 21 days stated in the Resolution.[29] In this case, however, the Board concluded that it needed more factual information on which to base a decision on whether an investigation should be carried out than was provided to it in the Panel's report.

The Panel submitted an additional report to the Board after Management had informed it of the status of the project's implementation (in particular on a remedial action plan agreed with the government of Brazil). Based on the Panel's additional report[30] and the comprehensive Management report[31] on the status of the project's implementation (which included a remedial action plan agreed with the government of Brazil), the Board decided in January 1996 not to authorize an investigation but to review the execution of the action plan after six to nine months with the assistance of the Panel. That review was completed, as envisaged, to the Board's satisfaction.

The handling by the Panel, Management and the Board of this request is important in two aspects. In one, it contributed to the above-mentioned Clarifications on the Resolution of the Inspection Panel. In the other, it foreshadowed debates calling for a second review of the resolution.

The Board's request for an additional review of the facts of the case by the Panel later prompted a discussion on an extension of the original 21-day period for the Panel's ascertainment of the eligibility of the request during the review process. The Panel argued in favor of such an extension that the Board had modified requirements of the Resolution by asking the Panel for additional information during the preliminary review stage, information which is sometimes equivalent to the contents of an investigation.[32] For the production of that information, the 21-day period provided for in the Resolution would not be adequate. Responding to the experience in the Rondonia case and following the Panel's arguments, the Board decided in the course of the first review of the Resolution that the first phase of the inspection process should

---

29 *See* Resolution Establishing the Panel, *supra* note 4, at para. 19.

30 *See* Request for Inspection – Brazil: Rondonia Natural Resources Management Project, Panel Report on Additional Review (INSP/R95-4), December 12, 1995.

31 *See* Brazil: Rondonia Natural Resources Management Project, Management Report on the Status of Implementation (SecM95-1271), December 20, 1995.

32 *See* Review of the Inspection Function – Practical Suggestions Based on Experience to Date, Working Paper for the World Bank Executive Directors prepared by the Inspection Panel in November 1995.

normally be completed within the 21 days as stated in the Resolution.[33] However, in cases where the Inspection Panel believes that it would be appropriate to undertake a "preliminary assessment" of the damages alleged by the requester (in particular when such an assessment could lead to a resolution of the matter without the necessity of a full investigation), the Panel may undertake the preliminary assessment and indicate to the Board the date on which it would present its findings and recommendations as to the need, if any, for a full investigation. If the Panel needs more than eight weeks from the date of receipt of Management's comments for its assessment, it should seek Board approval for the extension, possibly on a "no-objection" basis. What is needed at this preliminary stage is not to establish that a serious violation of the Bank's policy has actually resulted in damages suffered by the affected party, but rather to establish whether the complaint is prima facie justified and warrants a full investigation.

The other aspect, which was not discussed during the first Board review of the Resolution, but the occurrence of which took place for the first time in the course of the Rondonia request, concerns the conclusion of a remedial action plan by Management after Management was given the opportunity by the Panel to respond to the request and after the Panel had submitted its recommendation on an investigation to the Board. The taking of remedial action by Management at this point in time was not envisaged by the Resolution. By contrast, the latter provides that such remedial action would be taken by Management before the request for inspection is heard by the Panel which has to satisfy itself that "the subject matter of the request has been dealt with by Management and Management has failed to demonstrate that it has followed, or is taking adequate steps to follow the Bank's policies and procedures."[34] Nevertheless, Rondonia was not the only case in which Management came up with a remedial action plan only shortly before the Board had to decide on the Panel's recommendation, thus creating a dilemma for the Board (because the latter could of course not ignore the new facts presented by Management), while, at the same time, preventing it from being able to do full justice to the Panel's thorough report and recommendation.[35]

---

[33] *See* Clarifications, *supra* note 7, on the extension of the period allowed for the understanding of a preliminary assessment under the section on the Panel's function.

[34] *See* Resolution Establishing the Panel, *supra* note 4, at para. 13.

[35] *See* Shihata, The World Bank in a Changing World, Vol. III (1998), *supra* note 1.

5. Pangue/Ralco Hydroelectric Complex – Chile

The fifth request, received in November 1995, came from a Chilean NGO, representing people living in the area in which the Pangue/Ralco complex of hydroelectric dams on a river in Chile was to be built.[36] While the requesters alleged violation of a number of IFC and Bank policies, the Panel informed the requesters and the Board about its decision not to register the complaint because it found that the request was clearly lying outside its mandate since it concerned not an IBRD or IDA project but one financed by the International Finance Corporation (IFC).[37] IFC is a legally separate affiliate of the Bank which supports private investment through loans, guarantees and participation in equity. IFC's activities are not subject to the Resolution Establishing the Panel. IFC is however in the process of studying options for an inspection mechanism by which the Bank's private sector operations may eventually be covered.[38]

6. Jamuna Bridge Project – Bangladesh

In the sixth request registered in August 1996, failure of the Bank (IDA) to comply with the policies on environmental assessment, resettlement and participation of NGOs was alleged by a Bangladeshi NGO, representing people living on mid channel islands that emerge periodically from the Jamuna River bed as a result of accretion.[39] The complaint was brought in the context of the project financing the construction of a multipurpose bridge over the Jamuna River. In particular, non-compensation for the damages that the allegedly affected people incurred as a result of their resettlement was claimed.

---

36 *See* Request for Inspection – IFC Financing of Hydroelectric Dams in the Biobío River in Chile (INSP/SecM95-8), December 1, 1995.

37 *See* First Annual Report of the Inspection Panel, *supra* note 2, at 21.

38 The system for an inspection function, which IFC and MIGA are currently considering for their respective operations, could, once approved, be extended to all private sector operations of the Bank Group including those of IBRD and IDA. For the special issues involved in the proposal of an inspection function for IFC and MIGA, *see* Proposed Inspection Mechanism for Private Sector Projects: IFC and MIGA Inspection Panel (CODE96-40), June 27, 1996, and Consultations with Private Sector Clients and Co-financiers on the Possible Establishment of an Inspection Mechanism for IFC and MIGA (CODE97-50), August 19, 1997 (internal papers not available to the public). A concrete proposal on a suitable mechanism for IFC and MIGA is expected to be submitted to the Board in early 1998.

39 *See* Request for Inspection – Bangladesh: Jamuna Bridge Project, Panel Recommendation (INSP/SecM96-14), December 2, 1996 (including in Annex 1 the text of the request itself). For Management's initial response, *see* Annex 2 of the Panel's Report and Recommendation.

The Panel noted that the initial resettlement plan of the project did not even acknowledge the existence of the char people.[40] But Management's response referred to them on the basis of an erosion and flood policy which included a system of compensation of the char dwellers affected by river erosion.[41] This erosion and flood policy was adopted by the Bangladeshi Government and the Bank after the request was registered and while Management was drafting its response. In light of the erosion and flood policy, the Panel found that an investigation was not warranted at that stage because the erosion and flood policy constituted an adequate framework for compliance by Management with the Bank's policies and procedures.[42] The Board approved the Panel's recommendation, but asked Management to provide a progress report on the project's implementation for its review, to which it would invite the Panel to participate.

7. Yacyretá Hydroelectric Project – Argentina/Paraguay

In the seventh request registered in October 1996, a Paraguayan NGO claimed on its own behalf and on behalf of people living in the project area who wished to remain anonymous that the Bank (IBRD) had, among other things, failed to follow its policies on resettlement, indigenous people, wildlands, project supervision, and environmental assessment in the design and implementation of the Yacyretá Hydroelectric Power Plant.[43] This project is co-financed by the Bank together with the Inter-American Development Bank (IDB) through a loan to Argentina on whose territory the power plant is primarily built. The project under this loan is carried out by a bi-national entity.

In its response, Management challenged the eligibility of the request in a number of respects.[44] It argued, that since the Bank loans for the Yacyretá project were all made to Argentina, and the requesters were from Paraguay, they did not reside "in the territory" of the borrower, as required by the Resolution. Also, the Paraguayan NGO could not file a claim on its own behalf because it had not been damaged. It could only do so on behalf of the

---

[40] *See* Second Annual Report of the Inspection Panel, *supra* note 2, at 10.

[41] *See* Request for Inspection – Bangladesh: Jamuna Bridge Project, Panel Recommendation (INSP/SecM96-14), December 2, 1996 (reproducing Management's response in Annex 2).

[42] *Id.* at para. 56. (Panel Recommendation.)

[43] *See* Request for Inspection – Argentina/Paraguay: Yacyretá Hydroelectric Project, Panel Recommendation (INSP/R96-2), December 26, 1996 (including in Annex 1 the text of the request itself). For Management's initial response, *see* Annex 2 of the Panel's Recommendation.

[44] *Id.* reproducing Management's response in Annex 2.

residents living close to the project site. Finally, the anonymity of the requesters would make it impossible for Management to respond to their concerns.

In its report,[45] the Panel concluded that the request was eligible because, in its view, the project had a bi-national character and the Government of Paraguay, although not the recipient of the Bank loan, had also accepted some obligations. In addition, another different loan had been made to Paraguay with an element to address the resettlement of people living in the area next to the project site. A local NGO would have the right to file a request not only on behalf of residents affected by the project but also with regard to damage to the biodiversity and other environmental conditions caused by a violation of a Bank policy even in the absence of damages to people. Anonymity would not be a reason for declaring a request ineligible, since legitimate concerns by requesters of being subject to reprisals had to be taken into consideration by the Panel. The identity of anonymous requesters would usually be checked by the Panel on the occasion of site visits.

Besides these technical issues related to the requesters' standing, the Panel found Bank policies violated. It was particularly struck by the fact that the infrastructure works were almost completed while only a third of the housing in the resettlement component was finished. Other social mitigation measures also lagged behind. The Panel therefore recommended that the Board authorize an inspection.[46]

The Board, however, did not explicitly follow that recommendation, mainly because, for the second time, Management and the borrower had meanwhile agreed on an action plan designed to take care of the problems of project implementation. Instead, the Board invited the Panel to undertake a review of the existing problems of the Yacyretá project regarding environmental and resettlement issues in order to provide an assessment of the adequacy of the action plan agreed between the Bank and the countries concerned (Argentina and Paraguay) within the next four months. The Board also stated that it expected the Panel to review consistency of the Bank's actions with its procedures while reviewing the action plan.

In the course of its review of the plan, the Panel received a number of further requests asking for inspection of specific aspects of project execution which were allegedly detrimental to the people, communities and environment on the Argentine side of the reservoir. Because the substance of the issues raised in these requests were the same as in the original request, the Panel, in

---

45 *Id.* at paras. 13-39. (Panel Recommendation.) *See also* Second Annual Report of the Inspection Panel, *supra* note 2, at 11.

46 *See* Request for Inspection – Argentina/Paraguay: Yacyretá Hydroelectric Project, Panel Recommendation (INSP/R96-2), December 26, 1996, at para. 43.

consultation with the Board, incorporated them into the ongoing review. By then, the Panel's review was carried out in parallel with the investigation by the inspection mechanism of the IDB. In September 1997, the Panel presented the report on its review to the Board which in substance amounted to a full investigation of the complaints submitted by the requesters.[47] That report was discussed in the Board in December 1997. On the basis of the Panel's report, the Board noted that the implementation of the action plan had made significant progress towards resolving the environmental and resettlement problems of the project. The Board, nevertheless, requested Bank Management to continue its follow-up on the implementation of the action plan and to report to it on the further progress in the matter within six months. While the Board decided not to involve the Panel in the follow-up this time, it announced that it would determine later whether it wished the Panel to play a further role in this respect.

It should be noted that in mid-September about 50 brickmakers, who had been resettled during the course of the construction of the Yacyretá Hydroelectric Project, extended their original suit for damages against the bi-national entity serving as an executing agency for the project to the Bank and IDB. The basis for the brickmakers' action against the Bank is its involvement in the preparation of the resettlement and environmental action plan. The Bank filed a motion to dismiss the claims on the basis of its immunities pursuant to its Articles of Agreement,[48] the Specialized Agency Convention,[49] the Establishment Agreement between the Bank and Argentina,[50] and the arguments that there is neither privity of contract between the Bank and the plaintiffs nor another legal basis under the applicable law of Argentina (e.g. tort law) for a claim of the plaintiffs against the Bank. In this context, it must be emphasized that the Panel's assessment of a failure by the Bank to comply with its own standards does not imply any liability on the part of the Bank under the applicable law of a borrowing country. The Panel's assessment however may indirectly contribute to the determination of borrower actions which could constitute a fault under domestic law. While the borrower's actions clearly do not fall within the Panel's mandate under the Resolution, the Panel's determi-

---

[47] *See* Request for Inspection – Argentina/Paraguay: Yacyretá Hydroelectric Project, Panel Review and Assessment (INSP/R97-10), September 18, 1997.

[48] *See* Article VII of the IBRD Articles of Agreement (outlining the scope of the Bank's immunities).

[49] *See* Convention on the Privileges and Immunities of the Specialized Agencies, approved by the General Assembly of the United Nations on November 21, 1947 and Annex VI on the application of the Convention to IBRD (United Nations Publication, ST/LEG/4/Rev. 1, Sales No. C/E/F/R/S.75.X.2, 1974).

[50] *See* Agreement between the IBRD and the Argentine Republic Concerning the Establishment of a Resident Mission in Buenos Aires, signed on December 20, 1991 (on file with the Bank).

nation of Bank actions could provide an analysis that constitutes a factual basis for those who wish to present a claim against the borrower under domestic law.

8. Jute Sector Adjustment Credit – Bangladesh

The eighth request to be reported was filed in August 1996 by a group of owners of private jute mills in Bangladesh.[51] They claimed that they had suffered economic losses due to the Bank's (IDA's) failure to follow its policies and procedures on adjustment lending, supervision of programs and suspension of disbursements in the design and implementation of the Bangladesh Jute Sector Adjustment Program. The latter intended to restructure Bangladesh's jute manufacturing industry according to the needs of the world's market through a number of measures such as the elimination of excess capacity by closure and downsizing of a certain number of public mills, privatization of another number of these mills, and retrenchment of employees of closed, downsized, or privatized mills. As a result of political turmoil, the conditions for the disbursement of the second tranche of the credit, originally scheduled for March 1995, were not met and the tranche consequently not released. In fact, the project was tainted with a three-year delay in implementation.

In its formal response to the request, Management asserted that all policies and procedures had been observed, and that, in any case, acts and omissions in relation to the implementation of adjustment credits – in contrast to investment credits – were the sole responsibility of the borrower and the request, therefore, was outside the Panel's mandate.[52]

The Panel concluded that the request was eligible since, in its view, the requesters had suffered the alleged harm caused by the Bank's failure to ensure sufficient political commitment and to maintain certain macroeconomic policies as required under the Bank's adjustment lending policy, and to supervise the general macro-economic framework under the supervision of programs policy.[53] In the Panel's eyes, the Bank also failed to discuss remedies other than the non-release of the second tranche of the credit such as suspension and cancellation of the credit as prescribed in the policy on suspension of disbursement in order to sanction the non-implementation of the

---

[51] *See* Request for Inspection – Bangladesh: Jute Sector Adjustment Credit, Panel Report and Recommendation (INSP/R97-3), March 20, 1997 (including in Annex 1 the text of the request itself).

[52] *Id.* reproducing Management's response in Annex 2.

[53] *Id.* at paras. 87-89. (Panel Recommendation.)

program by Bangladesh. The Panel generally rejected Management's argument that it had no mandate to review the implementation of adjustment credits, a view which had been reinforced by a legal opinion from the Bank's Deputy General Counsel (Operations) who listed a range of remedies that would be available to the Bank in the case of non-compliance with implementation covenants of adjustment credits. However, because the new Government of Bangladesh and the Bank were negotiating a revised timetable for the implementation of the program and an extension for the credit's closing date, the Panel did not find an investigation useful at that stage and, therefore, did not recommend one to the Board.[54]

The Board agreed with the Panel's conclusion not to investigate, without determining whether it would follow the Panel's reasoning in all respects. In June 1997, Management allowed this loan to close.

In the absence of a Board decision on some substantive issues related to this request, some questions remain to be answered in future. Among them is the question of whether the Bank has a responsibility for the implementation of adjustment programs as the Deputy General Counsel (Operations) had suggested in his opinion on the basis of remedies available to the Bank in the case of non-compliance by the borrower with covenants in adjustment credit agreements. Another open question is whether the provisions in the Bank's policies on adjustment lending include provisions on rights or interests of individuals in the sense of the Resolution's eligibility requirements.[55] This question is legitimate because sectoral adjustment policies only address the sector as a whole and require the maintenance of a macro economic policy framework by the borrowing country's government without describing individualized rights. The Panel simply assumed that policies and procedures on adjustment programs would also include descriptions of rights or interests of individuals which could be adversely affected by the Bank's non-compliance with these policies and procedures. Were the Panel's reasoning correct, requesters could successfully challenge Bank actions in the context of an adjustment operation if they were part of the sector which the program addresses and if they suffered economic losses or failed to make expected profits as a result of the non-implementation of an adjustment program or the

[54] *Id.* at para. 89. (Panel Recommendation.)

[55] For a definition of rights or interests under the Resolution, *see* Shihata, The World Bank Inspection Panel, *supra* note 1, at 54. *See also* Bradlow & Schlemmer-Schulte, *supra* note 1, at 404 (analyzing the Bank's policies and procedures for their rights and interests contents in terms of formal and substantive due process requirements as well as emphasizing that the policies and procedures must include mandatory rules in order to create rights and interests of individuals in the sense of the Resolution's requirements).

non-adherence to the general policy framework guidelines.[56] It will be for the Board to determine whether ultimate beneficiaries of an adjustment program qualify as holders of rights or interests under Bank policies and procedures.

9. Itaparica Resettlement and Irrigation Project – Brazil

The ninth request, received in March 1997, concerned a resettlement and irrigation project in Itaparica, Brazil.[57] A local union of rural workers representing people living in the project area alleged the Bank's violation of its policies for dam and reservoir projects, on environmental assessment, involuntary resettlement, and indigenous people.

The Panel recommended investigation of the complaint but sought the Board's confirmation that it was not time-barred which, under the Resolution, is, among other criteria, the case when 95 percent of the loan financing the project is disbursed.[58] The project was initially financed by a Bank loan, which was fully disbursed. It was however later further financed by a supplemental loan – introduced through an amendment of the original loan agreement – which was almost, but not quite 95 percent disbursed. The General Counsel issued a legal opinion confirming that, in such a constellation, a request would not be time-barred.[59]

In September 1997, the Board, while avoiding the issue of time-limits on the eligibility of complaints, decided not to authorize an investigation, for the third time because of a remedial action plan, prepared after Management's initial response on the request to the Panel and to be fully financed by the Government of Brazil. The Board concluded that the Bank should help supervise the implementation of the Brazilian Government Action Plan which required the disbursement of an additional $290 million for the purpose of the project to ensure completion of works providing productive infrastructure and technical assistance to resettlers. It should be noted that both the action plan and the request for Bank supervision of its implementation were initiated by

---

56 The question of a violation of rights or interests of individuals in connection with adjustment programs has been raised earlier. *See* Enrique R. Carrasco & M. Ayhan Kose, Income Distribution and the Bretton Woods Institutions: Promoting an Enabling Environment for Social Development, 6 Transnational Law & Contemporary Problems 1, 45 (1996) (discussing whether the Panel's jurisdiction covers adjustment lending).

57 *See* Request for Inspection – Brazil: Itaparica Resettlement and Irrigation Project, Panel Recommendation (INSP/R97-7), June 27, 1997 (reproducing the request in Annex 1). For Management's initial response to the request, *see* Annex 2 to the Panel's Recommendation.

58 *Id.* at para. 46. (Panel Recommendation.)

59 *See* Ibrahim F.I. Shihata, Legal Opinion of the Senior Vice President and General Counsel, Time-Limits on the Eligibility of Complaints Submitted to the Inspection Panel (SecM97-693), July 28, 1997.

the Brazilian Government. The Board decided further that it would review the progress of the project in a year and invite the Panel to assist in that review.

It should be noted that the Board during its September 1997 meeting on this request decided to hold a further review on the general role of the Panel and the Resolution establishing it.

10. NTPC Power Generation Project – India

In the tenth case, received in May 1997, residents in the Singrauli area of India, where the National Thermal Power Corporation (NTPC) operates and is expanding a number of coal-powered generating facilities, claimed non-compliance by the Bank with its policies on environmental assessment, involuntary resettlement and indigenous people.[60] Management recognized its partial failure to observe some of the policies involved in its response to the request and submitted a detailed remedial action plan.[61]

Despite that plan, the Board, in September 1997, approved the Panel's recommendation for an investigation by the Panel of the Bank's role in the power generation project. But bearing in mind that the Panel had already undertaken a preliminary review at the project site, the Board decided that the investigation should be conducted at the Bank's headquarters in Washington. The Panel was asked to report its findings to the Board within three months. At that point, the Board would decide whether any further action would be deemed appropriate. The Board took also notice of the action program of corrective measures prepared by Bank Management and requested periodic progress reports on the implementation of that program.

The Panel presented its report on the limited investigation it conducted in the NTPC case in December 1997.[62] In this report, the Panel noted that it found the violations of Bank policies and procedures regarding the involuntary resettlement and associated aspects of the project (of which it had found prima facie evidence in its earlier recommendation) confirmed by its desk study. The Panel's report is expected to be discussed in the Board in early 1998.

---

[60] *See* Request for Inspection – India: NTPC Power Generation Project, Panel Report and Recommendation (INSP/R97-9), July 25, 1997 (including in Annex 1 the text of the request itself).

[61] *Id.* Memorandum on India: NTPC Power Generation Project, Management Response to Request for Inspection, June 3, 1997, reprinted in Annex 3 of the Panel's Report and Recommendation regarding this request.

[62] *See* Request for Inspection – India: NTPC Power Generation Project, Panel Report on the Investigation (INSP/R97-15), December 24, 1997.

III. Conclusion

It is interesting to note that, of the eight registered cases, the Panel recommended an investigation in five cases, while the Board formally approved the Panel's recommendation in favor of an investigation in only two cases (i.e. the first and the last case brought before the Panel).[63] In three cases the Panel did not recommend an investigation. In these three cases, the Board took notice of the Panel's recommendation against an investigation and approved of it, while, under the Resolution, it would have had the possibility to nevertheless direct the Panel to investigate the cases.

Aside from the existence of a formal authorization by the Board to the Panel to carry out an investigation as described in the Resolution, the Panel altogether played an active role in the supervision of the implementation of projects in six cases. (These cases are Nepal Arun, Rondonia, Jamuna Bridge, Yacyretá, Itaparica, and NTPC.) In all these cases, a remedial action plan had been adopted by Management. In four of these six cases, the action plan had been adopted after Management had had the opportunity to respond to the requests (Nepal Arun, Rondonia, Yacyretá, and Itaparica). In two cases (Jamuna Bridge and NTPC), the action plan had been taken at the same time that Management was drafting its response and was referred to in that response. The Panel's role in these six cases consisted either in assisting in the review of the implementation of the remedial action plan (Rondonia, Jamuna Bridge, Yacyretá, and Itaparica), or in carrying out the investigation itself (Arun Nepal and NTPC). Consequently, it may be said that, while the Board decided to formally authorize an investigation in only two cases, the Panel has had an impact in more than these two cases.

The cases have helped clarify a number of aspects under the Resolution. Among them figure the interpretations of terms in the Resolution such as "affected party, i.e. a group of persons with a common interest," "policies and procedures, i.e. those related to the design, appraisal and/or implementation of projects but not any policies," "projects, i.e. all types of Bank programs and activities," and "excluded procurement decisions, i.e. those by both the borrower and the Bank." The difficulties of interpreting other terms such as a requester "in the territory of the borrower," "rights or interests" of requesters, time-limits for requests under subsequent loans, and the follow-up on borrower's obligations in the context of the implementation of adjustment

---

[63] It may be noted that the Board's decision not to authorize an investigation but to undertake a review of the implementation of a project, provide an assessment of the adequacy of measures agreed between the Bank and the borrowing countries concerned, and review the consistency of Bank actions with Bank procedures in a third case did in fact amount to an investigation. *See* Shihata, The World Bank in a Changing World, Vol. III (1998), *supra* note 1.

loans have been discussed, while final decisions on the interpretation of these terms have not yet been made.

Procedurally, it has been interesting to see that the Panel's role to look into the subject-matter in the first stage of a request has been strengthened after the experience in the Rondonia case. Also, remedial action plans, while they have not been envisaged by the Resolution to be taken at the time they were mostly taken, have not in all cases prevented an investigation. One investigation has been approved by the Board and the Board asked for assistance in the supervision of project implementation under the action plan by the Panel in the other cases in which remedial action plans had been adopted. One of the tasks of the second review, which the Board decided to hold in September 1997 and which is expected to be completed in 1998, will be to decide whether the discretionary power which the Board exercised in handling the cases where Management had initiated remedial action plans should be kept, the approach which the Board took most often, i.e. not to authorize an investigation but to ask the Panel for assistance, be formalized, or the procedures be completely changed.

Institutional and Procedural Aspects of the Inspection Panel

Richard E. Bissell[*]

The creation and functioning of the Inspection Panel has become a singular and debated event in the evolution of the World Bank in the 1990s. The Executive Directors of the Bank established the Panel in response to growing public debate over the social and environmental effects of Bank lending, and especially the unresolved controversy surrounding the Narmada project in India. Instead of ending such debates over Bank projects, the Panel has become the visible focus of acrimony over the Bank's attempt to institutionalize and regularize the access of ordinary people to the corridors of power in the Bank. Given the essential characteristic of the Panel in attempting to fulfill the aspirations of the Executive Directors to democratize the World Bank, it may be understandable that the outcome is anything other than neat and orderly. For that reason one has to consider the Panel in the different contexts in which it was created and in which it now attempts to carry out its mandate. This paper will first examine those contexts, and then discuss three of the most important areas of disagreement that have emerged in the practice of the Board, Bank Management, and the Panel itself with regard to the inspection process.

The 50th anniversary of the World Bank in 1994 came amidst a global revolution, characterized by the collapse of communism, growing democratization, proliferating institutions of civil society, and a concomitant demand for accountability of public institutions. For the Bank, such a sea change became manifest in the public protests and the fundamentally different world in which it had to operate, as opposed to 1944, and has led to pressures for reform of its traditional operating culture. Indeed, a key element of that reform effort – the introduction of accountability and transparency of the World Bank to its grass-roots constituents – has engaged not only the Bank group itself, but now has the potential to alter the paradigm for governance of all international financial institutions.

---

* Richard E. Bissell was a founding member of the Inspection Panel from 1994 until 1997, as well as Chairman from 1996-1997. He is now Coordinator of the Interim Secretariat of the World Commission on Dams.

The essential question posed by this challenge to past modes of governance in the 1990s is whether a highly formalistic institution can find an avenue for structuring the dialogue with the most disorganized but democratic constituencies in the world – the grassroots – without damaging the essential characteristics and strengths of both sides. Put another way, the Bank group has always operated in a hierarchical structure that also sought consensus, with the incentive system designed to reinforce an internally-focused decision-making system. With the onset of the democratic revolution worldwide, the Bank has been reminded that it is a public institution, and that it needs to find a way to "democratize" itself through giving the ultimate beneficiaries of Bank-financed projects a "voice" in Bank operations. The task, then, has been to design a window for access to this internally-focused bank that the increasingly enfranchised grassroots were able to comfortably access in order to express their views about the work of the World Bank; at the same time, civil society had to play this role without losing its essential characteristic of reflecting public sentiments and being grounded in local public opinion. As a result, the two sides of the same coin, "participation" and "accountability," have recently taken on new meaning for the Executive Directors, management and staff of the Bank, as well as those engaged within borrowing countries.

Changing accountability at the Bank

The World Bank group has two different sets of accountability issues. On the one hand, those institutions focusing on public sector lending – the International Bank for Reconstruction and Development (IBRD) and the International Development Association (IDA) – have greater control over the design of the projects they fund and have more explicit public policy agendas to accomplish through the overall lending programs. On the other hand, the institutions focusing on private sector lending and guarantees – the International Finance Corporation (IFC) and the Multilateral Investment Guaranty Authority (MIGA) – have traditionally paid less attention to public policy issues and have significantly less leverage over their project partners. Many outsiders paid scant attention to this difference until it was highlighted by the need to increase accountability of the Bank group generally, and it was found that consistent practice might be impossible in the divergent approaches taken by component institutions towards questions of public interest.

Accountability based upon compliance with stated policies of the Bank also made a major shift in the early 1990s. Historically, the operational policies and procedures of the Bank were internal regulatory structures. They were not open for public review, and while they circulated widely among development specialists as widely admired standards for all development institutions, the Bank used them simply as formal parameters to guide the discussion between operational departments and central legal/policy staff about the wisdom of particular investments. Most policies were considered "confidential" and for many years it was a violation of Bank policy to release them publicly. With the decision to open them up and to tolerate public scrutiny of projects based on those policies, Bank management and the Board of Executive Directors changed the rules of the game. They apparently thought that the reassurances from staff that projects complied with all operational policies of the Bank would stand the Bank in good stead with the public; in hindsight, they may regret that decision.

The emergence of public accountability took place in a fashion to which Bank management was unaccustomed, demanded by outside groups and achieved through demonstrations, acts of national legislatures, and grassroots-oriented members of the Board at the Bank. A prolonged argument in the 1980s over the real contribution of the Bank – and especially its structural adjustment programs – to the development of aid recipients brought its activities under increasing scrutiny. Some of the arguments derived from well-established differences over what constituted "development;" others focused on the fact that certain regions of the world (especially Africa) were not showing sustainable improvements of broad-based measures of economic and social welfare expected in the wake of adjustment programs. The early years of that debate were largely characterized by "ships passing in the night," with outside critics making broad charges against Bank lending programs and related conditionality, and the Bank responding with its own data that failed to persuade those arguing a more general case without access to the Bank's information base.

Nevertheless, the Bank emerged in the late 1980s as the best-placed donor to drive development planning, owing to the relative shrinkage of the bilateral donors, and the Bank's focus on the economic decision-making nodes in borrowing governments. The Bank gradually built a formidable structure of economic decision-makers in many developing countries, either through training of host-country experts and/or through placement of expatriates, and yet continued to give lower priority to the effects of its endeavors on the ground. As a result, some bilateral donors and the growing civil society operating at the grassroots could only see the negative effects of Bank lending on the lives of ordinary people. The development world increasingly split into two camps, micro and macro, and the Bank became the symbol of everything right and wrong with the macro perspective. Bank leadership came to recognize the depth and bitterness of the grassroots complaints when a large coalition of NGOs called for dismantling the Bank on its 50th anniversary.

The Bank strongly supported, if in a *sotta voce*, the integration of accountability and transparency into national development planning within borrower countries.[1]

Public accountability became watchwords at the Bank. It was to be achieved, not only through the traditional mechanism of government representatives, but also through transparency and increased participation by the public in the affairs of the Bank. Special emphasis was placed on those members of the public who were identified as the intended beneficiaries of Bank projects. They were to be given a greater role in the entire development process, as well as more open participation in individual projects financed by the Bank. The Bank's policy on release of information to the public, for instance, was gradually reversed. Where the Bank had previously considered all information proprietary and confidential unless there were a compelling reason to release it, a 1989 directive from then-President Barber Conable stated that there was a "presumption in favor of disclosure, unless there were a compelling reason to withhold it."[2] Nevertheless, there were many reasons given for withholding information. A 1993 clarification and strengthening of the directive pushed Bank Management and staff in the direction of greater release of Bank information; yet to the present day, the Bank has yet to issue an Operational Policy on information disclosure. At the level of project design and implementation, new guidance from the top argued that increased participation by the beneficiaries of Bank projects should be involved. Consultation was valued for improving the design, and partnerships with the grassroots were essential for improving the likelihood of positive outcomes.

Nevertheless, the leadership at the Bank had no template for this process. What did it mean to "democratize a Bank?" In fact, would it be necessary to stop thinking about the group of institutions as a "bank," and instead to see them as "development agencies?" Concerns were expressed by many about this trend, especially among borrowing governments that now saw that power was being offered by the Bank to their own citizens who sometimes had little experience with democratic responsibilities. Among ministries of finance there was concern the Bank would fall into populist traps. Some Executive Directors argued for window-dressing, i.e., just enough grassroots participation to make local communities feel better, but not enough to give the public any real power. These issues all came to a head with the call for the creation of an Inspection Panel, to ensure that the people directly affected by a Bank-

---

1 See Samuel Paul, *Does Voice Matter? For Public Accountability, Yes,* Washington: The World Bank, Policy Research Working Paper 1388, December 1994.

2 The World Bank and International Finance Corporation, *Directive on Disclosure of Information*, July 1989, mimeo, p. 2.

financed project would have an enforcement mechanism to make the Bank live up to its policies and legal commitments.

CREATION OF THE INSPECTION FUNCTION

The support for establishment of an inspection mechanism came from a number of sources, both external and internal to the Bank, and without each of them, it is unlikely that this experiment would have been undertaken. Internally, the Bank installed new leadership in late 1991, when Lewis Preston took the reins as President. Preston saw immediately the need to find ways to bring fresh breezes to the old bank's hallways. With his encouragement, the Bank undertook a massive review of Bank supervision, implementation, and performance in 1992 directed by a former senior vice-president, Willi Wappenhans, whose series of reports to the President and the Board made it clear that the institution was suffering from hardening of the arteries. Old projects were clogging the passageways, and the existing mechanisms for supervision, audit, and evaluation needed strengthening at a minimum, although Wappenhans did not personally support an independent inspection function.

The rethinking within the Bank dovetailed with pressure from outside. The most vocal criticism focused on a single target, the Sardar Sarovar irrigation/hydroelectric project on the Narmada river in India, with the potential to displace more than 120,000 people from their homes at the proposed reservoir, and a similar number displaced by related irrigation works. An independent review of this project commissioned by the Bank, led by former UNDP Administrator Bradford Morse, began submitting its reports in mid-1992. The Narmada project, according to the Morse Commission, was the Bank's worst nightmare – badly designed, in violation of Bank policies on resettlement, inadequately supervised, and certain to inflict widespread misery on a quarter-million project-area residents who were going to be "victims" instead of "beneficiaries." The conclusion of this investigation – irrespective of the fact that India canceled further World Bank involvement in Narmada – was clear to the Executive Directors: (1) Bank-financed projects suffered from major implementation problems that might have been avoided with clearer, stronger design processes; (2) the Bank had inadequate internal corrective mechanisms; and (3) therefore, the Bank needed an ongoing mechanism to ensure compliance with Bank policies and to improve project quality. It was equally clear to some Executive Directors that they had to take greater responsibility for such follow-up without actually taking over management of the Bank. When faced with this challenge on the Indian project, however, the Directors found that they did not have the capabilities or the instincts for such a task; the Board had long relied on Management to such an extent that existing systems did not provide for real Board oversight of project implementation or compliance with policies. Protests over Narmada were damaging support for the Bank within their own governments; for example, the U.S. Congress attached a condition to the IDA X appropriation insisting on creation of an independent inspection function. The Board decided that they needed a permanent inspection panel to help them deal with these growing public disputes. As a result, after much discussion with the senior management of the Bank and consideration of various models from national governments (e.g., ombudsman, appeals commission, inspector-general), the Board felt confident to go forward with a tailor-made plan for an independent Inspection Panel, formally agreed to in resolutions by the IBRD and IDA Boards on September 23, 1993.[3] It would take another eleven months, however, for the President to recruit Panel members and for the Panel to become operational.

The application of the concept of accountability in the resolution creating the Panel was a source of much reflection and occasionally open debate. The variety of democracies and non-democracies represented around the Board table made for lively misunderstandings and compromises about the role to be played by the Bank vis-à-vis its larger constituencies. Ordinary people in borrowing countries, after all, were not those demanding the creation of the Inspection Panel; all they wanted was relief from a sense of being victimized. With regard to the Bank, they were so disenfranchised and distant that they were not consulted in the creation of this new mechanism for their benefit.[4] The most vocal representatives of the grassroots beneficiaries of Bank projects were international NGOs, generally based in North America or Western Europe, which had spearheaded the campaign to question the impact of Bank financing on the welfare of poor communities in the developing world. That very campaign, however, had antagonized many of the Executive Directors against the international NGOs, and those Directors were determined not to allow the creation of the Panel to unduly enfranchise that segment of the NGO community. At the same time, because Bank management was moving increasingly towards partnerships with many other NGOs for design participation and project implementation, there was an attempt to segregate "good NGOs" from "problem NGOs" in the debate. The argument was made that foreign NGOs could not legitimately represent local populations, which was

---

[3] Resolution of the Executive Directors establishing the Inspection Panel (No. 93-10 for the IBRD and 93-6 for IDA), September 23, 1993.

[4] By way of contrast, when the Bank group considered an inspection mechanism for the IFC and MIGA in 1996, it went out of its way to consult with their primary customer base – the private financial community that is instrumental in bringing projects to the IFC and MIGA for co-financing.

answered by the call to recognize that some countries were not democratic enough to permit local NGOs to represent communities at the grassroots. While the Resolution establishing the Panel framed a compromise, the issue was never laid to rest and continues to poison Board debates on specific inspection requests.

The solution for defining accountability was to focus on those directly affected by Bank projects, and empower them to bring a complaint to the Inspection Panel. To answer those who suggested that people at the grassroots might be too intimidated or unschooled to develop such a formal complaint, it was allowed that such affected communities could name a representative on their behalf, but that it should be a "local representative."[5] If local people wished to have an international NGO represent them, the burden of proof was on them to show that there was no local representation available.

Having focused on the target population for seeking relief from the Panel, however, the Board then delimited very precisely the scope of a possible complaint. What the Board wanted to avoid was the possibility that the Panel would be flooded with complaints. The Board thus put in place a series of eligibility hurdles, some of which turned out to be so formalistic as to discourage possible requesters from even approaching the Panel. There was thus some confusion at the beginning between "access," which was presumably universal among grassroots stakeholders, and "eligibility criteria," which were meant to enable the Panel to focus only on the most worthy requests received.

To deal with the issue of borrower sovereignty, the Board also wanted to reduce the likelihood that a mechanism at the Bank would become a means of addressing domestic complaints about borrowing governments. In this sense, the Board wanted to re-state its formal role as a bank, whose principal interest was in ensuring the application of sound, sustainable banking principles. A principal issue was to keep the Panel from investigating the actions of borrowing governments. Thus, it was intended to investigate only a possible "action or omission of the Bank as a result of a failure of the Bank to follow its operational policies and procedures with respect to the design, appraisal and/or implementation of a project designed by the Bank ... provided in all cases that such failure has had, or threatens to have, a material adverse effect."[6] It severely restricted the scope of any possible investigation undertaken by the Panel. And above all, it attempted to restore a formal relationship between the Bank and borrower governments that all observers knew had been breached for decades; there was in fact an unclear boundary between responsibilities of the Bank and a borrower, and yet to limit the potential liability of

---

5 Paragraph 12 of the Resolution.

6 *Ibid.*

each partner before the Panel, the legally-defined division of labor was restated. Again, the Board had muddled two different issues: with regard to potential "violation of policies," only the Bank could be at risk. On the other hand, with regard to real or potential "negative effects or damage" to the interests of requesters, the Bank, the borrower, and the implementing agency were inevitably going to be jointly under review by the Panel, and yet the Resolution of the Board made no provision for sorting out the effects of such findings by the Panel. By implication, the issue was left in the hands of Bank Management, thus putting the Borrower and the implementing agencies at a disadvantage. Borrowers have reacted to this issue by expressing hostility to the Panel mechanism itself.

PUTTING INDEPENDENT ACCOUNTABILITY TO WORK

The independent Inspection Panel based its initial actions on the Resolution passed by the Board, along with partial recollections of various Executive Directors and a published interpretation of the Resolution by the Bank's General Counsel.[7] As a result, the new Panel moved rapidly to convert these fragments of primary information into operational procedures, immediately published as a short booklet for use by the general public in August 1994. For the Panel, the first question was how to connect the newly-acquired "accountability" with an equally important and pragmatic issue of "accessibility." Reduced to its starkest image, how would a dissatisfied peasant in a rice paddy of Asia find out how to complain, and then deliver a cogent request for inspection, to this new Inspection Panel in Washington, DC?

Access is a major conundrum for modern democratizing movements. The very large political units in which people participate inevitably create a special class of constituents who are able to gain access to decision-makers. In some cases, money provides the access. In others, access may be limited to those with a special vocabulary. For instance, are non-economists ever treated seriously in open discussions of Bank structural adjustment programs? In this case, the Executive Directors stated that they wanted to enfranchise the weakest and most peripheral people in the global financial system, and yet laid out a legalistic blueprint for obtaining access to the Panel. How many people directly affected by Bank-financed projects would be able to obtain, read and understand Bank policy statements? And then understand how to "request an inspection" of a Bank-financed project?

---

[7] Later published by Ibrahim I.F. Shihata as *The World Bank Inspection Panel*, published for the World Bank by Oxford University Press, 1994.

The Panel faced a variety of issues in the first three years: some were derived from arguments over eligibility and access; some were fundamental differences over the nature of the Panel's task; and other issues focused on the outcomes and remedies to be sought in the Panel process.

a. Eligibility Issues

With regard to eligibility, the Panel attempted to maximize access within the terms of the Board Resolution. It was clear that many members of the Board had visions of more restricted access than was the view of the Panel members. Indeed, the price for some of the Executive Directors for creating the Panel appeared to be confidence on their part that most complaints would be determined to be ineligible. If applied restrictively, the provisions of the Resolution would surely have created barriers so high that only trained international lawyers would be able to leap over them.

In the first case brought to the Panel in October 1994, the Nepal Arun Hydroelectric Project, the petition was filed by "the Arun Concerned Group, the local residents of the Sankhuwa-Sawa District, and the citizens of Nepal." With the first case, therefore, the issue of access and eligibility was muddled. Unclear as to how to deal with the eligibility provisions of the Resolution, the principal signatories, Gopal Siwakoti and Ganesh Kumar Ghimire, had decided to claim various types of affected status in order to get their concerns about the Arun III Hydroelectric Project into an inspection. Questions were raised about the eligibility of those two individuals because they did not live in the Arun Valley. The signatories, however, also had power of representation from several people from the Arun Valley ("the Sankhuwa-Sawa District") with a request that they be treated anonymously – for fear of retaliation from neighbors with a hostile view of their filing the request.[8]

The Panel attempted to establish some precedents in this case that would help to sort out the tangled eligibility of these requesters while giving some guidance for the future. On the one hand, the Panel found that a request on behalf of an entire country was too broad in this case, and did not accept it as a justification for eligibility. On the other hand, an NGO located in the capital city of a country did appear to satisfy the criteria of a "local NGO," an interpretation accepted by the Board. The Panel also accepted the idea of anonymity for requesters, already implicitly accepted in paragraph 18(b) of the Panel procedures where the Panel agreed to withhold from publication the

---

8 The Requesters had a history of activism on this issue; see, for instance, Gopal Siwakoti and Adam Ma'anit, *The World Bank & Nepal's Arun III Hydro Project: A Case of Anti-Social Development*, Katmandu: Inhured International, June 1995.

names of requesters who might be in danger for having approached the Panel. Nevertheless, it was important at an early stage of the inspection process that the Panel confirm the identity and concerns of those who wished to have their names withheld. The Panel asserted, and the Board agreed, that the question of eligibility was essentially for the Panel to decide (despite an attempt by Management to assert that role for themselves).

Eligibility remained a contentious issue, with the inclusion in each of the Management Responses during the first three years a section explaining why the Requesters were ineligible. The Panel itself was discriminating in determining eligibility, a point demonstrated by the next several requests presented in 1995. The cases were in Ethiopia, Tanzania, Bangladesh, and Chile.

In Ethiopia, the complaint came from Greek nationals who had experienced nationalization of property following the 1974 revolution, and had never received compensation despite the creation of a structure for that purpose by the post-Dergue government in Addis Ababa. The role of the bank revolved around a little-known policy several decades old involving the responsibility of the Bank in lending to countries with outstanding nationalization disputes. While different observers of this case wanted to draw various lessons, the Panel chose to reject the complaint as it was written since it did not appear that the Requesters had exhausted local remedies before turning to the Panel, and that they had not made clear the projects financed by the Bank that might have contributed to their losses.

The second Request came from a group of Tanzanian citizens, who believed that the Bank financing of an Emergency Power Project had damaged their interests, as Tanzanian citizens and as employees/managers of a company that did not receive the contract for the power generator. They alleged that IDA Articles of Agreement had been violated in that private sector financing was said to be available on reasonable terms. The Panel, after a preliminary review, declined to investigate the concern, since it was clear that the Management and Board had been aware of the alternative private financing at the time of approving the loan to Tanzania, and therefore the decision could not be revisited. With regard to the more direct environmental effects, the allegations, even if true, could not be documented as having an impact on the requesters. On the latter issue, the Panel decided that the Requesters were not eligible.

In a third case, the Panel received a complaint from Bangladesh, alleging that the Bank staff had improperly supervised the awarding of contracts for road rehabilitation. When this arrived in February 1995, the Panel had not yet tested the extent of the prohibition in the founding Resolution against Panel involvement in procurement matters. In one sense, the complaint dealt not with the procurement itself (which is carried out by the borrowing country, not the Bank), but rather with the nature of Bank supervision, and the Bank's accountability for the conduct of the procurement, which occurs subject to Bank approval. The Panel, in looking at the complaint, concluded that the spirit of the Board prohibition was that the Panel should not delve into procurement matters, despite whatever legal construction developed by a Requester, and so declined jurisdiction. When the Board was notified of the Panel's decision, there was no objection.

The fourth case was presented in November 1995 by an NGO from Chile representing Indian groups (the Pehuenche people) who believed their heritage and welfare was endangered by plans for a hydroelectric project on the Biobio River.[9] The different element in this request was that financing came from the International Finance Corporation of the Bank group. The IFC was the largest creditor of the Pangue/Ralco Dam Complex, and had a 2.5% equity interest in Pangue, S.A., the utility owning the facility. Under the terms of the Resolution establishing the Panel, jurisdiction did not include the IFC or MIGA out of the Bank group institutions. The Requesters knew this beforehand, but wished to file the request in order to highlight the need for accountability in the private sector lending members of the Bank group (IFC and MIGA) similar to that in the IBRD and IDA. The Panel informed the Requester that it did not have the mandate to review the project, but forwarded the complaint to President Wolfensohn, who proceeded to appoint an independent investigation team to review the charges from the NGO. At the same time, he charged the management at IFC and MIGA to come up with a workable inspection mechanism that would bring them in line with the IBRD and IDA with regard to public accountability.

In other cases, the Panel determined, despite management opposition, in favor of the eligibility of the Requesters. In the Yacryreta Hydroelectric Project of Argentina and Paraguay, Bank Management presented numerous reasons for declaring the Requesters ineligible, but the Executive Directors rejected that viewpoint in authorizing the Panel's continuing role in reviewing that project. By and large, the Board of Executive Directors shared the Panel's disquiet over Management's advocacy of rejection of Requests on narrow, legalistic grounds when common sense indicated that there had been significant adverse effects on the local population and that the Requesters met the criteria of the Resolution. The standard thus became, over time, determined less by any restrictive interpretation of the Resolution, and more by a layman's

---

[9] Grupo de Accion por el BioBio (GABB) on Behalf of Pehuenches and other Chileans, *The Biobio Dams in Chile: Violations of World Bank Policies and Lack of Accountability at the International Finance Corporation. Claim before the Inspection Panel of the World Bank and Petition before the IFC Board of Executive Directors*. November 1995, mimeo.

interpretation of whether the community of requesters, having demonstrated damage from the project, met the intentions of the drafters of the Resolution on the Board.

b. Issues regarding the Scope of the Panel's Mandate

The expectations of the Executive Directors in founding the Panel, it is clear from the preparatory record, was that the Panel would focus on collateral damage to the environment and social structure from large, Bank-financed infrastructure projects. In fact, few of the ten Requests to date have been limited to those policy areas. Instead, the Panel and the Board have had to wrestle with many other aspects of Bank business, and the possible application of Panel resources to areas where unanimity did not exist among Executive Directors. Moreover, the frequent turnover of Executive Directors and their advisors meant that all too frequently new arrivals reviewed Panel actions without institutional memory of its founding or its prior work. Each recommendation to the Board thus became a matter of considerable controversy over the preferred mandate of the Panel when further action was recommended.

The Arun case served to limit the competence of the Panel in several ways. Care was taken by the Panel members in accepting the multi-faceted complaint to focus on those areas where the Panel thought it could make a difference. Some of the issues cited by the Requesters involved the economic analysis of the hydroelectric facility and the least-cost planning process of the power sector in Nepal. In the latter case, there were particular complaints about the likely high cost of the power from the Arun III facility. The Panel had to decide whether or not it wished to become a "technical review panel" along with its other functions, and decided that in large measure it could not, and certainly the Board's expectation was that it would not. The Narmada review panel chaired by Bradford Morse had made the opposite choice, and by becoming immersed in the technical issues of the Narmada project, had probably extended the work period by at least a year. The Panel believed that, while it could certainly apply some background technical knowledge to differentiate foolish arguments from sensible ones, it did not find its comparative advantage to the Bank to lie in areas of engineering, hydraulics, meteorology, or other "hard sciences." The Bank had already commissioned seven years of technical studies on these subjects in the project's design, and if opinion was already divided, it would probably remain divided after the investment of much time and consultant effort by the Panel. The Panel did, of course, read and profit from the existing technical studies commissioned by the Bank, where were badly divided on the issue of the project's feasibility.

Therefore, the Panel decided that in its current configuration, it would be best to focus accountability on those policy areas seen as highest priority by the Board, such as resettlement, indigenous peoples, the environment, and other social issues.

The Rondonia case that arrived from Brazil in June 1995 tested a very different set of issues for the Panel and the Bank. Flowing from lessons learned in the infamous Polonoroeste projects of northwestern Brazil, where Bank-financed highway projects had been a major cause of deforestation and uncontrolled homesteading by outsiders, the Bank helped the Brazilian government to launch the Planafloro – a development program for the state of Rondonia in the upper Amazon that would develop modern safeguards for the natural assets of the Amazon Basin as well as managed settlements to ensure the survival of existing communities such as the Amerindians and the rubber tappers. The Planafloro program was financed primarily from two sources: the external funding of the Bank in the Rondonia Natural Resources Management Project (approved March 1992) and internal funding from the Brazilian federal government.

The issue raised by the 20-25 non-governmental organizations requesting intervention from the Inspection Panel was not direct damage done by the Project or Planafloro. Rather, they objected to the fact that the promises of the project had not been met, in large measure because the Brazilians refused either to allocate their share of the project costs (thus immobilizing the entire project) or to follow through on enforcement measures at the state level to protect the natural and human resources targeted by the project. In effect, the Bank and the borrower appeared to have wasted three years, a costly delay in the life of the Amazon where each passing day meant more illegal settlers, more chain saws ripping down trees without permits, and continuing violent disputes over demarcation of borders. The project in question was designed to end such abuses, and by everyone's account, the project was accomplishing little and indeed, indirectly permitting growing damage to the region.

The question posed for the Panel, then, was whether the obligation of Bank management to carry out the operational policies on project supervision extended to the fulfillment of promises made and attainment of foreseen benefits in project design. In effect, was the Bank obliged to exercise as many remedies as possible when the borrower failed to carry out its contractual commitments to finish the project and to execute it in the fashion approved by the Bank's Executive Directors? The question was important, because some Executive Directors understood the role of the Panel to be to prevent harm to local populations and their interests, but had not yet seen the need for the Panel to ensure that Bank-financed projects were carried out with full benefits to the local population. As a result, the Rondonia inspection in its various stages caused repeated anguish about how far to sustain the role of the Panel in ensuring Bank compliance with all of its commitments.

As the Panel's experience moved beyond Arun and Rondonia, it became clear that the Board was less interested in examining the application of Bank policies – which they concluded were flexible standards – and more interested in identifying and remedying damage from projects. The Panel had difficulty meeting this change of direction, since the Board made no move to amend the governing Resolution appropriately. Eventually, the Panel recommended to the Board in 1996 that it amend the Resolution to eliminate the phase providing for investigation of policy violations. The Board was equally uncomfortable with that initiative, and chose to do nothing in response. The Board repeatedly turned aside Panel requests for investigations of policy violations and asked the Panel instead to examine and monitor damage to local people. This sensitivity by the Board is clearest in the Yacyreta case, where the Board excised "policies" from the mandate for review and assessment, and instead focused on "procedures." The Panel continued to have an impact on improving policy compliance within the Bank because Bank staff read the Panel reports with care; such sensitization about policies occurred despite, not because of, the direction taken by the Board. Finally, the Board reversed course radically in late 1997, when authorizing an investigation into the India National Thermal Power Corporation case. At that time, the Board directed the Panel to conduct an investigation based in Washington only, with no mandate to review the effects on people on the ground. The report was to be made only with regard to Bank compliance with its policies, and nothing more. This move by the Board reflected widespread unhappiness among the Executive Directors representing borrowers, who felt that the several years of prior investigations had focused too much on the effect of project implementation by the borrowers. Whether the new course taken by the Board will have a more positive impact remains to be seen.

c. Remedies Available through the Panel Process

In the design of the Panel, the Board took care to reserve to itself decision-making authority, and it was to be based, at the final step of a Panel investigation, upon recommendations from Bank Management as to how to remedy violations of policy and procedures confirmed by the Panel. In this regard, it can be argued that the actual implementation of the Resolution resulted in greater influence for the Panel over remedies to problems in the project.

In the first case, the Arun investigation took eight months in the second phase, owing to several changes of government in Nepal, a change of the

Presidency at the World Bank, and eventually a decision by the new President to withdraw the project from the Bank financing agenda.[10] Prior to its withdrawal, the project had been redesigned by the borrower and Bank Management, stimulated by two field-based fact-finding trips by the Panel members. The changes in the project's design were persuasive in terms of meeting the intention of Bank policies, even if there was undoubtedly limited capacity in Nepal to carry out the advanced design. Nevertheless, the Panel had made it clear that it could create the pressure needed to bring the Bank's work up to its policy standards.

Rondonia posed a different challenge. Bank management admitted[11] that it was true the project had not performed. The Planafloro program had been launched with great fanfare around the time of the Rio Environmental Summit of 1992, and it hardly enhanced the environment-friendly credentials of the Brazilian government or the Bank to have this project collapse.

As a result, there was an extraordinary increase in the supervisory activity of the Bank in the months following the request for inspection. Even though the Bank placed most blame on the Brazilian unwillingness to pay their share of the project costs, the actions of management indicated a strong sense of accountability to get the project moving. A much more proactive Plan of Action was negotiated with the Brazilians at the end of 1995: award of the contract for satellite-based mapping and monitoring, acceleration of the zoning process for Amerindian reserves, and a new approach to sustain health care in the Amerindian reserves, among others. When those measures turned out to be inadequate, the mid-term review of the project in the spring of 1996 turned into a design process for complete restructuring of the project and a new negotiating framework with beneficiary groups and NGOs.

The Panel accomplished all of this without ever launching an investigation of the project. The Panel on several occasions recommended to the Board that it was time for a formal investigation, under the procedural rules of the Panel, but did not press the case in view of the well-advertised reluctance of the Directors to authorize such a politically-charged process, and the accelerated effort of Bank management to show that progress was being made. On the final occasion, on January 25, 1996, the Executive Directors decided to give management six to nine months to conduct a complete review, to restructure the project, and to bring the improved project back to the Board, to be

---

[10] For the final record, see IBRD, *The Inspection Panel Investigation Report. Nepal: Arun III Proposed Hydroelectric Project and Restructuring of IDA Credit-2029-NEP*, Document INSP/SecM95-3, June 22, 1995; and IBRD, *ARUN III HYDROELECTRIC PROJECT. Management Response to the Inspection Panel's Investigation Report dated June 21, 1995*, Document INSP/SecM95-5, August 2, 1995.

[11] IBRD, *Management Response to the Request for Inspection, Rondonia Natural Resources Management Project, July 19, 1995.*

reviewed with the assistance of the Inspection Panel.[12] The motivation of the Directors in not authorizing an investigation (being accomplished in all but name through a "preliminary review") seemed to be to avoid aggravating perceived political problems for the government of Brazil, to ensure the government did not have an excuse to cancel the project, and to dampen the degree of public controversy that might arise from such a public step.

The Request dispatched to the Panel from the Jamuna Char Integrated Development Project in August 1996 raised many of the accountability issues already seen, such as the scope of the resettlement policy, the need for participation of local people in project planning and execution, and the institutional capacity of the borrower to carry out Bank policies in concrete programs. Even more importantly, however, it brought to the fore the wide gaps that may exist between policies of the Bank and those of borrowers with regard to sensitive social and environmental issues.

In this case, the question of resettlement of people who live in the widespread and shifting islands of the Jamuna river was not settled during project design. In social terms, these people who inhabit the chars (islands) are the lowest social class. On the other hand, the Bank was in the process of expanding its definition of "project affected people" in a project. Bank social scientists briefly raised the issue of the char people during design and dropped it in the face of borrower resistance. When it became known that local NGOs, representing char people and others in the Jamuna area, had submitted a request to the Panel, Bank staff moved quickly in September 1996 to obtain Bangladeshi acceptance of an Erosion and Flood Policy that would compensate everyone, including the char people. It was reluctantly accepted by the government, and even more ominously for future implementation, it was scheduled to run a year or more beyond the actual construction period. The question then had to be asked by the Panel: what was the likelihood of the government carrying out a policy in which they did not believe once all of the capital investment in the bridge was completed?

It was in such situations that the gap between policy directions of Bank and borrower becomes vitally important for the welfare of the beneficiaries. While a capital project is under construction, it is clear that Bank supervision can result in substantive compliance with its policies by borrowers; but after the Bank has left, what remedies are left? This is not a legal question (since under Bank legal agreements, all covenants apply until a loan is fully repaid), but rather a practical one – would a borrower listen to the Bank once all the money is spent? Most answer no, and in that pose a dilemma for Bank staff in

[12] The Inspection Panel, *Brazil: Rondonia Natural Resources Management Project*, Information Release, January 25, 1996.

terms of how far they can hope to change the behavior of borrowers on a sustainable basis with regard to social and environmental policies.

A THREE-YEAR TRACK RECORD

When the Inspection Panel was created in 1993, the Board created a trial period at the end of which it would review the record of the Panel and made recommendations for adjustments. That period was two years after the appointment of the members. Thus, the Board launched a series of discussions in 1996 that culminated in a resolution of "clarifications" with regard to the Inspection Panel's governing resolution.[13] First, the Board endorsed the work of the Panel, and terminated the trial period, thus endowing the Panel with permanent status in the Bank group. It then reaffirmed the scope of the Panel's work, in terms of the people and groups that would have access to the panel to make the Bank accountable, and provided the Panel with greater flexibility in working with those groups in order to make a preliminary determination of their complaint.

Does that mean that evident imperfections in the governing instrument of the Inspection Panel are now immutable? Apparently not, since the Board Chair, several Executive Directors, and the Inspection Panel's Chair went out of their way to stress the organic nature of the enterprise. The Panel was seen as an experiment to start, and has evolved into a permanent, but flexible, instrument. The virtue of that approach is evident in the changing atmosphere of accountability. One can see already in the life of the Panel the parallel development of accountability at the national and the international level. Just as the Bank has been pushing greater participation and accountability at the national level, so the Bank has been able to show by example what it can accomplish to enhance its own accountability. The nurturing of civil society has payoffs at both levels, and while sometimes such participation is inconvenient in the short run, it is increasingly evident that benefits in the long run justify such inefficiencies. At the same time, flexibility has its price – for instance, in the confusion between the "Management Response" provided for in the Resolution and the frequent "action plans" tabled by Management. There has been little reflection on the cost of allowing this imbalance to develop, such that Management is able to dominate the process through action plans and thereby diminishing the role of the Requesters.

Other international institutions have shown interest in the underlying principles of the Inspection Panel. It may have been the first, but it is no

---

13 Recorded in M-96-60, *Minutes of Meeting of the Executive Directors of the Bank and IDA held in the Board Room on October 17, 1996 at 11:10 a.m.* October 24, 1996.

longer the only mechanism of its kind. National governments have provided avenues of redress for individual citizens as part of their overall accountability in democratic systems. Even where governments were not democratic, carefully-crafted legal remedies may have existed to maintain certain enumerated rights. For international institutions, however, with their legal structure based on a Westphalian system of governments, it has been a painful process both legally and politically to provide citizens with direct access to international entities.[14] Human rights commissions and courts have generally initiated that trend, in Western Europe and in Central America. For financial institutions, the Inspection Panel was a complete innovation, and only slowly did the Inter-American Development Bank and the Asian Development Bank follow suit. In their own ways, the latter two banks adapted the idea to their own purposes.

The greater institutionalization and larger volume of cases at the World Bank's Panel gave it substantial influence over the other panels. The IDB received only one complaint by 1997, and the ADB had received none. The IDB became the focus of a substantial campaign to upgrade its investigation panel to a form closer to the World Bank's, particularly with regard to a permanent secretariat, and independence of the Presidency at the IDB. The contrast between the two panels received greater attention in the context of the Yacyreta request filed at both institutions as a reflection of their co-financing. Both Panels submitted reports to their respective Boards in September 1997.

The World Bank Inspection Panel has been unable to fulfill some of the central hopes of those who initiated it. The independence of the Panel is only partial at best, with the Board often divided in supporting the statutory independence of the Panel from Management. It is indicative that the Board has not restrained Management from commenting on eligibility (a matter reserved to the Panel, with confirmation by the Board, in the Resolution) and

---

[14] Various United Nations agencies have utilized the term "inspection" in review bodies. The UN operates a Joint Inspection Unit as an internal policing mechanism, and the UN Secretariat has an Office of Internal Oversight Services, with a Monitoring and Inspection Unit. The Office recently undertook a useful survey of all the internal oversight mechanisms in UN agencies, available as UN, General Assembly, A/51/801, 20 February 1997, *Enhancing the internal oversight mechanisms in operational funds and programs*. It found the most developed inspection units in UNHCR and the World Food Programme, but neither was developed for public access. For instance, the UN High Commissioner for Refugees has a Director of the Inspection and Evaluation Service, who works in the office of the High Commissioner to "provide the High Commissioner with an additional management tool which is flexible, independent, and directly responsible to her." For a survey of recent activities, see UN, General Assembly, A/AC.96/870, 13 August 1996, UNHCR Inspection and Evaluation Activities. The issue of individual access with grievances arises in UN bodies in other contexts, such as the appeal provided to individuals and groups under International Labor Organization rules. That issue is treated in a separate paper in this volume.

has not prevented recurrent and last-minute introduction of "action plans" that interfere with the Panel's work. The Board and Management, in their own ways and from different perspectives, are uncomfortable with the Panel being independent.

For the affected people in a project area – supposed to be the greatest beneficiaries from the Panel process – they have not played as central a role as they and their supporters have hoped. Perhaps as just one more reflection of their marginal status globally, the progress of an inspection under the current resolution treats them as objects at best, not as participants after the initial request. The fact that Management is allowed by the Board to table successive "action plans" without requiring or providing for further consultation with the affected people bespeaks a lack of real commitment to the principle of participation.

Nevertheless, the Inspection Panel has made a start in its stated mission. Until the necessity for a system of "checks and balances" is formally accepted in international institutions such as the World Bank, there will be discomfort with the existence and operations of the Panel. Out of that discomfort, leaderships can find an opportunity or they can try to make it go away. Given the underlying validity of the instinct that lead to the Inspection Panel's creation, the answer should be to build on the opportunity offered.

Some Lessons from the Inspection Panel's Experience

Alvaro Umana[*]

INTRODUCTION

There were a number of important reasons and a variety of factors that played key roles in the creation of the World Bank's Inspection Panel in 1993. These can be divided among internal and external actors and observers. Among the internal factors, the "Wapenhans Report" represented an important influence and raised critical issues. It was presented to the Executive Directors in November 1992, and one of its major concerns was that Bank Staff, responding to the promotion incentive system, were concerned primarily in increasing the volume of their lending programs, but less concerned about project execution, impacts and outcomes. Dr. Ibrahim Shihata, Vice-President and General Counsel of the World Bank, discusses some of the internal and external factors in his book: "The World Bank Inspection Panel".[1]

It is also evident that the role of civil society and non-governmental organizations played a fundamental role in what has been called "the most concrete step taken by the World Bank in the last ten years to establish public accountability and openness in Bank operations". Lori Udall, the author of that statement and of a recent review of the Inspection Panel, provides a more detailed account of the role of NGO's in the establishment of the Panel.[2] Richard Bissell, in his article "The World Bank in a Democratic Era" provides a perspective focused on the impact of the Panel toward democratization and openness. The crucial lesson to understand is that there are a number of different stakeholders involved ranging from the President and Board of the World Bank, through the Executive Directors and national governments, to the local affected populations that the Panel was intended to serve.

According to Dr. Shihata's book, the among the most important objectives that the Executive Directors had in creating the inspection function were:

---

* Chairman of the Inspection Panel

1 Shihata, Ibrahim; The World Bank Inspection Panel, Oxford University Press, 1994

2 Udall, Lori; The World Bank Inspection Panel: A Three Year Review, Bank Information Center, 1997

- Citizens of developing and developed countries increasingly ask for transparency and accountability of development institutions.
- The existence of an independent body will increase the credibility of the Bank.
- The cases where major conflicts arise with affected parties will be dealt with more efficiently and consistently by a permanent and independent structure than by ad-hoc bodies.
- The borrowers involved, if they wish, will have a better opportunity to present and defend their position and to get attention of the public and the media.
- The professional competence and integrity of management and staff will be protected if an independent investigations assess the facts and actions taken.
- Members of the Board, and directly affected parties, will have an additional, independent instrument to ensure that projects are fully compatible with the policies and procedures of the Bank.

At the internal level, the Wapenhans report had made clear that the Bank needed an independent look at projects that were experiencing implementation difficulties or causing harm to local populations and the environment. At the external level, the need for increased transparency and accountability was most significant, particularly in light of civil society's demands and the rising influence of NGO's on parliaments and governments of donor nations.

Although there were a number of alternatives discussed, the solution adopted took the form of a three member permanent and an independent structure, able to provide the Board with the only outside- and therefore truly independent- view of projects with potentially harmful impacts on local populations and the environment.

To date, ten formal Requests have been presented to the Panel. It is only through the analysis of these cases, individually and as a whole, including the related Board decisions, that a true picture of the Inspection Panel's role can be established. After over three years experience a number of fundamental questions can, and should be raised about the Inspection Panel. This is particularly relevant due to the inevitable impact that this experience could have on other multilateral development institutions and other international organizations. Among the most important questions are:

- Has the Inspection Panel met its objectives?
- How has the Panel affected Bank operations?
- How have the Panel's operations affected the different stakeholders?
- Has the Panel had an influence on project design, appraisal and implementation?
- Has the Panel dealt with affected parties more efficiently and consistently?
- Has the Inspection Panel increased the credibility of the Bank?

♦ Has the Inspection Panel influenced other similar efforts?

THE PANEL'S CASE HISTORY AND BOARD RESOLUTIONS

The Inspection Panel started functioning in August 1994, with a full-time Chairman and two additional Inspectors, as well as a small Executive Secretariat. An initial task undertaken by the Panel was the drafting of its Operating Procedures, to make the Resolution operational and obtain a common framework to approach all the cases.

As of September, 1997, ten formal Requests have been presented to the Panel (See Table 1). Eight were registered and two rejected. One, the Request relating to the Pangue dam in Chile, had to be rejected because it dealt with an International Finance Corporation (IFC) sponsored project. According to the Resolution, the Panel has no jurisdiction over IFC projects, only over IBRD and IDA projects.

Out of the eight Requests registered, the Panel recommended an investigation for five, namely those concerning the:

♦ Arun III Hydroelectric Project, Nepal
♦ Planafloro Project in Rondonia, Brazil
♦ Yacyreta Hydroelectric Project, Argentina and Paraguay
♦ Itaparica Resettlement Project, Brazil
♦ NTPC Power Generation Project in Singrauli, India

In each of these projects, potentially affected local populations could be suffering harm caused by lack of compliance by the Bank with its own policies and procedures. This was also the case in the Request relating to the Jamuna River Bridge project. Although the Panel did not recommend an investigation of this project, it did identify the "Char" or island people as a group that had been left out of resettlement programs, and this finding contributed to their inclusion in these programs. The Board instructed Management to report back to it on the execution of measures to compensate the Char dwellers and it invited the Panel to provide comments at that point.

In the five cases mentioned above, the Board did not approve an investigation in the terms provided for in the Resolution. It did, however, develop a "tailor-made" approach for each case. This is summarized briefly below and is dealt with in greater detail in the attached Appendix.

> ARUN III HYDROELECTRIC PROJECT: In October, 1994, a citizen's group from Katmandu, as well as people living at the Arun valley, submitted a request claiming actual or potential harm through alleged non-compliance by IDA with five of its policies and procedures. Bank Management responded to the request on November 22, claiming full compli-

ance. Following meetings with the requesters in Nepal, the Panel found apparent violations with three of the five policies and recommended an investigation. On January 5, 1995, the Board requested Management to furnish the Panel with more information on IDA's actions with regard to alleged violations of its policies. On January 20, after thorough consideration of the information received and discussions with Management, the Panel reiterated its original recommendation for an investigation in the three areas. On February 2, the Executive Directors approved the recommendation and instructed the Panel to take into account any action plans subsequently developed by Management. After receipt of the Panel's investigation report, Bank Senior Management reassessed the project and, upon their recommendation, the Bank President informed the Board on August 2, 1995 that he had decided to withdraw IDA support for the project.

RONDONIA PLANAFLORO PROJECT: On June 14, 1995, intended beneficiaries living in the project area, represented by local NGOs, submitted a request claiming that the project design of PLANAFLORO and the Bank's lack of enforcement of several project covenants had resulted in damage. In its response to the request on July 19, Bank Management acknowledged and explained a number of instances of lack of compliance with its policies. On August 17, following consultations with federal and state entities and people in the project area, the Panel recommended that the Board authorize an investigation. Instead of accepting or rejecting the Panel's recommendation, as called for in the Resolution, the Board on September 12 concluded that it needed more information. It instructed the Panel "to further substantiate the materiality of the damages and to establish whether such damages were caused by a deviation from Bank policies and procedures." At the end of November, while the Panel was conducting this additional review, Bank Management presented it with a "plan of action" designed to remedy past failures. On December 8, a few days after receiving this plan, the Panel sent the Board a report on its Additional Review. It found that the situation of many intended beneficiaries was worse than when the project started and it recommended that the Board authorize an investigation. On December 20, Bank Management sent the Board a plan of action that had been agreed by the federal and state governments to deal with the principal issues raised by the Panel. Later, on January 25, 1996, the Board decided that, in light of the agreed action plan, it would not be advisable to proceed with the investigation recommended by the Panel. However, it did agree to review Management's progress on the plan in six to nine months time and to invite the Panel to assist in this review. In January,

1997, the Board instructed the Panel to conduct its review and the Panel presented its report to the Board in March 1997.

YACYRETA HYDROELECTRIC PROJECT: On September 30, 1996, a group of people living in the project area in Paraguay and represented by a Paraguay NGO, filed a request claiming that they had been or may be directly and adversely affected by the Bank's omissions and failures in the preparation and implementation of the project. In its response of November 1, Management challenged the eligibility of the Requesters and claimed full compliance. The Requesters claimed that ten policies had been potentially violated, with a particular focus on the Bank's environmental, resettlement and project supervision policies. Following a review, the Panel concluded that the Requesters were eligible. On December 26, following a review of the situation on the ground, the Panel recommended an investigation. Subsequently, on February 3, 1997, Management sent the Board a progress report which included references to remedial action plans which had been recently agreed by the governments. Again, instead of accepting or rejecting the Panel's recommendation, as called for in the Resolution, the Board on February 28, 1997, decided to invite the Panel "to undertake a review of the existing problems of the project and to provide an assessment of the adequacy of the Action Plan as agreed between the Bank and the two countries concerned." The Panel was also expected "to look at the extent to which the Bank staff had followed Bank procedures…" (A concurrent review of the project was approved by the Board of the InterAmerican Development Bank.) The Panel completed its review and submitted its report to the Board in September 1997.

ITAPARICA RESETTLEMENT PROJECT: On March 19, 1996, the Panel received a Request from 121 individuals and an NGO representing people living in the project area. The Requesters claimed that their standards of living, health and economic well-being had suffered rather than improved as a result of the Bank's omissions and failures in preparation and faulty execution of the project. Bank Management responded to the claims on April 28, claiming full compliance. Following an extensive review, during which it again dealt with the issue of eligibility, the Panel submitted its report to the Board on June 24, recommending an investigation. Given the fact that the Government had recently approved an action plan to complete the project, and had requested continuing Bank supervision for two more years, the Board on September 9th decided not to proceed with an investigation. It further decided to review progress on the action plan within 12 months with the assistance of the Panel.

NATIONAL THERMAL POWER CORPORATION PROJECT (NTPC), Singrauli, India: On May 2, 1997, the Panel received a request from a group of residents in the Singrauli area of India, claiming actual or potential damage as a result of the Bank's policy violations in the preparation and implementation of the project. In its response of June 3rd, Bank Management acknowledged certain shortcomings in the application of its policies and procedures, ranging from "substantial" to "partial" compliance. It also submitted two action plans, one general and one specific. During July, the Panel reviewed the situation on the ground and found that the requester's concerns appeared to be well justified. It also reviewed the action plans and considered the specific plan inadequate. On July 25th, it submitted its report to the Board, recommending an investigation. On September 2nd, Bank Management submitted an updated specific remedial Action Plan designed to address some of the concerns raised by the Panel in its report. In light of this plan, which carried the support of the Government of India, the Board on September 8th decided to approve a limited investigation, restricted to a desk study in Washington. The Panel's findings are due in December, 1997.

Lessons from Experience

In 1996, the Board undertook a review of the Resolution based on two years experience. As a result, the Board issued a set of clarifications to deal with a number of issues that had arisen. In the year since the completion of that review, a number of developments have again raised the Board's interest in the nature of the Panel's work. First, the quantity of Requests coming to the Panel has grown: in the first two years only five formal Requests were received, but another five formal Requests were received in the third year (1996-1997) alone. Second, among those recent five requests were projects that raised significant political sensitivities among some of the Bank's largest borrowers. Third, only a few members of the present Board were Executive Directors in 1993 when the original Resolution was passed: as a result the perceptions and assumptions among Board members can more easily diverge.

Reviewing the above five cases where the Board has acted on the Panel's recommendations for an investigation, a number of important lessons emerge which might usefully lead to some further clarifications.

1. The Panel's *raison d'être* is to provide groups of private citizens who believe they are or could be negatively affected by Bank projects with direct formal access to an independent international forum where they can submit their complaints and have them addressed, with prompt disclosure of the

Panel's findings and the Board's disposition of those findings. This has been the focus of Board's attention to all cases where the Panel has recommended an investigation. In this sense, the establishment of the Inspection Panel is a clear advance in the development of international law of institutions and human rights. In terms of outcomes, the Panel has proven to be an effective instrument for starting a process to correct or avert damage.

2. The Inspection Panel was conceived as an instrument to improve transparency and accountability in Bank operations. In actual practice, however, some Executive Directors and Government officials have seen the Panel more as an instrument for pressuring Bank Management into insisting on borrower compliance with legal covenants agreed by the borrower for the projects in question.

3. The Resolution envisaged that the Panel would focus primarily on the Bank's adherence to its own policies and procedures. The Resolution is clear on this. In every case where the Panel has proposed an investigation, it has stressed that it is the Bank alone, and not the government or borrower, that is to be the exclusive subject of any investigation. Whatever the original intent, however, the practical result is that borrowing countries themselves feel under threat of an "investigation" and, given the perceived political implications of this, they have acted accordingly to block or avoid any further Panel involvement in the review of Bank-financed projects. The terms "investigation" and "inspection" seem to be difficult for borrowing countries to accept due to the negative connotations inevitably associated with them. The result has often been a sharp division among the Executive Directors , usually, for obvious reasons, along the so-called Part I and II lines.

4. According to the Resolution, the Panel has two main functions: on the one hand it is asked to check on Management's compliance with the Bank's operational policies; on the other, it is asked to assess "material harm" on affected or potentially affected populations. Of these two functions, the former, which can be described as a "policing" function, has proven to be less useful to the Board since the Panel's "verdict" does not lead to any action beyond correcting failures in project design or execution.

5. The Panel's report and recommendation for an investigation has repeatedly provoked Management into preparing an ad-hoc remedial action plans. The Resolution, however, did not anticipate that Management would act in this way, at least not prior to the Board addressing the Panel's recommendation to authorize, or not to authorize, an investigation. In acting in this way, Management has effectively preempted the process envisaged by the Resolution. In presenting its remedial action plans to the Panel and the Board just prior to the meeting, or at the same meeting at which the Board addresses the Panel's recommendations, Management has made it impossible for the Panel

(or the Board) to determine whether the plans do, in fact, address the concerns of the Requesters and the findings of the Panel. Furthermore, the Panel cannot determine whether the Requesters have participated effectively in the design of the remedial plans affecting them, as required by Bank policy. Given the speed with which these plans are developed, effective consultation seems almost to be precluded.

6. A review of past Board decisions reveals that the Panel's role in checking compliance with operational policies has been down played, while its role in addressing actual or potential harm to local populations and assessing remedial actions has been emphasized.

Panel's Impact on Stakeholders

Thus far, the analysis has focused almost entirely on the Panel's recommendations to the Board and the related Board decisions for each of the cases when the Panel has recommended an investigation. Nevertheless there are a number of additional stakeholders, both internal as well as external, that are impacted by the Panel's actions. Some may feel that they are directly impacted by being subjects of an "investigation", while others may see in the Panel a new instrument to redress harm or avert potential harm. Therefore the answers that may be provided to the fundamental question of the Panel's effectiveness depend on the perspective of the stakeholder in question. Table 2 summarizes the impact of the Inspection Panel on stakeholders and associated views on the Panel.

Among the internal stakeholders in the Bank are the President and Management. The President has a dual role as head of Management and Chairman of the Board. The President responds to a number of actors including the Governments of both lending and borrowing countries, the media, NGO's and in general is the interface to the outside world, where criticism of the Bank has been high, and demands for increased transparency and accountability have gotten stronger. The President has been a strong supporter of the Panel, and should have access to the Panel to use in a "preventive" mode in addition to the "corrective" mode based on investigations. During the first review of the Panel's experience undertaken by the Board, the Panel suggested that the Resolution be clarified to explicitly provide the President with access to the Panel. At the time, a considerable number of Executive Directors spoke against the proposal, and it was rejected.

Management is also directly impacted by the Panel since the latter was created to check on the former's compliance with the Bank's Operational Policies. Management has faced the existence of the Panel by utilizing every possible defense, including questioning the eligibility of the claimants and preparing "action plans", outside the terms laid out in the Resolution, to avoid an investigation. Management has consistently denied violation of policies, and only in one case it has recognized "partial " or "substantial" compliance. However, in every case has developed "re-action" plans (reacting to the Panel's reports to the Board) where solutions to existing problems are addressed, and therefore the need for an investigation is diminished or disappears altogether. By introducing these "action or reaction plans", Management has effectively pre-empted, delayed, or altered (as in the cases of Rondonia, Itaparica and NTPC) the Panel's further involvement. The last-minute preparation of action plans to correct or avert further damage has created "moving targets' for the Panel because these plans have been presented either at the Board meeting itself, or shortly before the meeting. Without the benefit of any previous knowledge of these plans, the Panel has been asked to give an opinion on the spot. In addition, the formulation of such last -minute plans has prevented any consultation with affected parties, as required by Bank policy.

The Executive Directors also have a dual role as Members of the Board and representatives of their National Governments. It is precisely this dual role and the fact that, by definition, inspections can only take place in borrowing countries, that has led to the split of the Board basically along so-called Part I and II lines. Since governments of borrowing countries feel under the threat of being "investigated", they attempt to stop or delay the process. Borrowing country governments largely see the Panel as an intrusion into their internal affairs, and as a pressure to fulfill legal covenants agreed upon under Bank loans. They also fear that interventions by the Inspection Panel may lead to additional liabilities.

Governments of some developed countries initially supported the creation of the Panel due to basic concerns about transparency and accountability, however they do not constitute a "block" in the same sense as the borrowing countries, and their support for the Panel's work has been more fractured. If, through the creation of voting "blocks", the Executive Directors lose the capability to analyze each case according to the facts and merits, the effectiveness of the Panel as a Board instrument will be irremediably lost.

Local governments are also important stakeholders since they often have to deal with the consequences and impacts of project implementation, and because of this fact, they may enter into conflict with National governments for increased attention to problems related to bank projects. Their active participation is often critical in finding appropriate solutions to local problems.

Non-government organizations, at the local, national, and international levels, have been important stakeholders. They initially supported the creation of the Panel for reasons of transparency and accountability. Although the Resolution clearly limits the participation of NGOs to cases where they can represent locally affected parties, the NGOs have gained access to the World Bank and have played an important role in helping local groups dealing with the formal requirements stipulated in the Resolution to make a claim eligible. Knowledge of the Bank's Operational Policies that may have been violated during project implementation is difficult to obtain for potentially affected local groups. Both national and international NGOs have been essential for local groups to present their cases adequately.

The last, and perhaps most important group of stakeholders, are the affected or potentially affected populations (PAPs). Despite the problems of access mentioned earlier, some have clearly gained due to the existence of the Inspection Panel as a new mechanism that focuses its attention on harm to local people, and its intervention has led to solutions and allocation of resources to solve project-related problems.

In each case considered, the Panel has made an effort to interview locally affected people directly, and assess their level of participation in the project and if adequate consultation, required by Bank policy, has actually taken place. In at least one case, a group of disenfranchised people were incorporated into resettlement plans through the Panel's intervention. In some cases, the Panel's attention has resulted in resources being made available to accelerate the solution of local problems. In other cases, the Panel has recommended urgent and immediate actions to avert further damage. It is clear that this heightened level of attention has been the result of the Panel's intervention.

FUTURE OPTIONS

With the perspective of hindsight, there a several important sources of conflict that could be corrected to make the Panel's work more effective. As mentioned earlier, the terminology chosen ("investigation") has proven difficult to accept, and the Panel has recommended that other terms be utilized, leaving "investigation" only as a last resort. However, the problem goes beyond terminology and is related to the Inspection Panel's role itself. The Resolution gave the Inspection Panel the role of checking on Management's compliance with the Bank's operational policies. The Panel is supposed to determine whether or not Management has been in compliance, but it is not supposed to provide recommendations on how to solve present problems. Even when the Panel provides evidence of clear violation of policies, there are no internal consequences. Past practice demonstrates that the Board has been more interested in finding solutions and assessing remedial actions. Therefore, the emphasis on compliance with operational policies could be complemented with an additional advisory role for projects that are experiencing difficulties and could lead to potential harm, as well as an specific role in assessing implementation of action plans developed by Management to correct harm in cases where formal Requests have been presented to the Panel.

It is also evident that the President of the Bank should be able to send projects that are experiencing difficulties or could pose particular risks to the Inspection Panel to utilize it in a "preventive' mode as discussed earlier.

Another important problem remaining is what to do about the "action plans". The Board could revert to the process and time frames envisaged by the Resolution as clarified in 1996.This would meet the current expectations of affected parties but, if it is to work, experience indicates that it would have to be accompanied by resolute determination on the part of Management to postpone preparation of remedial action plans until after the Panel's recommendation on an investigation has been acted upon.

If Management chooses to present a remedial action plan, the Board could formalize an alternative approach with extended deadlines for Management to submit its report. This time should be adequate for the Panel to asses the eligibility of the claims, but also enable Management to complete a remedial action plan to address those claims (including the required consultation with Requesters and other affected parties). Given the opportunity to review the remedial action plan, the Panel, in its report to the Board, could offer its view on the eligibility of the claims and on the adequacy of the action plan and consultation process related to the preparation of these plans. Therefore, in cases where Management chooses to present a remedial action plan, the Inspection Panel's role would be:

- To assess the consistency of plans with Bank policy, including participation by affected people and adequate consultation.
- To evaluate Management's supervision of remedial action plans.

In light of past experience and of the Panel's recommendation during its first review by the Board, it appears necessary to reconsider the Panel's mandate and its potential usefulness to the Board and Management and the outside world. The Panel has stated clearly that it would favor additional instruments besides the "investigation" and that it could also work on a "preventive" mode attempting to deal "upstream" with projects that are likely to develop problems under implementation. If the Inspection Panel's mandate is not broadened to include preventive measures, other instruments added, and the process reformed to provide access by the President, the work of the Inspection Panel will continue to be highly controversial and divisive.

There is also the danger that, if "action plans" continue to be the preferred course of action followed by Management, and the Board does not give the Panel the role of assessing Management's supervision, the Panel's position would be weakened. At the same time, there would be no independent assessment available. This might, in turn, lead to an additional request to be handled by the Panel, whose findings would be less and less relevant.

There is a real threat that, if the Board does not provide the Panel with a permanent and clear role during the "action plan" implementation, there would no independent follow-up by the Board and the Panel's role would be marginalized. In appearance, the Panel would be functioning, but in reality its influence would be considerably diminished and restricted to registering the Request and waiting for Management to prepare its "action plan".

CONCLUSIONS

In establishing the Inspection Panel, the World Bank created an innovative mechanism to enable groups who believe they are or could be negatively affected by Bank-financed projects to get an independent assessment of possible harm or damage stemming from the Bank's failure to apply its own policies and directives. By establishing the Inspection Panel, the Board took the lead in what has become recognized as a clear advance in the development of international institutions. At the same time, it improved the accountability of the Bank's Management and staff for the observance of its policies and procedures to enhance quality control in project design, appraisal and implementation

Although it is still too early to assess the Panel longer term impact on Bank operations, it is clear that the presence of the Inspection Panel has already had considerable impact, and, for example, contributed to a new term utilized by staff: "Panel-proofed project's", making sure that operational policies are clearly followed so that the project will not end up under investigation.

As the Lund meeting made clear, the lead taken by the World Bank is not only being observed with great interest by other international institutions, but also being adapted by some to their own situations. Both the InterAmerican Development Bank (IDB), as well as the Asian Development Bank have put in place inspection panels or mechanisms. The first inspection approved by the IDB, dealing with the Yacyreta Hydroelectric Project was conducted in parallel to the one carried out by the Bank's Panel.

It is still difficult to predict the development of mechanisms to guarantee transparency and accountability in international organizations, and whatever the difficulties experienced in its initial stages, the World Bank should be credited for having taken this initial step to create a truly independent body to check compliance with its own policies and procedures, and therefore opening up a new chapter in transparency and accountability of international organizations. However, it is not yet clear what the future role of the Panel will be. Given the Panel's case history, the fact that the Board has never been able to act on the Resolution as originally approved, and the second review of the Inspection Panel to be undertaken by the Board in 1998, there is a considerable risk that changes introduced to facilitate reaching Board decisions may end up significantly changing the mechanism as it has operated during its initial phase.

IMPACT ANALYSIS OF THE WORLD BANK INSPECTION PANEL

Key Questions:

- ♦ What is the fundamental objective? Harm / policy violation?
- ♦ Who are the stakeholders affected?
- ♦ What has been the impact of Panel actions on stakeholders and project design, appraisal and implementation?

Bank Levels

President

- Has been strong supporter of Panel
- Can respond to outside pressure by channeling NGO complaints to Panel
- Should have access to the Panel

Board of World Bank

- Created Panel in 93 Resolution, reviewed '96, only minor clarifications accepted.
- Panel reports have resulted in better knowledge of problem projects.
- Due to sharp divisions, unable to apply Resolution as approved, has pursued case by case, "tailor-made" decisions.
- Instrument for transparency and accountability in "abstract", too destructive to use in concrete applications. Investigation ̄atomic bomb.
- Panel has turned into a divisive issue generally along Part I and II lines

Management

- Has fought Panel at all levels and using "every possible defense", including eligibility claims and action plans
- Has consistently denied violation of policies; only in one case has recognized "partial" or "substantial" compliance

- Has found ways to pre-empt Panel through "action plans" strategy, creating moving targets and preventing consultation with affected parties

National Levels

National Governments and Executive Directors

Lenders

- Want transparency and accountability, supported Panel creation
- Support Panel reform but not a solid block Part I, some "free spirits"

Borrowers

- Largely see Panel as an intrusion into their internal affairs, and as a pressure to fulfill legal covenants for Bank loans, or fear of the creation of additional liabilities. "Cost-sharing"?
- Abhor to be "inspected" and create alliances to block "investigations". This has led to the formation of a solid Part II block.

Local Governments

- Sometimes support Panel to gain national attention
- May enter into conflict with national government, usually critical for solution of local problems

NGOs

- Have gained access to the World Bank through the Panel mechanism, have important role as "watchdogs"
- Have become representatives of affected parties/groups

Affected parties

- Despite access problems for most, some have clearly gained due to new mechanism which has led to solutions and resources to solve problems

⇒ Rondônia acceleration of project implementation, participation, deforestation control, grants to communities

⇒ Jamuna integrated disenfranchised "char" people into resettlement plans

⇒ Yacyreta implementation of plan to address environmental liabilities and lost resources

⇒ Itaparica proposed governmental allocation of $290 million promised to solve problems, Bank supervision

⇒ Singrauli immediate remedial actions to be implemented, Panel Report due December

Name of Request	*Registered*	*Panel Recommendation*	*Board Decision*	*Final Action*
Nepal/Arun III	yes	investigation	approved	report from Panel
Ethiopia/Exprop	no			
Tanzania/Power	yes	no investigation		
Brazil/Rondonia	yes	investigation	not approved	review by Panel
Chile/Pangue	no			
Bangladesh/Jamuna	yes	no investigation	review in 12 mos	due April 1998
Argentina/Paraguay/ Yacyreta	yes	investigation	not approved	review Sept 1997
Bangladesh/Jute	yes	no investigation		
Brazil/Itaparica	yes	investigation	not approved	review 1998
India/NTPC	yes	investigation	approved/limited	sent to Board Dec 1997

Access to Panel: The Notion of Affected Party, Issues of Collective and Material Interest

Michelo Hansungule[1]

General Remarks

Since the introduction of the Inspection Panel in September 1993[2], the World Bank has been busy trying to adjust to a rapidly changing environment. At the inception of the Bank over half a century ago, the drafters of its constitution seriously overlooked to provide for a mechanism for dealing with complaints from the general public which would arise from its operations and activities. The drafters of the Bank constitution could not foresee that the general public in the various countries in which the Bank officials would be carrying out its business might suffer harm as a result of their actions or omissions and might need to seek redress against the Bank. This serious anomaly has remained virtually uncorrected for the past fifty years of the existence of the Bank in spite of its implications on the integrity and general standing of the Bank as a whole.

But with the establishment of the Inspection Panel, the Bank is trying to send a clear signal that it will henceforth embrace the principles of accountability and transparency that previously only troubled states. Of course, this initiative should have come much earlier than this. There are many instances in the past in which the Bank's operations and activities have clearly harmed the interests of people in those countries in which it conducted its businesses. Various Bank projects in developing countries have been initiated without due regard to local needs and environmental concerns. Bank policies have been applied without taking into account the interests of local inhabitants, while Bank officials applying the Bank rules and procedures have frequently ignored the rights and interests of the people in affected areas – especially where these

---

1 Visiting Professor at the Raoul Wallenberg Institute of Human Rights and Humanitarian Law, Lund, Sweden. I am grateful to Ms. Inge Jacobs for the comments and changes she suggested to the draft copy of this paper. The paper was presented to a discussion jointly organised by the Raoul Wallenberg Institute and the World Bank in Lund in 1998.

2 The Inspection Panel was established by Resolution 93-10 of the Executive Board of 22 September 1993.

stood in the way of the project. The situation has not been helped by the local partner – the government. In the majority of cases, governments have joined forces with the Bank in favour of a project despite its severe implication on the rights and interests of the people. The harm and injury that may be inflicted on local people by the Bank either due to the failure of the Bank officials to adhere to the policies of the Bank or for any other reason would normally go uncorrected because there was no system of detection and redress within the Bank. If the victims belonged to the informed sections of the community with resources to embark on expensive litigations in their local jurisdictions, they still would usually not get at the Bank itself because it enjoys sovereign immunity from local process in the legal systems of the states which are party to the Bank Charter. One of the ancient principles of international law states clearly that a sovereign can not be compelled to submit to the legal system of another sovereign, which term extends to international institutions endowed with sovereign immunity in their constitutions, like the World Bank.

This immunity, an important attribute of the principle of sovereignty, would effectively operate to defeat any attempt by a victim trying to seek the liability of the Bank. A victim can only reach the borrower state, but even then, with great difficulty due to the complicated nature of internal redress systems in the majority of states and due to the difficulties involved in trying to prove that in a given case, the borrower state and not the Bank, which may have provided the bulk of the resources, should be held liable for the consequences of that process. This leaves a great number of Bank victims stranded and without any means of securing effective redress against the Bank in spite of the fact that the Bank clearly possesses the necessary means to effectively attend to most of the grievances arising from the application of its policies or from its operations. Judged against this background, the establishment of an Inspection Panel is, though only a token when viewed from the point of view of what could have been done by the Bank had it felt the need to, a giant step towards meeting the interests and concerns of the people in various countries. This being said, it is essential to point out that a lot more needs to be done to initiate further Bank reforms aimed at making the Bank an institution that cares with regard to the difficulties brought about on the ordinary people as a result of the implementation of its policies and procedures in those countries that borrow its funds. Today, the image of the Bank from the point of view of ordinary people in many of these countries is that it is an uncaring institution which takes no regard of the results of its actions or omissions however detrimental these may be to the local population. This image is certainly not good to the Bank. It is a widespread concern which the Bank can not afford to ignore, whatever the extent of its mandate. Victims of Bank policies and activities must be quickly addressed to rather than left to themselves.

Where the poor victims try to turn to their states for redress, they would most often be viciously met with harassment by state officials and politicians who as a rule do not tolerate such actions from their citizens. Politicians in developing countries very often view such litigants as ungrateful individuals bent on tarnishing the good image of their country to the Bank in particular and to the international community in general. Few politicians in developing countries can understand the importance of an individual or even a community raising complaints against a Bank project that has already received the blessing of the government "at the highest levels". Such protests are very likely to be viewed suspiciously as being motivated by political ends. It is common knowledge that ruling politicians in the majority of borrowing countries frequently urge their citizens to show gratefulness for what the Bank and other international donors are trying to do for them. Politicians in most of these countries are highly impatient with complaints from their people against projects because their largely vulnerable economies are too much dependent on them. Most of them do not understand the importance of balancing the objectives of the projects with the rights and interests of the people. Rather than worry about the welfare of the people in affected areas, they are eager to show off the results of the projects to their electorates at large as the results of their "governments". As a result, they have little patience with protests from one or two individuals or communities as might come from their citizens in their countries. Peoples' welfare comes second to their idea of public interest in their lists of priorities. Therefore, the government would be the first one to read the "riot act" to the protestors in a bid to shut them up. This is particularly the case in most of these countries, because due to the very high levels of poverty, victims of Bank policies are most likely to ignore the effect of these policies on the personal lives of the people and on the environment in general. In some of these countries, a World Bank project may be about the only active project for politicians to show the general populace about "their government" at work! There *are* very few projects in most of the third world countries if any which are solely developed from domestic resources sourced in those countries. This is one of the ancient dilemmas facing third world countries. Speaking as one from a third world African country, I can testify to the extreme vulnerability of the so-called economies of third world countries. They are not economies in the real sense but economies of sorts which can not stand by themselves if unsupported by international economic institutions and donor countries. They depend mainly on outside funding to finance their development projects, with the World Bank being among the most important sources of this funding. With this vulnerability in mind, it is easy to see why these states tend to over-react to any form of protest directed against such projects as those financed by the Bank.

However, the Bank has realised that since its establishment way back in 1944, many changes have taken place in society that it needs to appreciate in both its policies and the systems of work. It is true that the Bank is slow in picking up these changes while in some cases it has just refused to bend down in order to pick them up. The Bank is not used to being dictated from outside. Since its inception, it has become used to get its way. It has consistently ignored the numerous calls for change of its philosophy and its mode of operation. As far as the Bank is concerned, it has not seen any need for change. This has angered many people who feel there is plenty of things that the Bank could have done to influence changes in various countries, precisely because of its importance to the economies of these countries, particularly third world states. Human rights and democracy is one such area the Bank has flatly refused to involve itself in. As far as it is concerned, the World Bank looks at its work as not involving any responsibility towards human rights and democracy issues in borrowing countries. When deciding to lend some money to states for its various development projects, the Bank, as a rule, does not take into account the extent to which human rights and democracy are respected and observed by the borrower states. This new criteria which is increasingly becoming a typical subject of demand by western states in their relations with southern countries does not bother the World Bank in the same way it is beginning to bother western states today. Today, it is fashionable for western states, including those that had no integrity at all regarding human rights and democracy during colonialism, to insist on good governance, democracy and a good human rights record as the precondition for development aid. Isn't it common to hear the "holier than thou" tune being frequently played in the relations between the undeveloped South and the developed West in today's diplomacy? Developing countries, like first year graders on an assembly line, are having to account one by one about their human rights and governance records to western donors before they can be granted development aid. Those states that are lucky to be judged to be maintaining good records are of course rewarded; they get more than those without good records. What is a good and what is a bad record depends on the subjective judgements of the donors, which makes it quite difficult for some states (particularly those states not in good relations with a donor already at the time of judgement) to impress it however much it tries to develop a good record. To the contrary, the World Bank does not entertain this vocabulary in its language. It is said that the "Bank dictionary" does not contain this type of vocabulary but only the hard stuff on economics! In other words, a country's human rights record is of no consequence to World Bank programmes in that country. This means that the

Bank supports any member state whether it has any record of human rights or not. To some people, this means the Bank has no sense of morality, particularly since it can leave some money even next to "skeletons". Since it is not sensitive to human rights, it would not care really how many people a borrower of its funds may be sending to the gallows without due process at the same time as they conclude the loan agreement. As a rule, the Bank does not protest such excesses. It is not known to have withdrawn its support from a country in protest for that state's appalling record on human rights. While donors may do so in their individual capacity, the Bank can not apparently because such a course of action would be inconsistent not only with Bank practice but with the constitution of the Bank itself; so we are constantly told. The Bank constitution is said not to empower the organisation to have regard to political issues when carrying out its objectives. Therefore the organisation is only required to be guided by sound economic principles in its policies and practices and to avoid being political at all times in order that it does not violate its mandate. It is feared that human rights and issues of good governance could draw the institution to aspects for which it is not mandated to have regard. As an institution that is totally financed by governments across the world, the World Bank believes it has an obligation to carry out its mandate without any discrimination between those states that seem to comply with international minimum obligations on human rights from those that do not. To do so would be depriving some members of their resources as per the rules of the Bank on grounds not spelt out in the principal rules of the constitution of the organisation.

As pointed out before, this has drawn sharp criticisms from some quarters, and especially from human rights organisations and activists. To the advocates of human rights in developing countries, the Bank stance is only proving the West's lack of interest in the development of democratic processes in third world countries. It is alleged that there is a sort of a conspiracy between the Bank and developed western countries to keep a blind eye to the developments in third world countries. The question that has most frequently been asked with regards to the Bank policies in developing countries is why it is that the Bank has always failed to draw the simple distinction between the people in a developing country on one hand and the state on the other in the formulation and articulation of its policies? The Bank does not see that sometimes the interests of the people as expressed by interest groups and individuals do not coincide with the interests of the state: and even if these are clearly at variance, the Bank will still go on dealing with that state. This is troubling to many people. Some of those individuals have spoken out in very strong language against the Bank attitudes. For example, in the midst of a major constitutional crisis in Zambia, which led to an attempted military take over of the civilian government and in which several army officers and political leaders were held for a long time under preventive detention regulations before being charged with treason, a prominent Zambian lawyer and opposition political leader lambasted the World Bank for its insensitivity to issues of human rights violations in the country. He charged[3]:

> " (....) While the bilateral donors have assisted in ensuring that the government (....) makes some attempt to respect basic norms of democratic behaviour, the two Bretton Woods Institutions have done very little, if anything at all, in ensuring that the government respects the rights and freedoms of the Zambian people. When the bilateral donors who replenish the coffers of the International Development Association (IDA), insist on good governance on the part of the government, the Bank behaves as though nothing is happening. Even in the throes of the current state of emergency (....) the Bank has continued making disbursements (....)"

This has been the typical behaviour by the Bank in all those countries where it has conducted business. It is most often used by governments as an example of stability in a country which is falling apart. In these countries, it is quite common to find ministers of finance being shown in the public media signing agreement after agreement for the disbursements of new resources with Bank officials at the same time as basic rights and freedoms are being rudely confiscated from the population. The Bank behaves as if it has no conscience at all. It is not worried at all by the fact that people are being killed by state agents while they approve funding for so-called development projects. What message does this send to the government that badly needs such type of support it can not get from its people? And what does it mean to the victims of government excesses in respect to their views and perceptions of the Bank?

It is partly due to such perceptions that the Bank has decided to put some mechanism of redress within its system, although clearly not enough. The mechanism does not deal with human rights violations as such in the country of the Bank project. It only deals with complaints arising out of the Bank's failure to carry out its part of the project in connection with its policies and procedures. In this connection, the mechanism is too limited to be of any useful value to the majority of the people affected by Bank operations. But this being said, it must be pointed out that despite its limitation, the Bank must be commended for at least having seen the need to have an independent system of redressing complaints arising out of its operations.

Although limited in the scope of its mandate, the Bank, through the Inspection Panel, has no doubt been called upon to begin to honestly account to the general public for some of its activities, something which could not be possible before. There are many reasons for this change of attitude. Of course, the Bank staff tries to underplay the role of external pressures towards this

---

3 See Rodger Chongwe, Post Newspaper, (Zambia) 17th March 1998.

change. For example, when tracing the source of demands for change in the manner in which the Bank carried out its policies on the ground, Ibrahim Shihata begins from the Bank concerns itself. He does this by carefully tracing the concerns of the successive Bank presidents regarding the operations of the Bank, especially beginning from the mid-nineties. It may indeed be true that senior Bank officials were increasingly getting concerned about the manner in which the Bank staff in the field interpreted Bank policies and went about effecting those policies and procedures. However, this still does not exclude the crucial role played by outsiders in steering the process of change towards a regime that would provide for a system of public complaints. Shihata himself acknowledges this, though not as much as he acknowledges the fact that the Bank itself noticed and steered the need for this change. The role played by external pressures in bringing about this change is only grudgingly acknowledged and only in a few lines while attention is lavishly given to the Bank officials' roles. However, if we closely independently examine the developments leading up to the establishment of the Panel, it becomes quite clear that external pressures especially from the now famous Namada dam project in India represent the single most important case to have facilitated the initiative towards the establishment of the Panel. The international attention provoked by this dam project in which several local and international organisations publicly criticised the Bank for failing to have adequately prepared itself for the resettlement needs of thousands of the people that were going to be required to move from their homes after submerging an area of approximately 370 square kilometres (the size of many countries) clearly shook the Bank bureaucracy more than at any other time. The clumsy manner with which the Bank staff attended to the resettlements of the people involved in the Namada projects and the consequent environmental impacts that followed can not be denied as being the most important causes behind the Bank's sudden change of attitude, resulting in its decision to establish the Panel at about that time. It would be too much of a coincidence to be true that the Bank decided just at the same time the Namada dam catastrophe broke out to establish the Panel merely as a follow up to the earlier plans.

Lessons from the Idea of a Panel

With growing calls from the public for greater accountability and transparency in the world's biggest Bank, the fever of democracy which has previously only troubled states in developing countries has finally caught up with the Bank. Growing public awareness about fundamental human rights means that more and more people will try to get involved in the activities of such important organs of society as the World Bank in order to understand how it operates and find out if the Bank, in its operations, takes account of the interests of the people. This at once means that the World Bank must now more than ever before sit up and get ready to open up its doors to its operations and activities to the general public who wish to acquaint themselves and scrutinise them. The need for the Bank to increase its visibility in regard to its operations and conduct in today's rapidly changing environment can not be overemphasised.

The Inspection Panel is the idea of the World Bank to respond to complaints about the effect of its policies and operations in borrowing countries. It is intended that through this facility, people in borrower states will be afforded the rare opportunity, in addition to what they can do in their home countries, to see the inside of the Bank so many have just heard about, check its activities and policies and challenge them so far as these have adversely affected them. The Panel is of course not a court of law and not even like a court of law. Bank officials frequently like to stress this point as if to prove that it is in fact a kind of a court of law. The fact that it is not a court of law or like a court is sometimes denied so often by Bank staff as to suggest that this was in fact the idea behind its establishment. Otherwise, one would not spend so much time and energy trying to explain what the Panel is not if it was in fact not.

Another reason why the Panel is likely to be confused with being a court of law in the minds of ordinary members of the public in various countries who will reflect upon it, is that in the real everyday life of an average citizen, the mechanism that immediately springs to mind in connection with a facility for complaints is a court. Few people will envisage a different concept than a court when thinking of a complaint resolving machinery. The same occurs with international and national human rights protection bodies set up to protect human rights. Most people have time and again confused them with courts and therefore criticise their failure to deliver in the discharge of their objectives from this point of view. Courts are what are known best for resolving conflicts between subjects and national and international persons. Therefore, when the Bank announced its decision to establish the Panel, most people mistakenly believed that the facility would be some kind of a judicial body because this is what they are familiar with. Whereas Bank experts who set up the Panel may have had a non-judicial body in mind, the general public has another idea of what constitutes a complaint resolving system.

The third reason for the apparent mix up lies in the fact that the World Bank, though without a mandate to espouse human rights issues in its Constitution, is generally viewed as being one of the members of the United Nations family of institutions. This family has a long legacy of human rights protection as one of its primary tasks. In turn, human rights protection implies the idea of a judicial or quasi-judicial body ostensibly set up to redress human rights violations in a judicial way. As a result, the United Nations has been setting up a series of Committees with the task of protecting human rights more or less like courts do, although in a different sense. Therefore, when told that the World Bank had set up an Inspection Panel to deal with complaints arising out of the Bank operations, people immediately thought of it as being similar to the various UN human rights protection bodies if it was not like a court of law.

One possible way out of this "misunderstanding" is to avoid being extreme in interpretations of positions, especially for Bank officials with the task of operating the Panel mechanism. Bank officials need not overemphasise the non-judicial nature of the Panel while the public should avoid treating it like a court in every sense of the word. The Panel should be allowed to evolve in the light of the circumstances. If the circumstances will require it to follow the judicial way, it will do so even if this will not have been the original idea of the founders. If the nature of the problems the Panel will be required to deal with are such that it must judicialise its approach in order to be more effective, it will not be wrong for the mechanism to become more legalised, though this will make it lose track of some of its key objectives or even its original direction. The Inspectors are in fact going to find this out soon in the course of the operation of the facility. Most requesters will expect from them a certain way of behaviour as time goes on and they can not completely close themselves to the idea of being "judicial" in their work if this is what the public at large wants from them.

This being said, it is important to state again, for the sake of clarity, that the Panel should be regarded not so much for what it was intended at the time of its establishment than for what it can do in the current circumstances. It is understood that it was not to be a court of law. This much is clear, but it should not be said that it can not develop into a court of law, which it should if this is how it can best realise its objectives. On the other hand, we should fight the temptation to view it solely as a court of law. It should be regarded for what it is because it is only if we do this that it would be possible to prevent being tempted to entertain inflated expectations from the Panel which it can simply not render. If you look at it as a court of law, you would be looking forward to a procedure and remedies one would expect from a court process. Yet it is alien to the resolution creating the Panel to expect it to perform the function of a court however much we would expect it to deal with issues like a court.

In the real world, however, the Panel can not avoid behaving like a court of law in its operations. For example, it was tempted when dealing with the request for "Compensation for Expropriation of Foreign Assets in Ethiopia" in April 1995, to borrow from the rules of international law in order to reject a request for an inspection submitted by a requester. The Panel held that the request could not be entertained due to the fact that the requester had not yet "exhausted domestic remedies". What is interesting in this request is that the Panel resorted to the international law principle of domestic remedies purely in order to shut out this requester even though there is virtually no support for this stand in the Resolution. Indeed, the particular nature of this request may have prompted the Inspectors towards this conclusion and may somewhat have been justified in the position they took, but the point is that the decision demonstrates the fact that not even the Panel can afford not to behave like a court of law in some instances. In today's World, it is not possible to build a mechanism of a totally different kind from those we are already familiar with. It will be too controversial for the Bank to try and build an institutional arrangement on what are essentially disputes between parties in a different way. Ultimately, the process is bound to develop more or less the same features as judicial bodies, though not necessarily courts of law. This is not to deny the fact that the Bank is charting a new territory which it is entitled to.

If it is realised that in the present environment, more and more people will seek to enforce their rights through the various mechanisms created by the international system, the importance of the Panel becomes obvious. In cases where there lacks an international forum for redressing individual harm, people are likely to resort to self help and similar mechanisms. Therefore, the establishment of forums for redressing public grievances is a matter of a right. It is in this respect that the World Bank should be applauded for deciding to introduce an Inspection Panel as an independent facility with which to inspect its own policies, rules and operating practices. This forum is an important mechanism for private parties with complaints against the policies and activities of the Bank. Until September 1993, parties with such complaints had nowhere to go in the Bank system to seek redress, as the Bank did not have any independent provision for such grievances. The Panel, as an independent complaint redress system within the Bank, creates an opportunity to have the complaints attended to. In doing so, the World's biggest financial institution can now be made to account for its various actions or omissions so far as these harm people in borrowing states. It is true, as Shihata[4] points out, that this is a progressive step in the development of both international organisations and the international law of human rights.

However, it must again be stressed that the Bank, in creating the Panel, has not established a facility for redressing allegations of human rights violations

[4] Shihata, Ibrahim F. I. The World Bank Inspection Panel – A Background Paper on its Historical, Legal and Operational Aspects. A paper submitted to the Expert Meeting on the Inspection Panel held on 23rd – 25th October 1997 at Lund, Sweden, p. 36.

by the Bank in borrowing countries. While it must be admitted that the Bank, like other institutions, violates human rights when carrying out its operations or in not carrying them out, the Panel facility has not been designed for the purposes of affording redress to those who fall victim to the Bank policies and activities. It is important that this point is stressed to avoid the wrong conclusion that through the Panel, victims of human rights violations by the Bank can now seek redress. The Inspection Panel is an internal mechanism set up to afford the Bank the opportunity to examine its policies and how it has gone about implementing them on the ground as far as others, especially those affected, are concerned. It is from this angle that I intend to pick up the debate about the accountability of the Bank in the light of the Inspection Panel and in particular the aspects relating to access to the Panel.

Although the decision to create an independent Panel is purely an internal one, it is important that this is viewed in the context of its public nature. When deciding to establish the Inspection Panel, it must be realised that the Bank was not reacting from without. Shihata[5] has explained the origins of the source of the debate on the Bank's accountability as having been fuelled largely by the mistakes allegedly made by the Bank regarding two major projects in India. It is important therefore when analysing the Inspection Panel that this context is taken into account because it is the general background from where the decision to create an independent mechanism to inspect and investigate the policies and activities of the Bank stems from. The immediate motivation for an independent Inspection mechanism within the Bank therefore was to try and avoid mistakes such as those of the Namada dam project; a point I have stressed before.

But it must be stated once again that the Bank mistake in the two cases in India is not the only one. In developing countries, the Bank carries out several projects. As we pointed out before, the World Bank is an essential part of the social and the economic development of these countries. It provides most of the resources needed in most developing countries. Bank funded projects dominate the economies of third world countries to the extent that the Bank is a virtual household name. In both rural and urban areas, the Bank has projects. Schools are being built or rehabilitated with funding from the World Bank. World Bank funded dams and canals are being constructed together with water reticulation systems, hydroelectric projects, resurfacing of several thousands of kilometres of roads, etc. World Bank projects are a common sight in various countries in the third world. Take the case of Zambia, for example. In the period between 1992 and 1997, the World Bank was involved in a total of twelve different projects ranging from water reticulation and rehabilitation of water supply systems to agricultural marketing of produce;

---

[5] 4. *Ibid.*

from health sector projects to economic recovery and investment assistance; from mining investments to petroleum rehabilitation, etc. In urban restructuring and water supply projects, the World Bank, together with other western donors and governments have invested in the development and improvement of existing water supply systems in a total of ten municipalities and peri-urban districts in Zambia. The total amount of investments committed with donors input is as follows:

Cofinancing	*US $ (million)*
IDA	33.0
NORAD	11.0
Govt	2.4
Total	46.6

In the health sector, which aims at investment in the improvement of health, nutrition and family planning needs in urban areas in Zambia (including the capital city of Lusaka), the Bank alone has committed a total of US$50.0 million during the same period while in the field of enterprise development, aimed at the improvement of the financial sector, private sector development and poverty alleviation activities, the Bank alone has committed a total of US$45.0 million, again, in the same period. It is also taking part in the programmes designed to sustain the environment. Under this programme, the Bank has committed a total of US$20.8 million. Under the economic recovery and investment programme, the World Bank, together with other donors, has committed a total of US$27.20 million as follows:

Cofinancing	*US $ (million)*
IDA	23.00
ZCCM (local state miner)	3.48
Govt	0.72
Total	27.20

This funding is designed to help in Zambia's privatisation plan for the Zambia Consolidated Copper Mines, a state mining company which is now being sold by the government to the private sector. In the health sector, through which the government is being assisted to carry out the restructuring of the administration of the health facilities with a view of decentralising decision making to the communities from the Central Ministry of Health, the Bank and other donors have committed a total of US$557.0 in the period under review. The donor components of the funding are as follows:

Cofinancing	*US $ (million)*
ODA	24.9
SIDA	21.2
DANIDA	20.0
DUTCH	60.8
UNICEF	14.0
IDA	56.0
Govt	340.0
Total	536.9

Institutionally, the Bank is involved in such diverse activities as the reforming of the country's land tenure systems so that it converts from the traditional and more agrarian forms to the modern western type tenures and practices. It is involved in programmes dealing with judicial and public sector reforms in which the judiciaries and public services are being assisted in trying to cope with changing systems and practices. Under these programmes, public offices dealing with the delivery of justice, land titles and land reforms, taxation and various other aspects of government service are benefiting from Bank finance in order to improve their administrations, enhance the skills of the public officers through increased training, provision of technological capacities including computer soft wares, etc. In third world countries, especially the least developed countries, the World Bank completely dominates economic life. As we pointed out before, this fact is very visible in all of these countries, where the Bank and western donor states are most often the only pillars for social and economic development. Bank resources give these countries the psychological security they otherwise do not have. It is this aspect which makes governments in developing countries react negatively to such ideas as the introduction of an Inspection Panel. They fear that an inspection of the World Bank project which may be the only major project in the country may lead to the withdrawal of the Bank, which does not add well to the political chances of the ruling politicians.

The government resentment of any interferences with Bank funded projects was quite clear from our field work in Zambia. Senior government officials dealing with World Bank funded projects at the Ministries of Local Government and Housing as well as the Ministries of Mines and Health adamantly refused to entertain any questions on Bank projects from our research team as soon as the purpose of the research was explained to them. But what was even more disheartening was the reaction of the World Bank staff based in Lusaka and in some project sites. They too did not wish to co-operate with the research after they learnt that the purpose was to investigate the extent to which the Bank policies and procedures were being rigidly followed by Bank staff in the execution of the Bank projects so that if there were any lapses that constituted breaches which adversely affected people in material ways, such people would be advised of the possibilities of requesting for Inspection of the projects. The Bank head office refused to co-operate in the exercise and directed field staff to do the same.

They did admit though that the World Bank in Zambia does not issue the Bank policies and procedures to people in affected areas and neither does it ever explain these policies and activities of the Bank. None of the people living in affected areas were made aware of the existence of the Inspection Panel within the World Bank, let alone the method of how to approach it. The same question was put to ten NGOs dealing with human rights and development issues in Zambia and two each in Nigeria and Malawi. The response was the same. They had not even heard the concept of an Inspection Panel and so could not answer any of the questions put to them on the procedures of the Panel. In Malawi, Nigeria and Zambia, a total of fourteen human rights NGOs approached did not know of the existence of the Inspection Panel, the procedure for making a request for inspection, and had not even seen the book by Shihata on the World Bank Inspection Panel, although it has been on the shelves since 1994! It was even worse with the potential requesters. Some of those who really were in conditions that can be described as being affected parties in Zambia were so helpless they could not be expected to challenge the Bank, which is what they understood the idea of a request to mean. They pointed to the difficulties that such actions could bring them in the community, particularly in view of the fact that the local party leadership of the ruling party, who were also actually in the same position as the others, had not only publicly supported the project but were even employed on it as general workers in the mine that was partly funded by the International Development Association. Their first problem was that they did not even know that the World Bank was one of the funders of the mining project. They had vague ideas about government involvement only because the General Manager was appointed by the government. Second, it was difficult to enlist the support of the community to question the Bank because, quite apart from the difficulties of knowing how to do so, the mine was the only employer in the area and beyond it. Researchers concluded that it would be unproductive to engage the community in a discussion about the Inspection Panel and what possibilities it offered in an environment such as the project on Zambia's Copperbelt area.

Another aspect of the Bank funded projects in Zambia that merits attention is that the Bank had not carried out any environmental impact assessment on all the twelve projects covered in the research. For the entire five years of the lives of the projects, no environmental impact assessment reports had been done. Officials admitted this in an interview with assistants but explained that one project did not require an assessment because there were no environmental issues involved, while partial environmental assessment reports had been done on only two. The one that they claimed did not raise any environmental issues in fact involved investment in the mining and other extractives in copper and coal mines. No reasons were given for those projects for which there were no assessments done at all although they were required. On displacements of the people, Bank management in Zambia gave a thinly worded statement to the effect that "all projects listed above, DO NOT involve ANY displacement of people. In case of displacement of people, the WORLD BANK cannot be held responsible to compensate the victims but the government". It is quite clear from this wording that local Bank managements have not yet understood the new role of the Bank; that the Bank can in fact compensate people who have been displaced as provided for under the mechanism providing for the Inspection Panel. Whatever is known in the Bank about this mechanism, it has not flowed to the managers on the ground or perhaps they are simply unable to believe it.

Further, the Bank activities have frequently collided with certain private interests in Bank supported countries. Sometimes, the clash has had to do with the incompatibility of the values. As a rule, the institution has applied western values in carrying out its operations in the various countries it has had projects. Some societies in developing countries do not understand the reason for the Bank obsession with the market economy and the privatisations, deregulations and liberalisations that this entails. Some people in the South feel that the Bank does not have the interest of the people in southern countries in mind. Several times, the Bank has been accused of disrespecting non-western cultures and traditions and therefore acting in disregard of local means of protections of human dignity. These suspicions are as old as the Bank itself. In the ultimate, they have had the effect of creating suspicions between the Bank and the local population. Sometimes, though, the clash has had to do with a violation of vested rights and interests of private parties in the borrower country. Due to the concentrated nature of the Bank activities in these countries, as already pointed out, these clashes can not be avoided.

ACCESS TO PANEL

One of the most important features of the Panel is the eligibility requirements. The Bank does not deal with any type of complaint from any one who may wish to complain against the implementation of its policies and procedures. It is not like a High Court in a common law jurisdiction which has jurisdiction in all cases. Anyone in a common law jurisdiction can complain to the High

Court just about anything, although the court is not bound to entertain every complaint. The inspection Panel is different. It is closed with respect to certain complaints, either because complainants have no proper standing or can not prove connection between their complaint and the alleged violation. In this way, the Panel has limited jurisdiction and this is how it was intended to be by the Bank. To open the Inspection Panel mechanism to any type of complaint from any complainant would not only overcome the ability of the Bank but also lead to a flow of abusive complaints; it was feared. As a result, it was decided to include, in the Resolution, conditions which define the competence of the Panel and outline its jurisdiction. Paragraphs 12 to 14 of the Resolution provide for the jurisdiction of the Panel. Paragraph 12 reads:

> "The Panel shall receive requests for Inspection presented to it by an affected party in the territory of the borrower which is not a single individual (i. e. a community of persons such as an organisation, association, society or other group of individuals), or by the local representative of such party or by another representative in the exceptional cases where the party submitting the request contends that appropriate representation is not locally available and the Executive Directors so agree at the time they consider the request for Inspection. Any such representative shall present to the Panel written evidence that he is acting as agent of the party on behalf of which the request is made".

It further goes on to say:

> "The affected party must demonstrate that its rights or interests have been or are likely to be directly affected by an action or omission of the Bank as a result of a failure of the Bank to follow its operational policies and procedures with respect to the design, appraisal and or implementation of a project financed by the Bank (including situations where the Bank is alleged to have failed in its follow-up on the borrower's obligations under loan agreements with respect to such policies and procedures) provided in all cases that such failure has had, or threatens to have, a material adverse effect. In view of the institutional responsibilities of Executive Directors in the observance by the Bank of its operational policies and procedures, an Executive Director may in special cases of serious alleged violations of such policies and procedures ask the Panel for an investigation, subject to the requirements of paragraphs 13 and 14 below. The Executive Directors, acting as a Board, may at any time instruct the Panel to conduct an investigation...."

In terms of the above paragraph, a request may be submitted by:

(a) an affected party
(b) an Executive Director
(c) Executive Directors acting as a Board

To these three potential parties should be added the "anonymous requester", a later creation by the Bank.

These four are the only parties that can make a request for an inspection by the Panel. Of the four, the "affected party" and the "anonymous requester" can be said to be the "soul" of the mechanism. The success of the entire Panel process depends on these terms. It is these terms that will decide whether people affected by the World Bank activities will submit requests for inspection. What we call people in ordinary language are called "affected parties" or "anonymous requesters" in the Bank terminology. People in these areas of course don't know themselves by these terms. They know themselves simply as people, farmers, tenants, landlords, etc. But in order for them to use this mechanism, they are required to identify themselves with these artificial names. They must be able to understand, from the point of view of the Bank Resolution, who is an "affected party" and only after that should they send the request, otherwise the Panel will not entertain it even if they have a genuine complaint. They can not hide under the term "anonymous requester", for example, where they fail to define themselves in terms of "affected party" because even here the same conditions would apply, except that their correspondences will be treated with utmost confidence. A single person can not send an anonymous request because this will be declared ineligible for the same reason as in an ordinary non-anonymous request.

This technical jargon should at all costs be avoided by the Bank. If the idea behind the establishment of the Inspection Panel is simply to give the people a forum with which to air their views over the operations of the Bank in their areas, it must be done in such a way as not to frustrate that very objective. Experience tells us that technical terms very often intimidate the general public, especially the public of the kind who are normally affected by Bank projects. The Bank should find a more appropriate terminology which can fit in the language of an ordinary member of the public. All its efforts should aim at prodding the public to bring forth their complaints and they can only do so if no artificial restrictions are placed on the way to the Panel.

The term "affected party" as used in the Resolution introduces an unnecessary complication. An "affected party" is defined as a "community of persons such as an organisation, society, association or other group of persons." Earlier, the Panel had interpreted the term "affected party" to mean simply "any two or more people". But before long, the Bank Executive Board in 1996 "corrected" this by its own interpretation in which they construed an "affected party" as being "any two or more people with common interests or concerns". Though the Executive Board's construction has been described as a "clarification"[6], it in fact adds further doubts to an already doubtful term. The new "clarification" is in fact a violent departure from the earlier wording of the term by the Panel. It is one which will have severe implications on the access of requests from parties. The violence it introduces is clear from the new wording "with common interests or concerns" not pointed out in the Panel interpretation. In a sense, this extension deals a severe blow to those potential complainants who would like to request for inspection of the Bank policies and operations since they will now be required to prove the existence of

---

6 Shihata, *ibid.*

"common interests or concerns" among the group members – something not easy to achieve in practice for various reasons. This and the insistence on the "two or more people" in the Resolution as constituting the "affected party" effectively deprives the potential complainants of the very means with which to request for inspection. It departs from the idea behind the objectives of the Resolution, which is to give a voice to the people. The idea behind the Panel was for the Bank to recognise that it was wrong to operate the way it did, i.e. without giving the people affected by its operations the voice to air views whenever they feel they have been harmed by the Bank operations. It was also designed to act as a mechanism of the "last resort" for the victim. But the latter intervention by the Executive Board to give the term "affected party" a restricted interpretation in fact reverses all these bold objectives.

Two or More People

Any "affected party" – a group of people with this standing – can request for an inspection of a project. First, the term "affected party" in relation to the mathematics in the Resolution should be cleared because of its overall importance to the whole system and second due to the fact that it is a fairly unfamiliar term in the international system for complaint resolution procedures. Obviously, there are reasons why the Bank preferred this term over the usual terms although it is unclear from the Resolution. The problem of inserting a new term like this in such an important instrument as the Panel Resolution is that it is bound to create misunderstandings especially among the potential victims as well as the users of the mechanisms (the Bank Panel itself), which can ultimately affect the smoothness of the process. While it is not at all wrong to promote creativity, this should not be such as to catch those concerned by surprise. It should be possible to find in the new term more or less the same idea as in the usual terms.

The problem with the term "affected party" is not only with regards to its "newness" but more so with respect to the interpretational problems it tends to attract. It is not very clear who can not request for an inspection apart from the single individual expressly barred by the Resolution. Although organisations, societies, and associations as well as other groups of persons have been expressly provided for in the term "affected party", this is only by way of examples, as the term is drawn in an open ended fashion. It will not be absurd to interpret this term as intended for co-operatives, civil groups, incorporated bodies, and any number of people acting as a group, provided they of course are more than one person.

Significantly, the Panel is barred from receiving requests from individual victims, which sharply contrasts with the other international human rights protection systems. For example, only individuals can send communications to the UN Committee under the Optional Protocol to the Civil and Political Rights Covenant whereas under the Panel system the individual is not preferred. Second, the Panel has no mandate to entertain public actions submitted by actio popularis, unless the Executive Directors and the Board can be regarded as such.

The denial of the right of the individual to request for inspection is a significant anomaly which should be corrected. First, the rationale behind the difference between one person who can legally not request for an inspection on one hand and two people who can makes no sense. The only possible explanation is that the Bank arbitrarily fixed the meaning of the term "affected party" at "two" or more people. Otherwise, it is not clear why the Bank can not inspect a request from one person who may claim violation of material rights but carry out the inspection for the same claims if raised by this individual accompanied by someone else! The Bank can not say that it is not concerned with the effect on the individual of the failure of the Bank policies and operations yet this failure makes the individual a victim in the same sense contemplated by paragraph 12 of the Protocol.

Besides, some business organisations in some legal systems are made up of a single individual. In many common law jurisdictions, unincorporated organisations can be formed by only one person to run various types of businesses just like incorporated organisations only except when it comes to liability. Since such businesses would seem to qualify as "organisations" under the Resolution, it will be unfair to deny them the right to request for inspection and yet they are one-man organisations just like single individuals. This point illustrates the need to review the ban on single individuals under the Resolution. The Bank should not discriminate between complaints from individuals and those from groups. In the majority of cases, it is the individual who can bear the consequences of the failure of the Bank policy. Sometimes too, some individuals in a community may not want to complain because they do not have this culture. Most people in non-western societies still conduct their lives in accordance with their cultures. Though they may clearly be victimised in the sense of the Bank Resolution, their cultural background will restrain them from publicly complaining about the violation. Others will fear the political implication of the complaint against a project already formally endorsed by their government. In countries with lesser degrees of human rights, this is a real constraint. A complainant against a World Bank project in an area is unlikely to be allowed the freedom to exercise his or her rights to do so. Local politicians with little understanding of individual rights are likely to prevent the complaint. It happens daily that politicians in developing countries don't react kindly to attempts by citizens to seek international protection of their fundamental human rights. It is likely to happen even more in this case. What is being dealt with under these rules is the protection of the rights of the humblest of the humble among the members of the public. Those who are usually affected by dam or canal projects will most likely be the poorest of the poor. These are easily driven into fear by influential local politicians and can quite easily submit to their dictates because at that local level, they can not do without them. They rely on local politicians for their other needs or so they are made to believe. Therefore, they can not risk "biting the finger that allegedly feeds them". Only one or two who do not care about the consequences can decide to pluck enough courage to take on the Bank and the government. This should not mean that the individual victim who would want to ask for inspection should be denied this right only because some people in that community do not want to complain for various reasons. In the present case, the Resolution operates to the detriment of the individual who has been a victim of a specific act in breach of the Bank policies and procedures.

ACTIO POPULARIS

Alongside the above, public interest requests would be an important source of requests for the Bank inspection mechanism. In most of these countries where the Bank carries out its activities, people are unaware of their rights and how to go about seeking to protect them. They don't even know whether a project is a World Bank project. They can not find out this information on their own because most of them will be illiterate. It is even worse to expect them to know the policies of the World Bank and its operating procedures; as we have seen above. Even the so-called enlightened members of the public usually do not know this information either because it is too technical for them or is simply not available to the general public. We have clearly established this point above and that it is well known to the Bank itself.

The majority of the people who would usually be affected by such things as the negative effects of dam construction are those that have no education nor the means to resist such projects. To exclude actio popularis in the mode of the requesting system is in effect to leave such humble individuals without any form of protection. It is true that Article 1 of the Optional Protocol to the Civil and Political Rights Covenant limits the mandate of the UN Committee to individual complaints only. The Protocol does not permit the Committee to receive communications actio popularis. In A et al v. S[7] in which a communi-

[7] Communication No. 1 of 1976

cation was submitted to the UN Committee by 18 signatories on behalf of 1.194 alleged victims, including 14 of the signatories in which there were general allegations of violations of the ICCPR in state S together with a brief description of the violations in respect of each of the alleged victims, the Committee observed that the Protocol did not allow actio popularis and therefore declined to entertain the communication. On the other hand, the African Charter on Human and Peoples Rights does not exclude the use of actio popularis in its complaint mechanism. Most of the individual communications that have been submitted to the African Commission have in fact originated from Non Governmental Organisations acting in the public interest rather than from individual victims or their relatives. This is what has made the African system operational to the extent that it is. The low level of awareness of the fundamental human rights and the systems for their protection in the African region would have left the mechanism virtually unused if it had excluded actio popularis. This is one of the main criticisms generally levelled against the UN process. The World Bank should take cognisance of the actual conditions in borrowing countries when developing such mechanisms as the requesting process and stop pretending that it does not know that the majority of people in these countries lack the necessary means with which to find their way to such intimidating institutions as the World Bank by themselves. The concept of the "requester" should suit the circumstances of the area in order for the mechanism to have the confidence of the people for whom it has been designed.

Again, under the African system, the African Commission has decided in several communications that members of the public who can bring such communications to the Commission on behalf of victims need not even bring proof of authority from the victims, like is the case under the UN system. The reason behind this important decision is that victims in most of these countries where the degrees of enjoyment of human rights are very low will have died together with their kins making it virtually impossible to obtain their consent. Even the sheer task of collecting signatures from a thousand people or more who may be affected by a violation makes the requirement of consent unnecessary. The Inspection Panel can pick a leaf from the African system.

Besides shutting out the individual and the public from requesting the inspection, the term "affected party" is not at all clear. Although the Bank attempts to define the "affected party" as being a community of persons such as an organisation, association, society or other grouping of individuals, the full length of this term is not clear. As we pointed out before, since it is open ended, it would appear that it can cover other bodies than those suggested. It is not clear, for example, what is meant with "or other grouping of individuals" and especially what is not meant by it. But it is significant that it can include a local representative of such party. The idea of excluding international representatives of an affected party deprives the potential requesters of their usual tools. For example, a Western NGO can submit a complaint to the African Commission on behalf of an African victim but can not request to the Inspection Panel for the same victim under the Bank rules. More vague still is the term "another representative" in *exceptional cases* where the party submitting the request contends that appropriate representation is not locally available and the Executive Directors so agree. The difficulty of trying to determine which of the cases would apply in this case nearly makes the provision otiose.

The attempt to expand the list of requesters by co-opting the Executive Directors makes the Bank process unique. The Executive Director's power to request an inspection is however limited to "special cases of serious alleged violations of such policies and procedures". This limitation subtracts from the innovations the clause would otherwise have had. Even more, it is not clear who would determine the existence of conditions in which this power can be employed. Since it has not been used to date it is not possible to realistically speculate how it will ultimately develop. There is no doubt however that it is of limited value only. But the Executive Directors are empowered to "at any time instruct the Panel to conduct an investigation". This power which can only be exercised by the Board jointly can make up for the otherwise limited mandate of the mechanism if the Board was keen to use it. Up to now however, it has not been tested, which makes it largely academic.

Anonymous requests have not really made an additional improvement in accessing the Panel. The same reasons that would constrain open requests would apply to them. But the most difficult problem with anonymous requests is how the Bank would make sure that the requester in fact remains anonymous throughout the process. Their main fear is to be disclosed to the government and to local inhabitants. In various cases where anonymity has been applied in other human rights cases, it has been with guarded success. Often, when trying to investigate the complaint in the violating state, the government somehow gets to know the identity of the complainant. People know that when international bodies assure you of the anonymity of your identity, the assurance is fake and should not be relied upon as at some stage officials will get to know the identity of the complainant. It is not possible to imagine that this identity can successfully be withheld when in fact some details of the subject matter of the violation will be necessary to send to authorities to investigate the complaint at the local level and this can disclose the identity of the requester. Besides, if it is insisted that local remedies must first be exhausted, as the Inspection Panel has ruled in the Ethiopian request cited above, it renders the principle of anonymity essentially empty of any substance. The Bank must not dupe itself into believing this will not happen to it. State bodies in various countries have a way of finding out even the most secret of the information. It is important that the Bank deals with the government of the borrowing state on this issue directly rather than give the potential complainant a false sense of security.

COLLECTIVE AND MATERIAL INTERESTS

Paragraph 14 of the Resolution requires that the affected party demonstrates that its rights or interests "have been or are likely to be directly affected by an action or omission of the Bank as a result of failure of the Bank to follow its operational policies and procedures". Further, it is required that the requester shows that such failure "has had or threatens to have a material adverse effect". It is not enough under the rules for a party to merely claim to be victim of the failure. It must be showed how the group has been "materially affected" as a result of the failure. The idea that one must demonstrate how the failure has affected them in material terms is aimed at excluding psychological losses. In other words, a requester need not only reveal general allegations of fact in substantiation of the request for an inspection but should in fact raise issues under the Bank policies and operational practices as well as proving detriment suffered collectively as a result of the failure. But it is a matter of degree how concretely this requirement should be taken. While it seems the stress in the term "a material adverse effect" imposes a duty on the requesters to outline the circumstances that have produced the adverse effects, the group must also show how they, as a group, have been directly affected and that the effect has not only been material but adverse as well. How concretely should this requirement be taken? If it is a matter of degree, can there be any standards of effect that would surface from those that would not? This would be highly unrealistic.

As already pointed out, it is completely unrealistic for the Bank to insist on proof of collective harm rather than simply on harm. Any harm that results from the Bank policies, activities or its failure to act should be redressed by way of requests. A harm is a harm even if it has affected the parties variously. Some of the parties in the group may be affected materially while others not so materially. There will be different degrees of harm between individuals. Either because one's house is located further away from the dam or for another reason, the injury will differ. The Bank should not assume what is practically impossible in some cases. It is impossible to find the same degree of harm for all individuals in an area. This should not be the main condition for responding to a request. The Bank should revise the model form used for requesting inspection, especially in paragraph 5 which asks requesters to state that they believe their interests or rights have been or are likely to be "adversely" affected as a direct result of the Bank violation, by removing the word adversely. Further, paragraphs 2 and 4 of the same model requiring the requester to make reference to the Bank policies and procedures are extremely prohibitive since most people can not successfully fill in the form in an intelligible sense. Even the requirement to state the rights and interests of the requesters is such that very few of the potential requesters can fulfil it to the extent required. Rather, the paragraph should be redressed by a condition which may require requesters to describe their alleged violation. But most important of all, this information must be disseminated to the general public. The public at large must be taught how to use the requesting procedures as well as their rights under the Inspection Panel. Otherwise there is no need to have the Panel at all.

CONCLUSION

The Inspection Panel is an important mechanism for ensuring the monitoring by society of the conduct of the World Bank in relation to its own policies and rules. In today's society, the Panel adds substantially to the principle of accountability. It is important however that the system of rules governing the Panel is continuously being reviewed (as is already the case) to make it more effective in responding to growing concerns. The idea is to make the Bank more and more aware by other means of its shortcomings and how these may have affected the people who are supposed to benefit from the mechanism. It should be possible to find a mechanism which allows more and more people to come forward with such information to the Bank. We should not fear to be flooded with requests. This is what must happen in an institution which takes pride in being part of the society. A system can be abused even when strictly guarded by the most restrictive rules. This should not be the main concern of the rules.

The World Bank Inspection Panel: Amplifying Citizen Voices for Sustainable Development

*Dana Clark and David Hunter**

I. Providing Context: Why the Inspection Panel Was Created

A. Background – The Growing Demand for Sustainable Development

The World Bank Inspection Panel was created in 1993, as a result of the ongoing efforts of an international coalition of non-governmental organizations (NGOs) to transform the World Bank into a transparent and accountable sustainable development organization. Many ill-designed and controversial projects, such as the Pak Mun dam in Thailand, the Kedung Ombo dam in Indonesia, the Polonoroeste road project in Brazil, the transmigration project in Indonesia and the Sardar Sarovar dam on India's Narmada River, mobilized international NGOs and donor countries to begin questioning the Bank's way of doing business.[1] The international Bank reform campaign reflected a growing awareness that public tax dollars from donor countries were going to support projects in borrowing countries that had significant, adverse effects on the local and global environment, and that seemed to exacerbate rather than alleviate poverty.

After years of pressure, the transformation to sustainable development is far from complete, but many observers have noted the important successes of the reform campaign in pushing environmental and other reforms at the World Bank.[2] Among the most important reforms was the Bank's adoption of a set of environmental and social policies that aimed at improving the environmental, human rights and citizen participation record of the Bank. These included policies to ensure environmental assessment, consultation with indigenous peoples in projects that affected their rights, public access to

* The authors are working at the Center for International Environmental Law, Washington D.C.

1 For further information on the environmental critique of the World Bank's operations, see Bruce Rich, Mortgaging the Earth (1993); Catherine Caufield, Masters of Illusion: The World Bank and the Poverty of Nations (1996).

2 *See, e.g.*, Robert Wade, *Greening the Bank*, at 654, in Devesh Kapur, et al, eds., The World Bank: Its First Half Century (Brookings Institution, 1997).

information, and appropriate compensation for local people who are forcibly resettled by Bank-financed projects.

In short, these policies provided the fabric of rules for the Bank – the body of law in essence – for the transition of Bank activities toward sustainable development. The rules embodied the Bank's commitment to sustainable development and represented in many ways a new bargain between donor and borrower governments. In the future, money would be available not for old-style development that tended to impoverish people and to harm the environment, but for sustainable development that was based on tenets of environmental protection, respect for human rights, local participation, and broader transparency.[3] These new policies set the conditions by which donor countries could expect future Bank projects to be designed and implemented.

Although taken together the policies were an important step toward sustainable development, a major weakness plagued the Bank's reliance on a policy-based approach since the outset. Implementation of the policies depended entirely on self-policing, with no independent oversight. But the Bank's "culture of approval" encourages staff to process loans quickly and move large amounts of money, without adequate concern for the quality of implementation or the extent to which the projects are in compliance with Bank policies. As a result, policies that were supposed to ensure social and environmental sustainability have in many cases been routinely ignored by Bank staff, and the policies seemed to have little or no significant impact on improving the environmental and social profile of the Bank's overall portfolio.

The Bank's failure to comply with its policies was made devastatingly clear by its involvement with the controversial Sardar Sarovar dam on India's Narmada River. The Bank-supported project would affect over 200,000 people and have devestating environmental impacts. A grassroots uprising against the dam was supported by national and international NGOs. Human rights observers documented the social consequences of the project, and the world called for an evaluation of the World Bank's role.

In response, the Bank commissioned the first-ever independent review of a Bank-financed project. The review team, which became known as the Morse Commission after its Chairman Bradford Morse, published its findings in June 1992. The Morse Commission Report meticulously documented clear and routine violations of Bank policies on environmental impact assessment and involuntary resettlement, and the devastating human and environmental costs of those policy violations. The report concluded that the responsibility for

---

[3] *See, e.g.,* Declaration of the Copenhagen Social Summit, para. 6. For explanations of the relationship of sustainable development to issues of environment, human rights and good governance, see, e.g., Konrad Ginther et al, eds., Sustainable Development and Good Governance (1995).

improper resettlement of thousands of families appeared to "rest with the Bank" and that the "history of the environmental aspects of Sardar Sarovar is a history of noncompliance."[4] Indian NGOs called for the Bank to withdraw from the project, and ultimately the Indian government asked for cancellation of the Bank loan.

The Morse Commission's findings that the Bank largely disregarded its social and environmental policies and tolerated the borrower's violations of the policies, were soon confirmed more generally by an internal review of Bank projects. The Narmada policy violations were not an aberration, but a systemic part of the Bank's culture. The report, authored by Bank Vice President Willi Wapenhans, criticized the Bank's pervasive "culture of approval," in which the incentive structure encouraged staff to perceive the appraisal process as merely a "marketing device for securing loan approval."[5] This culture of approval led to the promotion of projects based on financial considerations, without adequate attention to the social and environmental implications of those projects. In essence, the failure of the Bank to ensure compliance with its environmental and social policies meant that the promise of sustainable development embodied in the policies was being sacrificed to the expedience of moving money through the pipeline.

B. Creation of the Inspection Panel

Spurred on by the international NGO reform campaign and the growing civil society consensus for sustainable development, member country governments called on the Bank to develop a transparent system of accountability, to try to ensure that public funds were spent more consistently with the Bank's mandate of sustainable development and poverty alleviation. The emphasis was now on improving Bank accountability for violating its policies and procedures. In response, in 1993 the Bank's Board of Directors passed an improved access-to-information policy and created the independent inspection panel.

The Inspection Panel, which formally opened in 1994, is an innovative forum for those people most directly affected by World Bank projects to raise their concerns at the highest levels of the Bank. Project-affected people can bring a claim to the Inspection Panel asking for an independent analysis of the Bank's role in the project, and the extent to which the Bank has complied with its own policies and procedures. The claimants must be directly and adversely

4 Sardar Sarovar: An Independent Review, xx-xxi (1992).

5 World Bank, Effective Implementation: Key to Development Impact, Report of the Portfolio Mangaement Task Force, at iii, 12 (Washington, D.C., 1992).

affected by the Bank's alleged policy violations, and the subject matter of the claim must have been brought previously to the Bank without a satisfactory response to the problem. The Panel is by definition an avenue of last resort, to be used when the staff of the Bank have been unresponsive to the concerns of the affected people.[6]

The Inspection Panel is a unique institutional development. It represents the first time that a global institution has created a direct line of access for citizens to monitor its own operations. By recognizing that nation-states are made up of individual stakeholders who have a legitimate role to play in international affairs, the Panel is a critical precedent for the democratization of international institutions generally.[7] The Inspection Panel does not only offer project-affected people a unique opportunity to enforce their rights to participate in the design, oversight and monitoring of Bank-financed projects; it also provides important opportunities for both the Board of Directors and Bank staff to improve their performance in moving the Bank toward a sustainable development model.[8]

Unfortunately, the Panel's role and value have not been fully internalized either by the Board of Directors or by Bank management and staff. The result is that for two years now the Panel has been under almost constant 'review' by the Board of Directors, and its recommendations and independence have been undermined by deep rifts at the Board level and suspicion from senior Bank management. As a result, the Panel has never been allowed to achieve its full potential for improving Bank performance. In the following sections we first revisit the potential benefits of the Panel process to the World Bank and then address some of the current impediments being placed in the way of an effective Panel.

II. The Inspection Panel's Importance for the World Bank

The Inspection Panel embodies a unique approach to increasing accountability at an international institution, in that it places the power to initiate oversight in the hands of citizens, often living and working at the project level. As a result, the Panel has the potential to bridge the gap between top-level decision

---

[6] For a further discussion of the elements for bringing a claim, see Dana Clark & Michael Hsu, A Citizen's Guide to the World Bank Inspection Panel (Center for International Environmental Law, 1997). *See also,* International Bank for Reconstruction and Development, *The World Bank Inspection Panel,* Res., No. 93-10 (Sept. 22, 1993); The Inspection Panel, *Operating Procedures* (Aug. 1994). <http://www.igc.apc.org/ciel/>.

[7] For a conceptual discussion of the need for greater civil society involvement in international affairs, *see, e.g.,* Philip Allot, Eunomia (1992).

[8] Ibrahim Shihata, The World Bank Inspection Panel 5 (1994).

makers at the World Bank and the people who actually feel the impacts of those decisions. By amplifying the voices of project-affected people, the Panel offers the Bank a critical avenue for moving toward a more sustainable development model and provides a surprisingly wide range of related benefits at every level of the institution – from the Board of Directors, which is provided unscreened, field-based information, to Bank Management, which is provided another tool to help ensure policy compliance, to the project task managers, who can use Panel investigations and findings as a way to improve project implementation, and to affected communities, who can ask that their interests under Bank policies be protected.

A. Facilitating a Culture of Results

As a mechanism for overseeing policy compliance, the Inspection Panel complements the Bank's other efforts to improve project implementation and move towards President Wolfensohn's stated goal of a culture of results. The very existence of the Panel helps to improve the incentive system within the Bank and should encourage Bank staff to be more careful in ensuring compliance with Bank policies and in being more responsive to the concerns voiced by local citizens. In several situations, local groups have decided against filing a claim to the Inspection Panel, because Management became more responsive to their concerns and took their suggestions into account at the project level. This heightened awareness of the need to ensure policy compliance or be held accountable will play a critical role in shifting the Bank from a culture of approval to a culture of results. As the Bank's General Counsel has noted,

> the mere presence of the Panel is likely to make the Bank staff more diligent in the observance of Bank policies. The usual zeal of presenting projects for Board approval in a manner and pace that meet the lending program's targets will be tempered, to a greater extent than in the past, by the zeal not to put the institution in the embarrassing position of being found in non-compliance with its own policies and procedures. Since these policies and procedures are meant to ensure quality in the Bank-financed projects and to serve broader institutional objectives approved by Bank members (through the Executive Directors), the greater attention paid to them can only serve the Bank, its members as a whole, and in particular the borrowers concerned.[9]

In addition, as with the findings of the Morse Commission, the findings of the Inspection Panel can play an important role in highlighting the consequences of pushing projects through based on loan targets rather than quality. For example, according to the Financial Times the Inspection Panel report for

---

9 *Id.* at 114.

its desk review of the Singrauli claim found that violations were even worse than initially thought and were primarily attributable to intense pressure from the bank's own management to accelerate the loan approval process. Further, the Panel reportedly concluded that "[t]here was no time to ensure that essential mechanisms and preconditions, such as state government commitment, capacity of implementing agency, etc. were in place or adequate" and as a result, "many local inhabitants lost their homes and livelihoods, while associated environmental problems damaged nearby farms and crops."[10] The Panel's independent analysis of the history of processing the Singrauli loan demonstates the continuing influence of the culture of approval.

Inspection Panel claims provide a context for evaluating the Bank's progress in improving the quality of project implementation. Indeed, most claims brought to the Panel have sought improvements in project design or implementation, not to stop or prohibit specific projects. Many claimants to the Panel have a shared objective with the Bank – ensuring that Bank funds are spent in accordance with the promises made in the loan agreement and in furtherance of the Bank's policies.

B. Identifying Systemic Policy Violations

Although neither the Board nor Bank management has yet reviewed the experience with the Panel with the aim of learning about the Bank's activities, the accumulating lessons of the Panel's investigations do highlight that the Bank is regularly violating certain policies. For example, nearly every legitimate claim that has come to the Inspection Panel has emphasized a failure of the Bank to meet the terms of its policy on project supervision. This policy is fundamental to the Bank's ability to transform itself to a sustainable development organization, because the components of the projects most frequently ignored are precisely those that mark the difference between development as it was practiced in the past and sustainable development. In short, social and environmental planning and mitigation have frequently not been implemented. Thus, for example, Brazil successfully built the roads contemplated in the PLANAFLORO project but neglected to demarcate the indigenous lands or rubber tapper reserves that were the 'sustainable' part of the project. Argentina was able to construct the Yacretá dam, but failed to provide the mitigation measures required prior to filling the reservoir, including providing adequate sanitation and housing to resettled communities. Most of the claims to date have thus sought to make the Bank fulfill its project

---

[10] Mark Suzman, *World Bank Accuses Itself of 'Serious Violation,'*, Financial Times, Jan, 7, 1998, at 5.

supervisory role and thereby ensure that the parts of projects meant to mitigate the environmental or social impacts are not forgotten during design, appraisal and implementation.

Similarly, most claims have also identified violations of the Involuntary Resettlement policy.[11] This is a critical issue for the Bank as a development institution, particularly given that current World Bank projects in process or in the pipeline are projected to displace more than two million people. As Theodore Downing has noted, "when people are displaced by development projects, social impoverishment seems incongruous, if not grotesque."[12] Recognizing the risks associated with development-induced displacement, the Bank's policy on involuntary resettlement requires that those who lose their lands or livelihoods to make way for a project should at least have their former standards of living restored, if not improved.

The Bank has historically maintained a dismal record of compliance with its policy on involuntary resettlement. This is borne out by the reality on the ground, and from internal and external critiques. A 1994 World Bank study of its experience with resettlement found that the Bank was failing in large part to rehabilitate the millions of people involuntarily displaced by Bank-financed projects.[13] Further analysis of problems with resettlement has been provided by the Inspection Panel's experience in several cases, such as Itaparica and Yacyretá. The Panel reports have documented and confirmed that large-scale resettlement leads to impoverishment of affected communities, and that the Bank has repeatedly failed to meet the terms of its policy on Involuntary Resettlement. The Panel experience could serve as a much-needed catalyst to force the Bank to re-evaluate its experience with involuntary resettlement. Any objective reconsideration of the issue should lead the Bank to change its lending portfolio to avoid large-scale resettlement. The focus should be on improving the performance of the Bank's portfolio, rather than on weakening the policy on involuntary resettlement.

---

11 *See, Involuntary Resettlement*, World Bank Operational Directive 4.30 (June 1990).

12 Theodore Downing in McDowell, *Understanding Impoverishment* 34 (1996).

13 Out of the 192 projects involving involuntary resettlement between 1986-1993, the Bankwide Review could identify only one where the Bank could claim that the resettled population had improved its standard of living, and even that claim is disputed by members of the identified community. The World Bank, *Resettlement and Development: The Bankwide Review of Projects Involving Involuntary Resettlement 1986-1993* (1994) 4, 2; *see also* Alex Wilks & Nicholas Hildyard, *Evicted! The World Bank and Forced Resettlement,* The Ecologist, vol. 24, no. 6, at 226 (Nov.-Dec. 1994).

C. Requiring the Bank and Borrower to Keep Their Promises

As noted above, many of the major Panel claims thus far have demonstrated significant problems with the Bank's supervision of project implementation. This is not simply an issue of a failure to follow Bank policies, however, but is an issue of whether the Bank can keep its promises – both to the donor countries and to the project-affected people. The Panel claims involving PLANAFLORO, Itaparica, Yaycretá, the IFC-financed BioBio project, and Singrauli have all demonstrated that promises made at the time controversial projects are designed (and in some cases made specifically to gain the support of Executive Directors and project-affected peoples) are largely ignored and forgotten during project implementation.

Most Panel claims at their root have simply asked that the Bank do a better job of keeping its promises and, when those promises also imply promises from the Borrower, that the Bank take its role of supervising the Borrower more seriously. Viewed in this light, it is hard to understand the deep resentment that Panel claims seem to instill in Bank staff and Borrower government officials. Having a mechanism that investigates projects that are not being implemented according to the approved terms and conditions allows the Bank to exercise it's fiduciary duty to its members and the affected people its projects are designed to help.

D. Bridging the Board's Information Gap

The World Bank's Board of Executive Directors is faced with a tremendous amount of paper and information that is passed up from the World Bank staff. However, this information is often filtered and packaged by the Bank management and staff in a way that facilitates smooth Board approval of proposed projects. The Board has little opportunity to gather independent information or to conduct any independent due diligence to check on the information. Moreover, the sheer amounts of information facing the Board means that the challenge of identifying problem projects is virtually impossible from their perspective.

The Inspection Panel process provides an important, alternative mechanism for informing the Board (and top Bank Management) of potential problem projects. By providing an impartial analysis of a particular project, the Panel provides the Board with timely information that can allow the Board of Directors to focus on challenges in project implementation and policy compliance, on both a project-specific basis and also systematically as certain patterns emerge from the various claims. The Board has a fiduciary responsibility to ensure that the projects it approves are implemented in accordance with the objectives and policies of the institution. The Board is also the appropriate organ within the Bank to take responsibility for problem projects, and to authorize and mandate steps to improve the projects. As the General Counsel has noted, the Panel simply "provides the Executive Directors and the President, through its findings, with independently ascertained facts which enable them to perform their duties and to ensure the Bank's compliance with its policies and procedures."[14]

The Inspection Panel thus provides an important opportunity for the Board to receive local-level information about the quality of project design and implementation and to hear directly from the people who are affected by projects approved by the Board. However, the claims are not the only process for facilitating this dialogue with project-affected people. A recent meeting organized by the Inspection Panel brought the Board together with individuals from Brazil, Paraguay and Nepal who had participated in the Panel process. This historic event illustrated the potential value of providing members of the Board with direct access to the experiences and insights of those affected by Bank projects. The Board should take increased advantage of such an opportunity in the future.

E. Increasing Bank Credibility

The existence of an impartial and independent forum for affected people increases the accountability, and thus credibility, of the Bank as an institution. This is true globally, as the international Bank reform effort has supported the Panel's mandate of increased accountability and transparency, and it is true locally, as claimants discover that they finally have a forum responsive to their concerns. For example, when Elias Diaz Peña of Sobrevivencia in Paraguay met with Executive Directors about the Yacyretá project, he explained that the visit of the Inspection Panel to the project area in response to a claim filed by the people, the attentiveness of the members of the Panel to the concerns of the people, and the fact that the people could expect an official response from the Bank, were all new and remarkable developments in the relationship between the local people and the Bank. Said Peña, "this was the first time that someone from the Bank actually listened to our concerns." Experiences like this are what build the credibility of the Bank amongst the local people.

---

14 *See* Shihata, *supra* note 7, at 117 (emphasis in original).

F. Channelling Local Opposition to a Project

The Inspection Panel has the potential to help reconfigure the relationship between the World Bank and people who are directly affected by the projects it finances. As explained above, the Panel can help to restore the credibility of the World Bank in the eyes of local people, who in many cases have viewed the Bank as a non-responsive entity that provided continued financial support for seriously flawed projects. The process of filing a claim can also help foster a sense of community empowerment. The people work together to develop a claim and then also to engage in what they hope can be a constructive dialogue with the Panel and the Bank, a dialogue which can take more than a year. The Panel process allows the community to articulate its concerns in a way that actually leads to a result rather than further neglect, and this helps to restore a sense of participation in the project.

This process serves an important role for the institution as well as the community, in that it helps channel the peoples' frustrations into a process that reinvigorates dialogue with the Bank. If the Panel process is allowed to operate as intended, it can provide an important means of constructively dealing with local concerns and dissatisfaction, potentially defusing mass protest. The oversight of the Inspection Panel stimulates greater openness and transparency by the Bank and borrower. The involvement of the Panel often compels project authorities to focus more seriously on the social and environmental problems in the project. Ideally, this should lead to greater communication flow between the institution and the affected people, and greater respect for and attention to their concerns.

The Itaparica claim illustrates what can happen when these lines of communication are closed. Hundreds of Brazilians affected by the Itaparica dam petitioned the Panel for a review of the Bank's role in a loan that was supposed to provide resettlement and irrigation benefits to the displaced population. The Panel found very serious problems in the project and recommended an investigation. However, the Board refused to authorize an investigation, approving instead an action plan promised by the Brazilian government – an action plan that neither the Board, the Panel nor the claimants had ever seen. Several more months passed without the claimants or other affected people receiving any action plan, but still continuing to suffer the ill effects of the failed resettlement effort. On March 11, 1998, 3,000 rural workers occupied the offices of the project authority in protest of the failures of the project and the refusal of the Brazilian government to meet with Polo Sindical, the peasants' organization that represented the claimants to the Inspection Panel. If the Panel had been allowed to conduct an investigation in the first place, or if the action plan had been vetted publicly as part of the response to the Panel claim, the energy expended in the social unrest could have been harnessed for developing an appropriate solution.

G. Improving the Plight of Affected Communities

Many of the reasons for the Panel described above have to do with how Panel claims can help the overall structure and operations of the Bank, but of equal or perhaps even greater importance is the value of the Panel as a mechanism for improving the day-to-day lives of project-affected people and communities. The experience with Bank-financed projects, particularly large infrastructure projects over the past few decades (and continuing today) is that these projects can have potentially devastating impacts on local communities that are either forcibly resettled or that have lost local resources vital to their economic well-being.

To be sure, no matter how well intentioned and no matter how well implemented, large infrastructure projects like those historically financed by the Bank will have negative impacts on some local communities. Mitigating those impacts is exactly the goal of many of the Bank's policies and many of the loan conditions that are made at the time of project approval. The Panel is not set up to reduce all harm to affected people, but only that harm exacerbated or caused by the Bank's neglect of its policies or the loan conditions. And who better than the project-affected people, themselves, to be empowered to bring these problems to the attention of the highest levels of the World Bank?

Nor should the Bank be overly concerned, as has been suggested by some Borrowing countries, about establishing islands of prosperity, where some local people seem to enjoy more rights and privileges than do the general population. To some extent, this is exactly the goal of Bank projects, and certainly it is the goal of the Bank's environmental and social policies and procedures – i.e. to establish a set of minimum standards for improving the treatment of projected affected communities. In this respect, projects financed by the World Bank may very well treat locally affected people better than projects financed from other means. That is the point, afterall of the environmental and social policies and related loan covenants, and indirectly of the Panel's oversight authority.

Ultimately, the Panel should be evaluated according to its ability to bring about improvements on the ground – to improve the lives of the affected peoples that have taken the difficult step to file a claim in the first place. It is frankly difficult at this time to evaluate the Panel's record in this regard. The filing of most of the claims has had an immediate positive impact on the plight of local communities, because the threat of independent oversight has led the Bank staff and the entities responsible for project implementation to improve their operations at least temporarily. Thus, for example, the Jamuna Bridge claim from Bangladesh led almost immediately to the inclusion of tens of thousands of people who had been inappropriately left out of the resettlement program. The filing of the PLANAFLORO claim led almost immediately to initial steps for demarcating indigenous lands – steps that were two years overdue. Similarly, shortly after the Yacyretá claim was filed, Argentina began its first modest steps toward providing the $300 million promised for resettlement and environmental mitigation. Unfortunately, long-term improvements in the communities seem to be less certain because as soon as the threat of transparent outside oversight is gone, the projects seem to revert back to many of the pre-existing problems.

III. Getting Back on Track: Returning to the Quest for Accountability

As of March 1998, ten claims have been filed with the Panel. The claims have successfully elevated the voice and concerns of project-affected people to the highest levels of the Bank and forced Bank Management and the Board of Executive Directors to confront difficult questions about the ground-level reality of certain controversial projects. But the experience thus far has not provided the range of benefits to the Bank described above, and in this section we explore some of the obstacles that have been placed in the way of the Panel process and offer specific recommendations for overcoming them.[15]

A. The Bank's Defensive Responses: Blocking Panel Investigations

Unfortunately, neither Bank Management nor the Board as a whole has viewed Panel claims positively and thus neither has risen to the challenges or opportunities presented by the Panel process. For example, rather than viewing the Inspection Panel as an important complement to improving project quality, Bank Management has responded to claims, claimants, and the Panel with suspicion and in some cases outright antagonism. Indeed, Bank Management's responses to claims have gone outside of the process envisioned in the Board Resolution creating the Panel. Management's responses

[15] These recommendations are adapted in part from an independent review of the Panel process conducted in 1997. *See* Lori Udall, The World Bank Inspection Panel: A Three Year Review (Bank Information Center, Oct. 1997).

and its tendency to disregard the intended process, have served to turn virtually every claim into a conflict situation. Rather than providing information and evidence about whether the Bank has complied with its policies as required under the Resolution, Management in Arun, Rondonia, Itaparica and Yacyretá responded by challenging the eligibility of the claim. In addition to violating the Resolution,[16] Management's adversarial and legalistic approach immediately placed the Inspection Panel on the defensive and led them to take the unanticipated role of being an advocate for the claim and the panel process. This has detracted from the Panel's role as a neutral fact-finder.

The legalistic nature of some of the responses from Bank Management also presents potentially significant issues regarding conflicts of interest in the multiple roles taken on by the Bank's Office of General Counsel. In fact, the Bank's legal department which answers to the General Counsel, is charged internally with reviewing the response to each claim. Then, as the claims are presented to, and debated among, the Executive Directors for their decision, the General Counsel provides additional legal interpretations. Thus, the General Counsel's office both represents Management in its response to a claim and provides legal advice to the decisionmaker (the Board). In some narrow circumstances, the Bank's Legal Department is even authorized to provide advice to the Panel regarding the Bank's rights and obligations."[17] The result is at least an appearance of a conflict of interest that significantly undermines the perceived credibility and objectivity in the overall Panel process. The General Counsel's response – that he is not personally engaged in responding to Inspection Panel claims on behalf of Bank Management – does not alleviate the conflict, particularly since the lawyers at least partly responsible for representing Management's interests in the claim process work directly for the General Counsel. To avoid the appearance of any conflict of interest and to increase the overall credibility of the process, the Board of Directors should engage independent, outside counsel when addressing legal issues raised in an Inspection Panel claim.[18]

---

[16] According to the Board Resolution and Panel Operating Procedures, Bank Management's initial response to a claim is supposed to be limited to providing the Panel "with evidence that it has complied, or intends to comply with the Bank's relevant policies and procedures." *See* Board Resolution, *supra* note 7, at para. 18; Panel Operating Procedures, *supra* note 7, at para. 27. Management is not authorized to provide legal interpretation of the Resolution or of the claimants eligibility. Initially, Bank Management provided their eligibility arguments directly to the Board of Directors, thus trying to bypass and undermine the Panel completely. This practice was stopped after complaints by NGO observers.

[17] Board Resolution, *supra* note 7, at para. 15.

[18] Note that there is precedent within the World Bank Group for using independent counsel. When President Wolfensohn was facing difficult legal issues relating to the release of the independent report he commissioned to investigate the Pangue Dam on Chile's BioBio River,

For its part, except for the very first claim, the Board has significantly modified, conditioned or outright rejected every single recommendation the Panel has made to investigate a claim. Before the investigation can proceed under the Panel Resolution, the Board must authorize a full investigation, after receiving the recommendation of the Panel based on a preliminary review. In practice, the Board's decisionmaking has been plagued with delays and has been highly politicized. In some instances, for example in the case of PLANAFLORO, the Board asked for additional information from the Panel as an obvious way to delay making any decision. Overall, the Board's reluctance to authorize investigations in cases that clearly meet the eligibility requirements set forth in the Resolution has infringed on the Panel's independence and diminished the Panel's (and the Bank's) overall credibility.

The Board should take itself out of this initial stage, and empower the Panel to determine whether a claim warrants an investigation. The Board could continue to have a role in that decision, but the presumption should be more clearly in favor of upholding Panel recommendations. One suggestion is that the Panel could submit to the Board a memorandum summarizing its decision whether or not to investigate, and the Board could review that on a "no objection plus" basis – in other words, if there was an objection by a certain number of Board members, then a full Board meeting would be convened to determine by majority vote whether to reverse the Panel's decision.

In recent claims where the Board has rejected a full investigation, but authorized a "review and assessment" (Yacyretá) or a "limited investigation" (Singrauli), the Board has collectively determined the terms of reference for the Panel's investigation. Thus, in Yacyretá, the Board asked the Panel to look at current problems in the project and to assess the adequacy of the action plans. This restricted the Panel from examining the history of policy violations in the project, which is critical both for understanding how the project got to its current state and therefore how to design an appropriate remedy, and also for purposes of accountability. Even more seriously, in the Singrauli claim, the Board restricted the Panel to a "Washington" review and prohibited the Panel from going to India, where the project is located. This decision effectively cut the affected people out of the investigation process and prevented the Panel from exercising many of the investigatory measures outlined in the Panel's Operating Procedures (such as meetings with the claimant, Bank authorities and NGOs in the country where the project is located; visiting the project site, etc.). The Panel should be empowered to set the terms of reference for any investigation. After having evaluated all of the evidence presented in the claim and submitted by Bank management and having visited the site as part of the

---

he engaged the law firm of Wilmer, Cutler & Pickering to provide him with legal advice independent of the IFC General Counsel.

preliminary review, the Panel is in the best position to issue its own terms of reference for an investigation.

B. The Claimants Want Action, Not Action Plans

Management's suspicion and lack of support for the Inspection Panel has also been demonstrated by the way Management has developed action plans in response to many of the claims – particularly when one considers that for a claim to be eligible it means Management must have failed to respond adequately to the same complaint previously. Indeed, at this time one of the almost certain outcomes of filing a claim is that management and the borrower will develop an action plan. The development of action plans is conceptually a positive step, as they offer an opportunity for fixing the specific problems raised in the claim. In practice, though, the action plans have been developed without participation of the claimants, other project-affected people or the Panel; they have been introduced at a time and in a way that tends to undermine the Panel's ability to conduct an investigation; and they have been used to shift the focus of the claim process (and thus the blame for policy violations) from the Bank to the borrower country governments.

The way in which Management has developed and provided action plans also contravenes the Resolution creating the Panel mechanism. Under the Resolution and the Panel Operating Procedures, any action plan developed in response to a claim should be presented either when Management provides its initial response to a claim[19] or when it submits final recommendations after the Panel's full investigation is over.[20] Instead, Management and/or the Borrower have submitted action plans directly to the Board of Directors, offering them as an alternative to authorization of an inspection into the specific claim. In several cases, the Board has used approval of Management's Action Plan as an excuse to deny an Inspection Panel investigation. When this happens, no independent mechanism is left to ensure that action plans are translated into action (unless the Panel is invited to monitor implementation of the plan).

Moreover, under the ad hoc practice developed by Management, action plans have not been developed in cooperation with the claimants, nor do they necessarily address the specific problems raised in the claim. Perhaps more importantly, the claimants have demonstrated that the problems they have

---

[19] *See* Board Resolution, *supra* note 7 at Para. 18; Panel Operating Procedures, *supra* note 7, at para. 27 ("Management shall provide the Panel with evidence that it has complied, or intends to comply with the Bank's relevant policies and procedures.").

[20] Board Resolution, *supra* note 7, at para. 23; Panel Operating Procedures, *supra* note 7, at para. 54 ("Management will submit to the Executive Directors for their consideration a report indicating its recommendations in response to such findings.").

identified in Bank-financed projects deserve action – not action plans. The claimants have often seen multiple action plans by Management that promise change but accomplish little on the ground. For example, there had been several action plans to fix problems with the Yacyretá dam project before the claim, but little had actually been done to provide closed sewers or otherwise improve the plight of the resettled people.

Outside observers and some Board members have noted that, if properly developed and introduced, action plans and Panel investigations need not be mutually exclusive. Indeed, most of the claimants thus far have filed their claims specifically to catalyze action to improve the projects, but the action plans should be used to respond to, not undermine, the claims. If Management is designing a plan in response to a claim, Management should consult with the claimants and other affected people in the preparation of the plan and the final plan should be publicly available in the local language before the Board makes any decision.[21] The Panel should also be allowed to comment on the action plan before it is finalized and should be authorized to oversee the plan's implementation, with both the Panel and Management jointly and periodically reporting back to the Board on the plan's implementation. Such Panel review and oversight would provide the Board with an objective evaluation of the extent to which the action plan is responsive to the concerns identified in the claim, as well as the extent to which the plan itself is in compliance with Bank policies. It would also provide the claimants with greater confidence that their claim will be addressed through the action plan. Continued Panel oversight would give Management and the Borrower the incentive to actually implement the plan, and would provide a forum for both the claimants and the Board to ensure that implementation was satisfactory.

C. Politicization of the Panel Process at the Board Level

The single most important threat to the Panel at this time is the split between borrowers and donors at the Board of Directors. This split explains why the Board of Directors, once it created the Panel, has been unable to simply let the Panel operate with respect to individual claims. The split has also led to the current state of essentially permanent 'review' of the Panel, in which the

[21] The fact that many of the action plans have never been made publicly available is particularly disturbing. Claimants from Itaparica and Yacyreta have been unsuccessfully requesting a copy of the action plans that were developed in response to their claims. The Board of Executive Directors approved Brazil's action plan for Itaparica in lieu of authorizing an inspection, and never even saw the proposed document. Bank Management has also thus far refused to release the Yacyreta action plan, claiming that it is the property of the borrower.

Board of Directors, unable either to endorse or indict the Panel by consensus, muddles along effectively crippling the Panel's ability to operate.

The borrowing countries' general opposition to the Panel has been articulated in several ways – (1) a distaste for the word "inspection," (2) resentment of Management's tendency to blame the borrowing country government for problems identified by the claims; and (3) concern about who will pay for the costs of remedial actions which might be identified as necessary by the Panel process.

The concern about the language is one that could be fairly easily addressed. At least conceptually, the Panel could be authorized to 'review' a project, without any substantive changes in the Panel's mandate. In the one example where this was tried, however, in the 'review' of Yacyretá the Board actually reduced the substantive parameters of the Panel's investigation.

The concern about the borrowing government being blamed for project failure is more complex. Often, the problems in the project stem from poor design or planning and poor implementation, by both the Bank and the Borrower. In particular, if a claim challenges the Bank's failure to supervise its Borrower, the inquiry inevitably shifts to one that explores the relationship between those parties. Nonetheless, the very purpose of the Inspection Panel is to evaluate the Bank's role and to determine the extent to which the Bank has undermined a particular project. The Panel has been very careful to focus on the Bank, and most claimants to the Panel have insisted that they consider the Bank, rather than their government, to have primary culpability for project problems. Yet, the focus on the adequacy of action plans has tended to shift the Board discussions away from Bank responsibility and toward the Borrower's conduct.

The borrowing countries should endorse Panel oversight of the Bank's role in project design and implementation, because the Panel analysis can help clarify that many of the key problems in a project are attributable to the Bank, rather than the Borrower. The Bank is responsible for supervising and monitoring the project, and for ensuring that the Borrower is applying the proceeds of the loan or credit consistently with the loan agreement and Bank policy. The Bank should also be responsible for ensuring that the Borrower has the necessary capacity and resources to meet the terms of World Bank policies. In practice, however, projects are often designed in such a way that the Bank takes responsibility for financing the construction of the civil works and shifts the technical and financial responsibility for the social and environmental mitigation to the borrowing country government. The Bank also has the responsibility to ensure that social and environmental assessment and mitigation are fully incorporated in the design and implementation of projects. The Bank has a wealth of technical expertise to assist in these aspects of a project. It also has legal tools that it can utilize to ensure that these responsibilities are met at an early stage. All too often, though, the Bank has refused to utilize its resources or its remedies to correct obvious social and environmental devastation associated with projects. This can have economic, ecological, social and political ramifications for borrowing countries, which ultimately are left to cope with the consequences of failed development projects.

The third concern, regarding whether the Borrower will be forced to pay for additional costs of remedial actions that might be identified during a Panel investigation, is also potentially complicated. On the one hand, an investigation may find (such as was the case in Yacyretá) that the Bank failed to supervise the project effectively, and as one manifestation of this failure the Borrower simply did not contribute to the environmental and social mitigation that was promised at the time of loan approval. In such a case, the Borrower might reasonably be asked to fulfill the earlier promises. In other contexts, however, where the Bank's negligence has harmed affected people, the Bank (not the Borrower) might very well be the entity that should provide funds to fix the problem.

Note, however, that in most cases neither the Borrower nor the Bank should be surprised by the costs that may result from a Panel investigation. The Panel is simply enforcing operational policies and procedures that were in effect at the time the project was developed and implemented. These are not new costs, but costs about which both the Bank and the Borrower were fully informed all along. The only reason these costs may be a surprise is if they were not taken seriously at the time when the project was being designed. The Bank, for its part, must show the courage and the commitment to tell the Borrowers that projects cost more to do right – i.e. to do them according to the operational policies and directives.

The three reasons for opposition as articulated by the Borrowing countries tend to shroud deeper, more fundamental, concerns about the Panel process generally, and indeed about the Bank's commitment to the goal of sustainable development. In essence, the Borrowing countries oppose the Panel because they do not welcome the additional oversight into project implementation within their territory. This is seen both as a donor-driven infringement on their sovereignty and as an unnecessary condition on development assistance.

To some extent, this deeper borrowing-country opposition seems to misconceive the driving force behind Panel claims. The Panel process is not driven by donor countries or northern NGOs, but rather by project-affected citizens of borrowing countries. In this respect, Panel investigations are not donor-driven infringements on borrowing country sovereignty. They are rather an outlet for borrower-country citizens to ensure that their rights are not infringed upon by international institutions that they otherwise have limited access to or control over. This may still make borrowing country governments uncomfortable, but such discomfort has less to do with north-south politics than with concern that project-affected people may undermine top-down development decisions in their countries. Empowering local communities to participate in this way in development decisions is a hallmark of the sustainable development model.

The Panel mechanism has also brought to the surface a lingering lack of commitment among some borrowing countries to the Bank's environmental and social policies – policies adopted by the Bank in order to move toward sustainable development. Some borrowing country representatives now openly reject the benchmarks mandated by policies, for example, on involuntary resettlement. There is concern that the Bank's standards are often higher than the country's standards, resulting in disparity between the treatment of people affected by Bank projects and those affected by other development projects.

In the past, the Bank has been sympathetic to these concerns about the practicality of achieving the objectives of its policies. Rather than modifying the scale of its projects to comply with the policies, Bank staff has given a wink and a nod to policy violations, allowing project implementation to proceed. By providing a mechanism for enforcing the policies, the Panel has tightened the system and forced those who never took the policies seriously in practice to resist both the mechanism and the policies themselves. In response, Bank Management has suggested weakening some policies, such as involuntary resettlement. By weakening the policies, Management would not only deprive project-affected people of procedural and substantive rights, but also reduce the Panel's jurisdiction. This is a wrong-headed response to the serious problem of pervasive policy violations. As an institution dedicated to facilitating sustainable development and alleviating poverty, the Bank should change its portfolio, not its policies.

Essentially, the Board of Directors and top Bank officials must decide whether the Bank is going to take seriously the challenge of sustainable development and hold its projects to appropriate social and environmental standards. Is the Bank a standard setter, and will it only loan money for those projects that can meet its standards? Or will it water down its toughest policies, thereby undermining the shift toward sustainable development and place at risk the future support of donor countries?

To some extent, the borrowing countries' concerns with the Panel reflect the inherent unfairness of an oversight mechanism (the Panel) that operates only in borrowing countries; no similar institution operates in donor countries to ensure that their projects meet international standards. On the other hand, the Panel is established to monitor compliance with policies that now reflect the conditions under which donors are politically able and willing to continue providing financial support to the World Bank Group. In short, the policies and Panel may very well be the price of admission to future World Bank development assistance.

D. Impediments to Filing Claims

In bringing claims, locally affected people have overcome significant hurdles and in many cases demonstrated exceptional courage. Numerous factors block access to the Panel process, including a lack of knowledge of the existence of the Panel at the field level and the enormous risk that comes from challenging a Bank-financed project. Other hurdles include the fact that local people often do not have access to Bank policies and procedures, and that even when those policies are available they have not been translated into the local language.

More telling perhaps than what the Bank has done in opposing certain claims, is what they have not done to facilitate awareness of and access to the Inspection Panel. Despite a 1996 pronouncement by the Board that "Management will make significant efforts to make the Inspection Panel better known in borrowing countries,"[22] Bank Management has not taken any concrete steps to educate Bank staff regarding the Panel's role nor have they taken steps to inform project-affected people of the existence and role of the Panel. For example, the Bank organizes regional meetings with NGOs throughout the world, but has never invited the Panel to attend nor have they distributed at the meetings any significant information about the Panel's existence.

World Bank regional offices should actively disburse information relevant to the Panel process including the Resolution, Panel Procedures, Panel forms on how to file a claim, and Panel Annual Reports in local languages. World Bank policies and any claims and Panel reports from that country should also be available in local languages in all regional Bank offices and public information centers. The Panel should also more actively initiate meetings with affected people and communities to increase understanding about the Panel and its operations. Additionally, the Panel should ensure that relevant documents are translated into the language of the country from which the claim originated.

Simply expanding information about the Panel will not overcome what is perhaps the most significant impediment to filing an Inspection Panel claim: the danger associated with raising concerns about projects in some countries. Bank-financed projects often have a significant impact on borrowing countries' economies, and the governments of the countries are by definition

---

[22] Clarification of Certain Aspects of the Resolution, Oct. 17, 1996.

supportive of the projects and often unwilling to entertain criticism from locally affected people. The political dynamic inherent in a large-scale development project, particularly one involving resettlement, is that the government authorities have determined that a certain local population will have to undergo enormous upheaval in the name of the greater economic good of the country. To file a Panel claim would in many cases be considered anti-development and hence anti-government, a position that could lead to reprisals by the project authorities or the government. This can be highly risky for claimants. As a result, many claimants have opted, pursuant to Paragraph 18(a) of the Operating Procedures of the Inspection Panel, to request that the Panel keep their names confidential.

Three recent claims illustrate the dangers people face when they take a public stance regarding problems in Bank-financed projects. Fulgencio Manuel da Silva, one of the lead organizers of the claimants from the Itaparica project in Brazil, was shot and killed on October 16, 1997. Although it is not clear that his death was related directly to the claim, Mr. Da Silva's murder has been linked more generally to his efforts to organize and protect the rights of the peasant communities uprooted by the Itaparica project. On November 21, 1997 Madhu Kohli, the designated representative of claimants from Singrauli, India, was beaten as she tried to prevent a bulldozer from destroying the crops of a family that has not agreed to shift from its lands. The contractor assaulted Madhu Kohli in the presence of four officials of the National Thermal Power Corporation. The NTPC is the World Bank's largest-ever beneficiary, and its representatives reportedly did nothing to prevent the violence. Subsequently, Senior Bank management refused to investigate the incident, because a site visit would be "inconvenient" and would only "raise expectations."[23] Ultimately, Bank pressure led to the creation of an independent monitoring panel in the region. Finally, in February 1998 local people affected by the Yacyretá Hydroelectric Project, also the subject of a claim to the Inspection Panel, were beaten by police as they demanded that their concerns be addressed by the project authorities and the multilateral development banks.

[23] In a letter dated November 25, 1997 to Dana Clark of CIEL, Mieko Nishimizu, Vice President South Asia Region, wrote regarding the attack on Madhu Kohli: "I have instructed our Director in India [Edwin Lim] to advise me on this situation by obtaining a first hand report, on an urgent basis and in whatever manner he deems necessary." In a meeting one week later, Ms. Clark asked Mr. Lim what steps had been taken to obtain this urgent, first hand report. Mr. Lim responded to Ms. Clark that he had not gone to the field, had not discussed the incident with Madhu Kohli, and had not interviewed the NTPC staff involved. He further stated that no one from the Bank staff would be going to the field to investigate the alleged attacks because it was "inconvenient for Bank staff" and because Bank visits to the field "raise expectations of compensation." Dana Clark, Notes of meeting with Bank staff (Dec. 1, 1997).

Bank staff seem insufficiently aware of the risks that are assumed by claimants to the Inspection Panel in their quest for accountability. The Bank must consider the threats faced by people who are trying to argue for the rights guaranteed by Bank policies. As noted by Professor Daniel Bradlow, one of the early architects of the Panel concept, Bank policies often create the political space for local people to either participate in or protest a particular project. Often, by exercising – or attempting to exercise – the rights articulated in Bank policies, local people become exposed to repression by the State.[24] Even when disturbing events are called to the attention of Bank management, the Bank has refused to take a strong stand against such human rights abuses and has refused to provide any sort of institutional shield to the people who have invoked their rights under Bank policies or the Panel process.

CONCLUSION: EXPANDING THE ROLE OF THE CLAIMANTS

Despite the many problems that have beset the Inspection Panel process, one very clear message has emerged from the claims: the claimants have a perspective and ground-level understanding of Bank projects that the Bank desperately needs to hear, whether or not Management or the Board likes the message. By amplifying, rather than obstructing the voices from the project areas, the Bank could recapture the inherent value of the Panel process. The Inspection Panel was created to provide the Board and top Bank Management with an effective feedback loop to test the impact of their policies and projects on the ground and to assist in the broader effort to make the Bank's activities more sustainable. In practice, however, the early history of the Panel process shows insufficient support for learning from the experiences of project-affected people. Thus, expanding the effectiveness of claimant participation must overcome a strong institutional skepticism toward the value of hearing the voices from the field. It requires a cultural shift in the institution, but one that would reinforce the Bank's other steps toward a culture of results aimed at sustainable development.

The Panel process was designed to provide an effective voice for locally affected people. Yet, under current practice, once a claim is filed, the claimants disappear from the equation. The current Inspection Panel process lacks participation by the very people who initiate the inquiry and who are most directly affected by the outcome (or absence thereof) of the Panel review. For example, claimants have no opportunity to comment on Management's response, or the Panel's preliminary recommendation or final report

---

[24] Daniel D. Bradlow, "The World Bank, the IMF, and Human Rights," Transnational Law and Contemporary Problems 48, 50 (Spring 1996).

before it goes to the Board. Second, claimants have no opportunity to advocate for their interests or concerns at the time when the Board is determining whether to authorize an investigation or designing remedies based on the Panel's final report. In contrast, Management is present during these Board deliberations and actively tries to influence the decision making process. Third, the claimants have not been involved in the design or implementation of action plans, and in several cases have even been denied access to the action plans. Fourth, the claimants have no way to appeal decisions of the Panel or the Board, nor are they able to request that their claims be heard in a timely manner. These shortcomings should be considered and addressed as the Board evaluates its experience with the Inspection Panel.

Modest changes in the process can relatively easily increase the process's responsiveness to the rights and interests of claimants. Specific steps could be taken to extend the role of the claim and to provide greater fairness and due process to the claimants, including steps to ensure that the claimants have an opportunity to comment on the terms of reference for an investigation, the Panel's initial report and recommendation, Management action plans, and the Panel's final report. The claimants should also receive copies of all memoranda, letters or reports generated from Bank management, the Panel or General Counsel which are directly relevant to their claim. Finally, the claimants or an appointed representative should be allowed to attend any Board meeting (or part of a meeting) that specifically addresses their claim (particularly since Bank Management and the Panel can attend Board meetings where a claim is discussed).

If the claimants role is thus enlarged, the community-based aspect of the Panel process will be preserved and the shift from top-down development to development that considers the concerns and aspirations of local people will be advanced. In short, the Panel will be allowed to further its potentially unique and profound role in moving the Bank toward sustainable development.

The Inspection Policy of the Asian Development Bank

Eugenia McGill[*]

INTRODUCTION

The inspection policy of the Asian Development Bank (ADB), which was approved by its Board of Directors in late 1995, represents an important milestone in ADB's history. For the first time, people who are directly affected by development projects supported by ADB have a formal channel through which to raise concerns about the Bank's involvement in these projects. ADB's inspection policy also represents a variation on the concept of an "inspection function" first introduced at the World Bank in 1993 and then at the Inter-American Development Bank (IDB) in 1994.

This paper first provides background on ADB. It then traces the development of ADB's inspection policy and reviews key elements of the policy, pointing out similarities and differences with the World Bank and IDB approaches. Next, the paper discusses some of the concerns that nongovernmental organizations (NGOs) have expressed about the policy, and steps that have been taken or are being considered to address these concerns. Finally, the paper comments on ADB's experience with the policy and some of its implications for ADB's general operations.

BACKGROUND ON THE ASIAN DEVELOPMENT BANK

ADB was established in 1966 to support economic growth, development and co-operation in Asia and the Pacific.[1] It is a multilateral development finance

---

[*] Senior Administrative and Policy Officer, Asian Development Bank. The views expressed in this paper are those of the author and do not necessarily represent the views of the Asian Development Bank or its member countries.

[1] Asian Development Bank. 1966. *Articles of Agreement of the Asian Development Bank*, Article 1. Manila: Asian Development Bank. From its founding, ADB's development operations have extended to developing member countries in East Asia, South Asia, Southeast Asia, the Mekong area and the Pacific. With the admission of the People's Republic of China (1986), Mongolia (1991), Kazakstan (1994), the Kyrgyz Republic (1994) and Uzbekistan (1995) as

institution owned by 56 member countries, including 40 countries in the Asian and Pacific region and 16 countries from outside the region.[2] With its headquarters in Manila, Philippines, ADB has permanent missions in 11 of its developing member countries, as well as representative offices in Frankfurt, Tokyo and Washington, D.C.

In its first 20 years, ADB acted primarily as a project financier, helping member governments build basic infrastructure through loans and technical assistance. Since the mid-1980s, ADB has increasingly played the combined role of project financier and policy advisor. Its operations now include ongoing policy dialogue with member governments; program loans aimed at broad policy reforms in sectors such as agriculture, education, finance and health; and capacity building in key development institutions. In addition, ADB promotes a number of initiatives for regional and subregional cooperation. It also provides direct support (through loans and equity investments) to private enterprises on a selective basis.

Since the 1980s, ADB has paid increasing attention to environmental and social concerns in its operations. ADB's strategic development objectives include, in addition to the promotion of economic growth, poverty reduction, support for human development (including population planning), improvement in the status of women and environmental protection.[3] These strategic objectives are supported by a number of policies and/or staff instructions, including those relating to environmental considerations,[4] social dimensions,[5] gender and development,[6] involuntary resettlement,[7] indigenous peoples,[8] and

---

developing members, the Bank's "region" for purposes of development assistance now extends to North and Central Asia as well.

2 ADB's highest policy-making body is its Board of Governors, which is composed of representatives of each of its member countries who meet annually. ADB's general operations are directed by its Board of Directors, which is resident in Manila and includes 12 Directors (each with an Alternate). The President, who is elected by the Board of Governors, conducts the business of the Bank with the assistance of three Vice Presidents. The President and Vice Presidents are often referred to as the "Management".

3 Asian Development Bank. 1995. *The Bank's Medium-Term Strategic Framework (1995-1998)* [the MTSF]. Manila: President's Office, Asian Development Bank.

4 *Operations Manual*, Section 20 ("Environmental Considerations in Bank Operations", issued 7 January 1997). Manila: Strategy and Policy Office, Asian Development Bank. ADB's Operations Manual codifies operational policies approved by ADB's Board of Directors, as well as staff instructions and other directives issued by ADB's Management.

5 *Ibid.*, Section 47 ("Incorporation of Social Dimensions in Bank Operations", issued 7 January 1997).

6 *Ibid.*, Section 21 ("Gender and Development in Bank Operations", issued 7 January 1997).

7 *Ibid.*, Section 50 ("Involuntary Resettlement", issued 7 January 1997).

8 Memorandum of the President to All Professional Staff, *Staff Instructions on Certain Policy/Administrative Issues*, 15 February 1994.

cooperation with NGOs.[9] To link its strategic objectives with its public sector operations, ADB has set general targets for its project and lending mix: at least 50 percent of all new projects, on a three-year rolling basis, should have social or environmental goals as a primary or secondary objective; and by the end of the decade, at least 40 percent of ADB's lending volume should be directed to social or environmental objectives.[10]

In recent years, ADB has also taken steps to improve the general quality of its development assistance, and to increase its own transparency and accountability. Prompted by concerns about the effectiveness of some ADB-supported projects, in April 1993 the Management appointed a Task Force on Improving Project Quality chaired by one of its Vice Presidents. The Task Force reviewed ADB's existing loan portfolio and consulted with ADB staff, member governments and NGOs. In its report published in January 1994, the Task Force made a number of recommendations, including that greater attention should be paid to the institutional constraints of developing country sectors and agencies, and the possible need for capacity building; that governments and intended beneficiaries of development projects should be fully involved in all stages of the project cycle, beginning with project identification; and that greater attention should be paid to monitoring the implementation of projects.[11]

In September 1994, ADB's Board of Directors approved a new policy on information disclosure, the objective of which was to increase the availability of ADB documents and other information to the general public.[12] While recognizing that there are some practical and legal constraints on the disclosure of certain types of information, the policy endorses a presumption in favor of disclosure of information relating to the Bank's operations. A wide range of operational documents are now available to the public through the Public Information Center at ADB's headquarters, through ADB's resident missions and representative offices, and through depository libraries in its member countries. Information on ADB, its publications and operational documents is also available through its Internet Web site <http://www.asiandevbank.org>.

To complement and reinforce these initiatives, in 1994 ADB's Management also undertook to establish an "inspection function". The development of this initiative is discussed in the next section.

---

[9] R79-87: *The Bank's Cooperation with Non-Governmental Organizations*, dated 25 June 1987 and approved on 16 July 1987.

[10] MTSF, para. 24.

[11] Asian Development Bank. 1994. *Report of the Task Force on Improving Project Quality*. Manila: Asian Development Bank.

[12] R134-94: *Confidentiality and Disclosure of Information*, dated 18 August 1994 and approved on 9 September 1994.

Development of an Inspection Policy

As part of a general move to improve the effectiveness and transparency of ADB's operations, and its own accountability for results, in early 1994 the Management began work on a proposal to establish an "inspection function". This function, which was to be independent of the Management, would review complaints from parties affected or potentially affected by ADB-supported projects (or from members of ADB's Board of Directors) about ADB's potential noncompliance with its own operational policies and procedures.

The initial precedent for creating such a function was the September 1993 resolution of the Boards of Directors of the International Bank for Reconstruction and Development (IBRD) and International Development Association (IDA) establishing an independent Inspection Panel (the World Bank Panel).[13] As discussed in other papers, the World Bank Panel is a permanent three-member panel appointed by the IBRD and IDA Boards of Directors to receive requests to investigate allegations that IBRD or IDA has failed to follow its own operational policies and procedures. By early 1994, the Inter-American Development (IDB) was also developing a proposal to establish a similar function, which was approved by its Board of Directors in August 1994.[14] While IDB's Independent Investigation Mechanism (the IDB Mechanism) mirrors the World Bank Panel in many respects, it includes two key differences. First, in place of a permanent panel of outside experts, the IDB Board of Directors has appointed a roster of 10 outside experts, from which it will form panels to investigate particular complaints. Second, whereas the World Bank Panel initially screens requests for inspection and makes recommendations to the IBRD or IDA Board of Directors as to whether an inspection is warranted, requests for investigation of IDB-supported projects are made to the President of IDB, who forwards them to the IDB Board of Directors for consideration.

In developing an initial proposal for an inspection function, ADB's Management considered carefully both the World Bank and IDB models already in place, as well as the United Nations Joint Inspection Unit, "inspector general" and "ombudsman" offices established by some member country governments, and other possible mechanisms. The Management also took into account ADB's existing supervision, audit and evaluation systems, in order to avoid duplicating their activities.

---

[13] Resolution No. IBRD 93-10/Resolution No. IDA 93-6: "The World Bank Inspection Panel", approved on 22 September 1993.

[14] IDB Board Resolution : "The IDB Independent Investigation Mechanism", approved on 10 August 1994.

A working paper was submitted to ADB's Board of Directors in September 1994, and was discussed by the Board in October. The paper weighed the relative advantages of the World Bank Panel and IDB Mechanism, and concluded that, on balance, the IDB approach would be better suited to ADB's circumstances. In particular, the paper noted that ADB's experience did not suggest the need to establish a permanent outside panel. The paper also noted that the establishment of a roster of experts would allow for a greater diversity of backgrounds and expertise than a single panel of experts, and that the participation of Board members in the entire inspection process, including the initial review of inspection requests, would reinforce the Board's responsibility to direct ADB's general operations. However, as a variation on the IDB Mechanism, the paper proposed the creation of a new standing committee of the Board (the "Inspection Committee") as well as a roster of independent outside experts.

Under the proposal, the Inspection Committee would initially review inspection requests (in consultation, as needed, with an independent expert from the roster) and recommend to the full Board whether an inspection was warranted. If the Board authorized an inspection, the Committee would select a panel of independent experts from the standing roster to investigate the matter and make a report, which would be considered first by the Committee and then by the full Board. The Inspection Committee would consist of six members, including four from the Asian and Pacific region (of whom at least three would be from borrowing member countries) and two from outside the region. Both the Committee and any panel of experts would receive administrative support from the Office of the Secretary, which is the general secretariat for the Board of Directors and Board committees.

The working paper noted that the establishment of a Board committee to deal exclusively with inspections would demonstrate the importance of the function to ADB and its Board of Directors. Such a committee would also facilitate the Board's consideration of inspection requests, and would provide an effective link between the Board and any panel of outside experts conducting an inspection.

In discussing the working paper in October 1994, some Board members strongly supported the general proposal, while others voiced certain concerns. It was also suggested that ADB should proceed cautiously, and might benefit from observing the experience of the World Bank Panel before establishing its own inspection function.

Fortuitously, in October 1994 the World Bank Panel received its first inspection request, relating to the proposed Arun III Hydroelectric Project in Nepal. Under the circumstances, ADB Management concluded that it would be appropriate to observe the progress of the Arun III inspection before finalizing ADB's own proposal for an inspection function. Over the following months, ADB staff followed the World Bank Panel's consideration of the Arun III request, as well as developments at IDB relating to the appointment of its roster of experts.[15] In November 1995, ADB Management submitted a final policy paper to its Board of Directors, which considered and approved it in early December.[16]

The general structure of the inspection function approved by the ADB Board in December 1995 was substantially the same as that originally considered in October 1994. However, the final policy paper included some technical changes and clarifications added in response to comments on the earlier proposal.

As contemplated in the Board policy paper, the President appointed the members of the initial Inspection Committee in March 1996. After reviewing close to 100 expressions of interest, the President nominated 17 individuals to be included in the initial roster of experts. The Board approved these nominations in early October 1996. By this time, the Inspection Committee had developed and approved a set of detailed Inspection Procedures based on the policy paper. (The Inspection Procedures are included in an Appendix to this paper.) These procedures were provided to ADB's main NGO contacts and distributed to ADB's resident missions and representative offices. The Inspection Procedures were also issued to ADB staff in the form of staff instructions. Later in 1996, these procedures were published in a guidebook for the general public[17] and were posted on ADB's Internet Web site, together with the names of the Inspection Committee and roster members.

Overview of ADB's Inspection Policy and Procedures

1. Purpose

The purpose of ADB's inspection policy – similar to that of the World Bank Panel and IDB Mechanism – is to establish a formal channel through which

---

[15] *The World Bank Inspection Panel*, by Ibrahim F. I. Shihata, Senior Vice President and General Counsel of the World Bank (published in 1994 by Oxford University Press), provided very useful background on the establishment of the World Bank Panel. Eduardo Abbott (Executive Secretary to the World Bank Panel), Antonia Macedo (Assistant Executive Secretary to the World Bank Panel), and Gay Davis Miller (Senior Counsel of IDB) were also extremely helpful in sharing information about the World Bank Panel and IDB inspection procedures.

[16] R225-95: *Establishment of an Inspection Function*, dated 10 November 1995 and approved on 5 December 1995 (the ADB Policy Paper).

[17] Asian Development Bank. 1996. *ADB's Inspection Policy: A Guidebook.* Manila: Office of the Secretary, Asian Development Bank.

local communities, organizations and other groups (and, in special circumstances, members of ADB's Board of Directors) can request independent review or "inspection" of ADB's role in certain development projects.[18]

2. Scope

ADB's inspection policy extends to both proposed and ongoing projects. For this purpose, "project" is defined as any public sector loan, guarantee or technical assistance grant financed or to be financed in whole or in part from ADB resources, or administered or to be administered by ADB.[19] (Direct investments and loans to the private sector were initially excluded from the scope of the policy. The possible application of the policy to ADB's private sector operations will be considered as part of a general review of the policy after two years.)[20]

A "proposed" project is one under preparation that has not yet been approved by the Board of Directors (or a technical assistance project still to be approved by the President under his delegated authority). An "ongoing" project is one that has been approved and is being implemented, but that is not yet "substantially completed". A project is considered "substantially completed" if 95 percent or more of ADB's financing has been disbursed and/or cancelled, or the closing date for withdrawals or disbursements has passed.[21] (The resolutions establishing the World Bank Panel and IDB Mechanism include similar definitions of "substantially completed" projects, and also exclude them from review.)

The inspection policy is intended to ensure that ADB's operational policies and procedures are followed in the formulation, processing and implementation of ADB-supported projects. For this purpose, "operational policies and procedures" are defined as the Bank Policies and Operational Procedures set forth in ADB's Operations Manual (the OM) and, if applicable, corresponding sections in earlier editions of the OM.[22] (The reference to earlier editions of the OM would be relevant to the inspection of a project that has already been

---

[18] *Inspection Procedures*, as approved by the Inspection Committee of the Board of Directors of ADB on 9 October 1996 (the ADB Procedures), para. 1.

[19] *Ibid.*, para. 5.

[20] The decision to initially exclude private sector operations was based on a recognition that ADB's private sector loans and equity investments differ in a number of ways from its public sector loans and grants, and that the inspection procedures developed with public sector operations in mind might not be effective or appropriate for its direct private sector activities. Therefore, it was considered wise to revisit the issue after two years, by which time ADB would have gained experience with the application of its policy to public sector operations.

[21] ADB Procedures, para. 6.

[22] *Ibid.*, para. 4.

approved. In that case, the operational policies and procedures that apply are those that were in effect on the project approval date. Depending on the circumstances, it might be necessary to look to earlier editions of the OM for the relevant policies and procedures.) The definition also includes staff instructions relating to the formulation, processing or implementation of projects, and which are intended to be incorporated eventually in the OM. (This would include, for example, ADB's Staff Instructions on Indigenous Peoples, which were issued by the Management in 1994 and are still in force pending the ADB Board's adoption of a formal policy on indigenous peoples, and the incorporation of this new policy in the OM.)

3. Parties Who Can Request an Inspection

ADB's inspection policy is substantially similar to that of the World Bank and IDB in terms of the parties who can request an inspection. A request can be made by a community, organization or other group residing either (a) in the borrowing member country where the project in question is being implemented or is proposed to be implemented, or (b) in an adjacent member country, if the group is affected or likely to be affected by the project.[23] (The resolutions establishing the World Bank Panel and IDB Mechanism do not expressly refer to parties in adjacent countries.) A request can also be made on behalf of such a community, organization or other group by either (a) a representative residing in the same country, or (b) in exceptional cases when no appropriate local representative is available, and ADB's Board so agrees at the time it considers the request, by a representative from outside the country.[24] In either case, the request must include reasonable evidence that the representative has been authorized to act on behalf of the group. Finally, in special cases involving allegations of particularly serious violations of ADB's operational policies and procedures in connection with an ongoing project, one or more members of the Board of Directors may also request an inspection.[25]

The resolutions establishing the World Bank Panel and IDB Mechanism contain similar provisions relating to inspection requests by representatives and by Board members, except that they allow Board members to request the review of proposed as well as ongoing projects. In addition, the IBRD/IDA resolution provides that the full Board may at any time instruct the World Bank Panel to conduct an investigation. ADB's inspection policy limits inspection requests by Board members to those involving ongoing projects on

---

[23] *Ibid.*, para. 12.
[24] *Ibid.*, para. 13.
[25] *Ibid.*, para. 14.

the basis that any concerns a Board member might have about a proposed project can be raised and addressed at the time the Board considers the project for approval.[26]

4. Requests That Will Be Considered

ADB's inspection policy is also substantially similar to the World Bank's and IDB's in terms of the types of requests that will be entertained. In general, a request for inspection must assert that:

(a) ADB has failed, in formulating, processing or implementing a project, to follow its operational policies or procedures;
(b) this failure has had or is likely to have a direct and material adverse effect on the requester's rights and interests; and
(c) this failure was brought to the attention of ADB's Management, which failed within a period of 45 days to demonstrate that ADB had followed, or was taking adequate steps to follow, its operational policies and procedures.[27]

While they include similar elements, the resolutions establishing the World Bank Panel and IDB Mechanism do not specify a time limit within which the Management must demonstrate that the institution is following or taking steps to follow its operational policies and procedures. (ADB's inspection policy includes somewhat more detail on both the steps an affected group should take to raise its concerns initially with the Management, and the manner in which Management should respond.[28] However, as discussed later in this paper, these more detailed provisions have been criticized by some NGOs.)

ADB's inspection policy is also similar to the World Bank's and IDB's in terms of the matters that will not be investigated. These include:

(a) complaints relating to actions that are the responsibility of parties other than ADB, or that otherwise do not involve an act or omission by ADB in violation of its operational policies and procedures;
(b) complaints against decisions made by ADB, a borrower or executing agency concerning the procurement of goods or services, including consulting services;
(c) complaints relating to completed or substantially completed projects;
(d) complaints relating to matters already considered under the policy, unless new evidence is presented that was not known at the time the original request was made;

---

[26] *Ibid.*
[27] *Ibid.*, para. 15.
[28] *See ibid.*, paras. 20-27.

(e) complaints about the general adequacy or suitability of ADB policies and procedures;
(f) complaints that relate to personnel or other nonoperational matters; and
(g) as mentioned above, complaints that relate to private sector operations (although this exclusion will be reconsidered as part of a general review of the policy).[29]

The resolutions establishing the World Bank Panel and IDB Mechanism also expressly exclude items (a) through (d). Moreover, the exclusion of (e) and (f) can be inferred from other provisions of those resolutions. As noted above, only ADB expressly excludes (g) – private sector operations.[30]

5. Structure

As indicated in the previous section, the main differences among the World Bank, IDB and ADB inspection functions relate to their organizational structures. While the World Bank has established a permanent Inspection Panel to initially review requests for inspection and carry out any investigations approved by the IBRD or IDA Board of Directors, ADB and IDB have instead established rosters of independent experts who can be called on to carry out inspections approved by their Boards on a case-by-case basis. In addition, ADB has established a permanent Board committee, the Inspection Committee, to initially review requests for inspection, make recommendations to the full Board relating to these requests, and coordinate any inspection authorized by the Board to be carried out by independent experts from the roster.

6. Inspection Process

These structural variations lead to some differences in each institution's inspection procedures. In ADB's case, the inspection process includes the following basic steps:

(a) a party makes a complaint to the President about a project;
(b) Management responds to the complaint within 45 days;

---

[29] *Ibid.*, paras. 5 & 18.

[30] Thus far, much of the World Bank Group's private sector operations has been effectively exempt from inspection, since the original resolutions establishing the World Bank Panel apply only to IBRD and IDA operations, and not to those of the International Finance Corporation (IFC), the World Bank affiliate mandated to carry out direct private sector operations, or the Multilateral Investment Guarantee Agency (MIGA), which supports foreign direct investment in developing countries by providing guarantees and other services. This situation would obviously change if the Boards of Directors of IFC and MIGA established their own inspection functions or agreed to extend the World Bank Panel's mandate to cover IFC and MIGA operations.

(c) if the complaining party is not satisfied with this response, it can then send a request to the Inspection Committee for an independent review or "inspection" of the project;
(d) the Committee will ask Management to respond to the request within 30 days (unless the Committee concludes that the request is clearly frivolous or ineligible), and may seek additional information from the requester or Management, as well as seeking the views of an independent expert from the roster;
(e) the Committee will then recommend to the Board whether an inspection is warranted (within 14 days of receiving all necessary information), and the Board will decide on the recommendation;
(f) if the Board authorizes an inspection, the Committee will promptly select a panel of experts from the standing roster to investigate ADB's role in the project and make a report to the Committee;
(g) the inspection panel's investigation may include a review of ADB documents, meetings with ADB staff and Management and, with the consent of the relevant government authorities, a visit to the project area and meetings with the requester, project managers, government officials and others;
(h) following receipt of the panel's report, the Committee will ask Management to respond to the report within 30 days, and may request additional information or clarification from any party; and
(i) the Committee will then forward the panel's report and its recommendation to the Board (within 14 days of receiving all necessary information), and the Board will take a decision on the matter.[31]

ADB's policy – like that of the World Bank and IDB – requires that the requester be notified promptly of the Board's decision whether to authorize an investigation.[32] Following an inspection and the Board's consideration of the inspection panel's report, the policy also requires that the requester be provided promptly with copies of the inspection panel's report, Management's response, the Inspection Committee's recommendation and any Board decision thereon. At the same time, these documents will become publicly available.[33]

The Inspection Committee is required to prepare annual reports covering the inspection requests received, their disposition, the investigations undertaken and their results. These annual reports are also publicly available.[34]

---

31 ADB Procedures, paras. 19-64.
32 *Ibid.*, para. 43.
33 *Ibid.*, para. 63.
34 *Ibid.*, para. 69.

Finally, under the terms of the Board paper approved in December 1995, ADB's inspection policy is to be reviewed by the Management within two years of its effectiveness and the results submitted to the Board. This review should consider, among other things, the possible application of the policy to ADB's private sector operations.[35]

NGO Concerns About ADB's Inspection Policy

In informal exchanges with ADB staff over the past two years, representatives of regional and nonregional NGOs have voiced concerns about certain aspects of ADB's inspection policy. This section attempts to summarize some of these concerns and ADB's responses.

1. Private Sector Exclusion

First, NGOs have objected to the initial exclusion of ADB's private sector operations from the scope of the inspection policy. In response, ADB staff have noted that this issue will be revisited as part of a general review of the policy, and that in any case private sector loans and equity investments represent a very small portion of ADB's total operations (e.g., less than 5 percent of the total amount of loan and investment approvals in 1996). Thus, the great majority of ADB-supported projects are already covered by the policy.

2. Independence and Impartiality

Second, NGOs have expressed concern about the independence of ADB's inspection process. In particular, they note that the Inspection Committee is comprised of Board members who are representives of member country governments, and who might therefore be inclined to support the Management's position when considering complaints about projects, especially ones the Board has already approved. Concerns have also been raised about the impartiality of the Office of the Secretary, which provides administrative support to the Committee and any inspection panels, since this office is part of the Bank and reports to the President. (This is in contrast to the World Bank Panel, which is separate from both the IBRD/IDA Boards and Management

---

[35] ADB Policy Paper, para. 51(d).

and has its own secretariat staff, although its budget is provided by the World Bank and it functions as an advisory body to the IBRD/IDA Boards.)

In response to these concerns, ADB staff have pointed out various features of ADB's policy that are intended to ensure that all requests for inspection are considered fairly. For example, the policy requires that a member of the Inspection Committee not participate in the consideration of a request if the member has any personal or financial interest in the subject matter, or if there is even the appearance of a conflict of interest.[36] In addition, the Committee must consult with an independent expert (from the roster) before it can recommend that an inspection request should be denied, unless the Committee has concluded that the request is clearly frivolous or ineligible.[37] Any inspection of a project authorized by the Board is carried out by a panel of independent experts selected from the roster. An expert cannot serve on an inspection panel if the expert has a conflict of interest, or if there is even the appearance of a conflict of interest.[38]

Regarding the Office of the Secretary, the Inspection Procedures expressly provide that the Office cannot participate in any way in the preparation of the Management's responses to initial complaints and requests for inspection, nor on the other hand can the Office help parties to prepare complaints or requests. However, staff of the Office are available to answer questions and provide clarification on the Inspection Procedures to any interested parties outside ADB, as well as to ADB staff and Board members.[39]

3. Initial Complaint to Management

Some NGOs have also objected to the procedures for making an initial complaint to ADB's Management. They note that the requirements for making an initial complaint (outlined in paragraphs 20-23 of ADB's Inspection Procedures) are substantially similar to the requirements for requesting an inspection (described in paragraphs 28-34 of the procedures), except that the initial complaint should be addressed to the President, while the request for inspection is addressed to the Inspection Committee. NGOs have suggested that this two-step process is burdensome for project-affected people, who are likely to have limited time and resources to prepare such submissions, and who therefore may be discouraged from using the process.

---

36 ADB Procedures, para. 36.
37 *Ibid.*, para. 40.
38 *Ibid.*, para. 46.
39 *Ibid.*, para. 67.

In response, ADB staff have pointed out that the two-step process is not unique to ADB. The resolutions establishing the World Bank Panel and the IDB Mechanism also require affected groups to first bring their concerns to the Management's attention before requesting an independent inspection of a project. As noted in previous sections, ADB's Inspection Procedures are more detailed in explaining the steps that should be followed to raise these concerns. At the same time, the procedures make clear that no elaborate form is required; a simple letter is sufficient.[40] The procedures also specify that the Management must respond to any initial complaint within 45 days.[41]

Ironically, the intention in specifying the requirements for making an initial complaint, and in providing a time period for the Management's response, was to make the process more transparent and certain. The critical reaction to these provisions illustrates the challenge of developing procedures that on the one hand are clear and unambiguous, but on the other hand are simple enough to be followed by parties with limited resources and little experience with administrative processes. The upcoming review of ADB's inspection policy will provide an opportunity to reexamine this and other aspects of the policy for possible improvement.

4. Anonymous Requests

NGOs have questioned whether and how the Inspection Committee would consider requests for inspection made on behalf of groups who wish to remain anonymous. They maintain that people living in the vicinity of a government-sponsored development project may be reluctant to openly criticize aspects of the project for fear of being harassed or retaliated against by supporters of the project. They suggest that indigenous, landless and other vulnerable groups would be particularly reluctant to step forward. To overcome this problem, they argue that an affected group should be able to request an inspection through a local NGO or other representative without disclosing the identities of the group members.

Although the resolutions establishing the World Bank Panel and IDB Mechanism do not address the issue of anonymous requests, both the World Bank Panel and IDB Management have accepted requests for inspection made on behalf of individuals or groups who wished to remain anonymous. For example, in the case of the inspection request relating to IBRD's loans to Argentina and Paraguay for the Yacyretá Hydroelectric Project, the Paraguayan NGO making the request sought anonymity on behalf of various

---

[40] *Ibid.*, para. 21.

[41] *Ibid.*, para. 26.

people in the project area. In this case, a member of the Panel interviewed most of the individuals during his initial visit to the project area, and confirmed that they could be treated as representative of various categories of people allegedly affected by the project.[42] When IDB, a cofinancier of the Yacyretá Project, received a similar inspection request made on behalf of anonymous people in the project area, IDB engaged one of the independent experts from its standing roster to visit the area and verify the circumstances of the individuals being represented in the request.[43]

ADB's Inspection Procedures do not expressly address the handling of requests made on behalf of anonymous individuals. However, as discussed in the previous section, the procedures do permit a local NGO or other party to request an inspection on behalf of an affected group. Ordinarily, the representative must supply proof that it is authorized to represent the group (e.g., by providing a signed copy of instructions or authorization from the group).[44] However, the Inspection Procedures also state that, if any required information cannot be provided, the party making the request should give an explanation.[45] Thus, the procedures already contemplate that there may be situations in which a requester cannot provide all the information ordinarily required. In these cases, the Inspection Committee can still review the request and decide whether an inspection seems warranted, notwithstanding the omission of certain information.

The treatment of requests for inspection made on behalf of anonymous individuals is another issue that may be considered in the upcoming review of ADB's inspection policy. In their current form, however, the Inspection Procedures are sufficiently flexible to allow the Inspection Committee to consider such requests on a case-by-case basis. If the Committee were to receive such a request, and concluded that there were plausible reasons for the requester to withhold the identities of those he/she represents, the Committee could verify the existence of the group by taking steps similar to those taken by IDB for the Yacyretá request. That is, the Committee could designate a member of ADB's roster of experts to visit the project area, meet the affected individuals and then confirm their existence and circumstances to the Committee (without disclosing their identities).

---

42 *See* Attachment 1 to INSP/R96-2: Request for Inspection – Argentina/Paraguay: Yacyretá Hydroelectric Project – Panel Report and Recommendation to the Executive Directors of the International Bank for Reconstruction and Development, dated 24 December 1996.

43 This was confirmed by Gay Miller, Senior Counsel of IDB, who was involved in the processing of the inspection request for the Yacyretá Project.

44 ADB Procedures, para. 32.

45 *Ibid.*, para. 34.

5. Translations in Local Languages

Finally, it has been suggested that the Inspection Procedures, the Operations Manual, and other ADB documents should be translated into the languages most frequently spoken in ADB's developing member countries. It is argued that this would promote broader awareness and understanding of ADB's inspection policy in developing member countries, and would widen access to the inspection function.

The issue of translating documents into local languages is a general one that has relevance beyond the inspection policy. This issue may be addressed in the upcoming review of ADB's inspection policy, or in connection with more general proposals to translate ADB documents into the main languages of its developing members.

ADB's Experience and Implications

At the time this article was submitted for publication, ADB's Inspection Committee had received two submissions from the same group. In November 1997, the Chairman of the Committee received a letter from a group in Pakistan calling itself the Citizens Alliance in Reforms for Efficient and Equitable Development (CREED). The letter raised certain concerns about the Korangi Wastewater Project, an ADB-supported project in Karachi, Pakistan, which had been approved by ADB's Board in September 1997. After reviewing the letter, the Committee concluded that no formal complaint had yet been made to the Management. The Committee therefore forwarded the letter to the President to be handled as an initial complaint under paragraph 37 of the Inspection Procedures. Thereafter, the Vice President (West Region) sent a reply to CREED, which was the subject of further correspondence between CREED and the Bank. In February 1998, the Chairman of the Inspection Committee received a second letter from CREED requesting an inspection of the Korangi project. As of the end of February, this letter was being reviewed by the Committee.

Although ADB's experience thus far with its inspection policy has been limited, the establishment of the policy in itself has implications for ADB's operations. First of all, the inspection function underlines the importance of ADB's operational policies and procedures. Since the focus of any inspection will be on ADB's adherence to these policies and procedures in a specific project, ADB staff now have an additional incentive to make certain that all relevant policies and procedures are being followed in the projects under their responsibility.

The inspection policy also reinforces other ADB policies and procedures, in particular, the information disclosure policy and the requirement to consult with affected or potentially affected groups at all stages of the project cycle. Project-affected people can only make effective use of the inspection process if they have sufficient information about the project in question. The policy therefore underlines the importance of making information about a potential or ongoing project available to people in the project area. Moreover, if local communities are adequately informed about a project under consideration – or about the status of a project in implementation – many of their possible concerns about the project may be allayed. It can also be expected that most project-affected people would not go to the trouble of seeking an inspection unless they believed their interests or needs had not been sufficiently considered. Thus, ADB staff now have an additional incentive to consult regularly, and in a meaningful way, with groups affected or likely to be affected by a project, in order to solicit their views, keep them informed and ensure that their concerns are being addressed.

From this perspective, ADB's inspection function not only provides an additional means to encourage accountability among ADB staff and Management, but also can serve as an indirect tool to improve the quality and effectiveness of ADB's development assistance.

The Independent Investigation Mechanism of the Inter-American Development Bank

Gay Davis Miller[*]

The Inter-American Development Bank (IDB) Board of Executive Directors approved establishment of an Independent Investigation Mechanism policy for the Bank on August 10, 1994.[1]

The Mechanism was created in the context of the negotiations for the Eighth General Increase in Resources of the Bank where the IDB's Governors asserted the desirability of further increasing the transparency, accountability and effectiveness of the IDB's performance in its operations. The Mechanism was intended to further that goal.

As approved by the IDB's Board of Executive Directors, the Mechanism was intended to "apply in cases of complaints that the Bank ha[d] failed in the design, analysis or implementation of proposed or ongoing operations to follow its own established operational policies, or norms formally adopted for the execution of those policies (including enforcement of compliance with borrower's obligations required by such policies and/or norms), when material adverse effects have or might reasonably be expected to occur as a result of such failure by the Bank."[2]

For the purpose of the Mechanism, Bank operations were defined to include loans, technical cooperation or guarantee operations, at the design, appraisal and or implementation stages. The Mechanism specifically excludes from its application i) actions for which other parties, such as borrowers or funding recipients are responsible, and which do not involve any action or omission on the part of the Bank; ii) procurement matters, because provision is made under other Bank policies to resolve any questions or disputes; iii) any action which does not constitute a Bank-supported operation as defined by the Mechanism policy; iv) for loan operations, any request filed after the project has been 95 percent disbursed; and v) matters over which a recommendation has already been made under the provisions of the Mechanism, unless new

---

* Senior Counsel, Corporate Affairs, Inter-American Development Bank.

1 The Statute defining the procedures for the Mechanism was distributed on August 15, 1994.

2 Article 1.1

evidence, information not known at the time of the prior request, or new circumstances are introduced.

The IDB's Investigation Mechanism differs most from that of the World Bank in its support structure. Partly for reasons of cost saving, and partly for the purpose of assuring the continued independence and objectivity of the review panels, the IDB decided against establishing a permanent panel. Instead, a roster of individuals, representing a broad range of technical expertise and skills, is appointed by the Board of Executive Directors for five-year terms. When the Board determines that an investigation is warranted, the Mechanism provides that a panel of three individuals is to be named from the Roster to conduct the investigation. Criteria for appointment to the Roster include "integrity and recognized competence in areas related to socio-economic development...[and familiarity] with Latin America and the Caribbean."[3] The Mechanism requires that all ten individuals appointed to the Roster be of different nationalities. When the initial Roster was appointed in 1995, considerable effort was expended to assure a broad range of technical expertise from which to draw in appointing investigative panels, and though the Mechanism does not so specify, efforts were made to assure the inclusion of women on the Roster.

In recognition of the fact that former staff of the IDB may have special expertise which would be of benefit in the event of an investigation, the Mechanism permits appointment of former staff to the Roster after two years following termination of their Bank services. The initial Roster appointed by the Board of Executive Directors included one former staff member of the Bank. Appointment to the Roster does not serve as a permanent ban to subsequent Bank employment, but former Roster members are prohibited from employment by the Bank in other capacities, including any consulting work, for a period of two years following termination of their terms on the Roster.

INVESTIGATIONS

Investigations pursuant to the Mechanism can be generated in two ways. Although a Director may request that a panel be convened to conduct an investigation without a request having been received from outside the Bank, this avenue would be applied only in very exceptional circumstances. In the normal course of events, is contemplated that the request would be received from a community of persons, or their representative, who can demonstrate that they are likely to be directly and materially affected by an action or

3 Article 2.2

omission of the IDB in relation to its operations. The requesting party must offer some reasonable evidence that its members' rights are likely to be negatively affected as a result of a failure of the IDB to follow its operational policies or norms. The Mechanism is intended as a safety net for individuals directly affected by a Bank operation. The language was drafted to provide access to the procedure to local groups or their local representatives; the policy permits accepting a request from a non-local representative of an affected group only in very limited and exceptional circumstances, when no appropriate local representative is available, and when the Bank's Directors agree to accept such a representative.

Provided that the request meets all of the required criteria, the Bank's Board of Executive Directors may authorize an investigation. The formal requirements for the request are intentionally simple, to not preclude access to the process by the individuals whom the policy was intended to protect. The complaint must be in writing, and must state all relevant facts known to the complaining party. It also must include any supporting evidence, or a reference to where such evidence might be obtained, if known. It must include an indication of steps taken to bring the matter to the attention of the Bank's management, and any response to such attempts.[4] The policy also requires that the request specify the policy or policies of the IDB which are alleged to have been violated, and more importantly, that it specify how such violation has caused or will cause material adverse affects on the complaining party.[5]

Under the Mechanism policy as originally approved by the IDB's Board of Directors, a request for an investigation is sent to the IDB's President for review and a recommendation by the President to the Board whether the request should be granted.

The policy prescribes that IDB Management will be asked to prepare a response to a request for an investigation unless the request is clearly frivolous. The response is forwarded to the Board with the President's recommendation. In the first formal request for an investigation received by

---

4 In this, the IDB's Mechanism differs somewhat from the procedure established for the Asian Bank in that no formal set of communications between the requesting party and the Bank's management has been prescribed by the IDB. While the Mechanism presumes that some effort should have been made to resolve the matter directly with the Administration, the policy does not establish a specific requirement for such communication, and it is possible in some undefined circumstances that the Board could accept a request for an investigation without such communication having been made. In contrast, the Asian Bank makes such communication a specific prerequisite to acceptance of a request for an investigation.

5 Although the requirement of an allegation of violation of Bank policies helps to define the scope of the Mechanism, the purpose and value of the policy is not to assign blame for policy violations, but to guide the Bank to better design and administration of its operations. If policy violations are found to have occurred, determining the reasons for the violation may provide valuable insight for better planned projects, and even for establishing better policies.

the IDB following approval of the Mechanism, the recommendation of the President was based upon the clear possibility of material adverse effects of the project on the individuals making the request, and upon a genuine concern that continuing problems with compliance with preconditions for disbursement of the final loan, which was designed to remedy many of the recognized problems, indicated a possibility that the loan was not adequately designed or analyzed. The complexity of the project,[6] the possibility of serious adverse environmental and human consequences of continuation of the project without an adequate remedy for the problems known to exist, and the desire for transparency in efforts to resolve pending issues were the basis for the President's recommendation for an investigation with reference to the adequacy of the design of the final loan.

PANELS

The Mechanism policy provides that the Board of Executive Directors will nominate a panel of no fewer than three individuals from the permanent Roster to conduct an investigation in the event that the Board determines that an investigation is warranted.

The panel is given a great deal of independence in deciding how its investigation will be conducted within the terms of reference approved by the Board. The Mechanism policy prescribes that the panel will choose its own coordinator,[7] and that it will be free to determine the procedures it will follow in conducting its investigation. The policy guarantees to the panels access to any IDB staff and to any pertinent Bank records they may deem necessary to conduct their investigation. The panels are given full authority to consult with any Bank office they deem necessary to contact, and for the purpose of the performance of their functions, panel members are declared to be officials of the Bank, entitled to all of the privileges and immunities of Bank officials granted pursuant to the IDB's charter, the Agreement Establishing the Inter-American Development Bank.

The policy takes into account the sovereign independence of the member country involved, by requiring that the Director representing that country on the Bank's Executive Board be consulted as part of the investigation, and specifically that such Director will be provided an opportunity to record the

---

[6] The project, which began in 1978, involved funding from both the World Bank and the IDB, and included four loans approved by the IDB. At the time the request was received, three of the IDB loans had been fully disbursed.

[7] Following the first review conducted pursuant to the policy, panel members suggested that in the interest of having more time to devote to their investigative role, such administrative details as naming the panel coordinator might be provided by the Bank.

views of that office as part of the panel report. In addition, the policy specifically prescribes carrying out any part of the investigation in the territory of the subject member country without that country's prior consent, such consent to be confirmed in advance through the office of the Executive Director.[8]

Findings

The Independent Investigation Mechanism policy encourages investigative panels to arrive at their findings whenever possible by consensus. In the absence of a consensus, any dissenting views are to be specifically recorded in the panel's final report to the Board.

The policy prescribes that the end product of an investigation will be a written report addressed to the Executive Directors and to the Bank's President. The report is expected to address all facts and to state the panel's conclusions on whether the Bank has complied with all relevant Bank operational policies and norms. The Panel may include any recommendations it deems pertinent. Confidential material which is included in the report is required to be segregated into an annex to the report to facilitate later public release of the non-confidential portions. No format for the report or definition of its length or content is otherwise prescribed.[9]

The IDB's Management is required to submit to the Board a reply to the panel report within 30 days after it has been received. The Board is then expected to consider the report and Management response and to determine what preventive or corrective actions, if any, should be taken by the Bank in response to the information provided by those documents. There are no preestablished indicators of what the Board response might be, nor is there any established time frame for either the Board decision or the implementation of any measures taken. It is intended that in each instance the Board's response to the information should be based on the circumstances of the specific operation in question. The policy provides that the Board will designate the period in which Management will be expected to implement the decision of the Board, and specific provision is made to require Management to report back to the Board on the measures taken in response to the Board decision,

---

[8] The Yacyretá hydroelectric project which was the subject of the first formal request for an investigation received by the Bank, involved both Paraguay and Argentina though the request was received from a group in Paraguay. Both countries were consulted and visited in the review which was conducted by the panel.

[9] The first investigative panel was faced with the question of resolving on its own the issues of length and format. Some guidance in this area by the IDB may prove helpful to subsequent panels.

and to ensure compliance with the applicable operational policies or norms of the Bank.

PUBLIC INFORMATION

Public access to information about projects which may become subject to investigation is provided in the Bank's Information Disclosure policy.[10] The Independent Investigation Mechanism policy makes specific reference to direct communication with the requesting party following the Board's decision whether an investigation should be conducted, requiring direct notification to the requesting party whether an investigation has been authorized within 15 calendar days after the Board's decision. While the initial request requires a response to the requesting party, and Bank practices suggest that information about formal requests received and investigations authorized will be posted on the IDB's Internet information pages, specific provision in the policy for general public access to information about an investigation is made only with reference to the final report of the panel and the final Management response to those findings. The policy requires making those documents available to the public after they are submitted to the Board.[11]

The panel is required to maintain as confidential all information to which it has access, but which is considered confidential in accordance with the Information Disclosure policy. Findings of the panel which would be considered confidential are required to be segregated and submitted separately

[10] The Independent Investigation Mechanism could not function without the existence of a policy permitting public disclosure of information about Bank operations and operational policies. The Bank adopted a policy on Information Disclosure in October of 1994, based on the premise that the transparency and accountability to be achieved by public disclosure of information about the IDB's operations would increase the effectiveness of IDB-supported projects. Profiles of proposed projects are released at various stages in the design process beginning as soon as a project is sufficiently defined for the Bank's internal review process to begin. Environmental documents, which are perhaps the most critical to the expected application of the Mechanism, are required to be released for local review and comment before the Bank undertakes its formal loan analysis mission. Operational policies are made available on the Internet and through Bank information offices as soon as they are approved by the Board.

[11] The current policy requires such materials to be made public 15 days after their receipt by the Board of Executive Directors. It appears to be more practical to have such documents released to the public following their consideration by the Board. A package of amendments to the policy under preparation may include a proposal for an amendment to align the IDB's practice more closely with that of the World Bank, and require the public release of such materials within a very short time following their consideration by the Board.

as an annex to the final report. Confidential material which has been included in annexes to the report will not be released.[12]

The Mechanism contemplated, when approved by the Board, that an annual report would be prepared to cover the requests received and the investigations undertaken. As of the end of 1997, only one formal request for an investigation had been received. As a consequence, the first such annual report is expected to be prepared early in 1998. This report will be submitted to the President and to the Board and will be available on request to interested parties outside the Bank.

THE FIRST REQUEST

The first request for an investigation pursuant to the IDB's Independent Mechanism policy was received by the Bank late in September of 1996.[13]

The request was submitted by Sobrevivencia, an NGO located in Asunción, Paraguay, which claimed to represent a group of individuals affected by the Yacyretá hydroelectric project on the border of Paraguay and Argentina. The request was submitted simultaneously to the World Bank, which had financed part of the project. In addition to the complicating factors of the involvement of two member countries, and co-financing by another international institution, Sobrevivencia indicated that the individuals which the organization claimed to represent wished to remain anonymous. The Bank was able to resolve the specific problem of determining the eligibility of Sobrevivencia to act as a representative of the affected individuals by sending a member of its permanent Roster to interview the individuals making the request, to verify that Sobrevivencia did represent them. The member of the Roster was asked to certify to the Bank's President that such representation authorization existed without revealing to the Bank the identity of the individuals represented.

Evaluation of the first formal request was further complicated by the fact that the Bank had approved four loans to the bi-national entity administering the project over a 19-year period, and that three of the loans had been fully disbursed. No monies had been disbursed under the fourth loan, which was designed to address many of the problems which were the subject of the investigation request. Because of the apparent magnitude of the problems remaining to be resolved in relation to the project, and the objective compliance of the request and of the requesting party with the required criteria for

[12] Material which has been annexed to the panel report rather than being included in the main body, but which is not considered confidential may be released to the public following review of its content to verify that the content is not confidential.

[13] By the end of 1997, no other completed requests had been received by the Bank.

making a request, the President recommended to the Board that an investigation be authorized even though the Bank's Management denied any indication of violation of any of the cited Bank policies or norms in place at the time the various actions of the Bank complained of in the request.

In a close parallel with the decision of the Board of Executive Directors of the World Bank, the IDB's Board of Directors determined that while a full investigation was not warranted, a panel should be convened from the permanent Roster to review the existing situation and to determine with reference to specifically listed aspects of the project, whether the action plans then being formulated in cooperation among the two countries, the executing agency, and the two financial institutions were adequate to address the known problems with the project. Although the panel was not authorized to conduct a full investigation within the meaning of the Mechanism policy, the panel was instructed to follow as closely as possible the administrative procedures established for the Mechanism in carrying out its functions, and in submitting its final report to the Board.

The panel appointed by the Board was instructed to conduct its review in a time table whose completion date was a close match to that of the World Bank Inspection Panel, which was authorized to review the same project with very similar terms of reference. The two panels cooperated closely in conducting their reviews, and the IDB panel benefitted from the experience of the World Bank Inspection Panel, which was well established and had completed several previous investigations. As of this writing, the final reports have been submitted to the respective Boards of the two financial institutions, but no final decisions by the Boards have been published. The Executive Board of the IDB has instructed Management to engage in further contact with the two governments and the executing agency, and to report back before making its final determination.

Looking to the Future

In its first request for an investigation, and in its response to that request, the IDB learned a great deal about the ability of the Mechanism policy to function in the Bank's culture. Some adjustments will be necessary in the near future, and undoubtedly, further adjustments will be made as the Bank's experience with the Mechanism grows.

The Bank was handicapped in its evaluation and administration of the first request by the lack of a specific assignment of responsibilities for internal support functions for the Mechanism. In the original policy, provision was made for support functions during a panel investigation to be provided by the

Secretariat Department during an investigation, but no provision was made in the policy for assigning responsibility for necessary support at other times. In practice, the necessary administrative support has been divided among the Bank's Secretariat office, the Office of the President, the Legal Department, the External Relations Department, and the Administrative Department of the Bank. While this has been adequate for the Bank's needs with a small volume of work for the Mechanism, a more centralized approach will be necessary for efficient administrative support and response with an increased volume of work related to the Mechanism. A variety of solutions to address this concern are under consideration.

One idea being explored is that a member of the permanent Roster be designated to serve as a procedural advisor to the process in the absence of a constituted panel. While budgetary considerations in the IDB prevent establishment of a full time permanent panel like that of the World Bank, the designation of a member of the Roster to serve in an independent capacity to resolve procedural questions for the Mechanism would carry the establishment of an independent review process one step further. To this point, any procedural questions have been resolved internally, but the use of a member of the Roster to review the representation authorization given to Sobrevivencia for the first request was a successful precedent.

The panel which conducted the Yacyretá investigation was unanimous in suggesting that greater administrative guidance be provided to panels. Consequentially, the Bank is examining ways to provide further support to the panels to reduce the time they must devote to administrative decision-making.

The President's role in recommending whether a panel should be constituted to conduct an investigation concerning possible policy violations by the Bank conflicts with his role as titular head of management, when Management's initial response to an investigation request may be a denial that such violations have occurred. The Asian Bank, which modeled its inspection policy on that of the IDB, did not include the requirement of a recommendation by the President. Rather, after a required exchange of correspondence directly with management, the requesting party's request is submitted to a committee of the Board of Directors for a decision. A similar approach would be possible for the IDB, following a review within the Bank of compliance of the request with the objective requirements for a formal request. A committee of the IDB Board of Executive Directors, the Board Matters and Evaluation Committee, has assumed responsibility for analyzing the requests and the panel reports following an investigation, and that Committee in turn reports on its deliberations and makes recommendations to the full Board, so simply eliminating the step of a presidential recommendation may prove appropriate.[14] The division between purely administrative functions of reviewing the criteria for a request and the substantive consideration of such a request is being studied within the Bank for a recommendation to the Board for an appropriate adjustment to the Mechanism policy.

In addition to issues related to timing of the public release of the panel reports noted above, details of the policy which relate to the direct responses required to be given to the requesting parties are also being reconsidered. The policy requires notification to the requesting party when the Board has reached a decision whether to conduct an investigation, but does not thereafter require any specific response to the requesting party. A provision that the final report of a panel and the management response will be "made available to outside interested parties on request" does not appear to be an adequate means of addressing the concerns of the individuals who have undertaken the effort of presenting a formal investigation request. While it is the Bank practice to respond to all correspondence received from a requesting party, a specific set of provisions for direct formal notification to the requesting party of decisions taken by the Board at specific points in the process may be in order, provided that the Board agrees that those decisions should be made public.

Finally, the Bank must also address the question of application of the Mechanism to its private sector operations, which by nature are different from the operations conducted solely by the Bank or by the Bank in cooperation with other public entities. Private sector operations have enabled the Bank to increase the scope of resources available to the benefit of its member countries, but the needs of private entities working in cooperation with the Bank differ from those of a governmental institutions. The Bank is presently reexamining the appropriate levels of disclosure of information concerning private sector operations to protect the continued ability of the institution to work in cooperation with these enterprises, and in so doing will inevitably be required to examine the special problems of application of the Investigation Mechanism to projects in which these entities are participants as well.

---

[14] A means will still be required to address the early elimination of clearly frivolous claims and those which do not meet pertinent criteria for submission of a request for an investigation to the Board under the Mechanism. Those functions are delegated to the panel at the World Bank and to a Board committee at the Asian Bank, but whether these primary review responsibilities should remain with Bank staff, perhaps with guidance from a member of the Roster as necessary, remains to be determined.

The Independent Inspection Panel of the World Bank – Comparison with other International Complaints Procedures

Jakob Th. Möller[*]

THE WORLD BANK PROCEDURE COMPARED WITH UN COMPLAINT MECHANISMS

At first glance, the World Bank Inspection Panel procedure may not seem to have much in common with any of the existing UN procedures for dealing with alleged violations of human rights. Dissimilarities outnumber similarities by a wide margin. This may be perfectly acceptable. The World Bank procedure is today sue generis, a first of a kind, and was not intended to copy or imitate any other procedure. A comparison, therefore, may have limited practical value. Nevertheless, we will venture to compare the newly established World Bank procedure with some existing UN procedures, basically for the purpose of identifying some of the strengths and weaknesses that emerge. In spite of the obvious differences, the ongoing review of the World Bank procedure could perhaps draw on the experience gained in the application of other complaint mechanisms, at least in so far as the weaknesses of the latter may be avoided in the refinement of the new procedure. Some of these weaknesses are inherent or intentional (e.g. the result of a political compromise) while other are artificial or unintended and hamper the effective and efficient use and application of the mechanisms in question.

Broadly speaking, existing UN procedures may be divided into two main categories, i.e. those governed by resolutions (e.g. the 1503 procedure and the so-called "special procedures", country oriented or thematic) and those governed by international treaties (at present, the individual complaints procedure governed by the Optional Protocol to the International Covenant on Civil and Political Rights (the Optional Protocol procedure) and two similar procedures governed, respectively, by the Convention against Torture and Other Cruel, Inhuman or Degrading Treatment of Punishment (the CAT procedure) and the International Convention on the Elimination of All Forms of Racial Discrimination (the CERD procedure). For the sake of simplifica-

[*] Retired staff-member of the UN Centre for Human Rights, Geneva.

tion, we have chosen the 1503 procedure and the Optional Protocol procedure for the comparison with the World Bank procedure. A nutshell comparison reveals the following:

Legislative basis:

World Bank procedure:	Resolution of the Board of Directors.
1503 procedure:	Resolution of the Economic and Social Council.
Optional Protocol procedure:	International treaty (the Optional Protocol to the International Covenant on Civil and Political Rights).

Target of petition procedure:

World Bank procedure:	World Bank.
1503 procedure:	Any Government (global application).
Optional Protocol procedure:	States parties to the Covenant and the Optional Protocol.

Nature of allegations examined:

World Bank procedure:	Serious violations of World Bank policies and procedures.
1503 procedure:	Gross violations of human rights (Universal Declaration of Human Rights used as yardstick).
Optional Protocol procedure:	Any violation of the individual rights protected by the International Covenant on Civil and Political Rights.

Knowledge of procedure, availability and accessibility of the law:

World Bank procedure:	Poor.
1503 procedure:	Poor.
Optional Protocol procedure:	Poor.

Form and language of petition:

World Bank procedure:	Written (in English or local language of petitioner/requester).
1503 procedure:	Written (any language).
Optional Protocol procedure:	Written (any language with which the petitioner feels comfortable)

Who can file a petition (standing of petitioners):

World Bank procedure:	Any group of two or more directly affected individuals.
1503 procedure:	Anyone claiming to have reliable knowledge of alleged violation (actio popularis).
Optional Protocol procedure:	Anyone claiming to be victim of violation.

Permissible representation:

World Bank procedure:	Locally appointed representatives. Foreign representatives, exceptionally.
1503 procedure:	Unrestricted.
Optional Protocol procedure:	Any duly appointed representative, or close family member.

Other remedies to be exhausted first:

World Bank procedure:	Bring to attention of Bank's Management.
1503 procedure:	Domestic remedies, if effective (rarely found applicable).
Optional Protocol procedure:	All available domestic remedies.

Timeliness:

World Bank procedure:	Before 95% of loan for disputed project is disbursed (i.e. not applicable to past projects).
1503 procedure:	"Within a reasonable time".
Optional Protocol procedure:	No time limit specified for filing complaint (but not retroactive for events prior to entry into force of Covenant/ Optional Protocol for country concerned).

Stages of procedure:

World Bank procedure:	(1) Preliminary review and recommendations to Board of Directors as to whether the matter should be investigated (admissibility stage). (2) Investigation (merit stage).
1503 procedure:	(1) First review as to admissibility (Working Group on Communications). (2) Second review as to admissibility (Sub-Commission).

	(3) Draft recommendations on the merits (Working Group on Situations).
	(4) Consideration of the merits (Commission on Human Rights).
Optional Protocol procedure:	(1) Admissibility stage.
	(2) Merit stage.

Consultations during procedure:

World Bank procedure:	Fairly extensive with the borrowing country and all relevant Bank authorities at both stages of procedure.
1503 procedure:	Apart from soliciting written replies/observations from Government concerned, non-existent unless country visit is undertaken.
Optional Protocol procedure:	Apart from soliciting relevant written information/observation from both parties at both stages of procedure, non-existent.

In situ investigation:

World Bank procedure:	Subject to Government consent, normally in most cases.
1503 procedure:	Envisaged as possible, with Government consent, but never applied.
Optional Protocol procedure:	Not envisaged in procedure.

Participation by third parties:

World Bank procedure:	Open to any member of the public who wishes to furnish supplementary information.
1503 procedure:	Not permitted.
Optional Protocol procedure:	Not permitted.

Final action of implementing body:

World Bank procedure:	Recommendations/Report (findings) to World Bank Board of Directors (who decide whether to act or not).
1503 procedure:	Confidential decision of the Commission on Human Rights (made known to Government concerned only).

Optional Protocol procedure:	Views on the merits, or decision declaring the petition inadmissible.

Publicity:

World Bank procedure:	Panel's report/recommendations, Management's recommendations and Board's decision made publicly available and publicity given to results of Panel's investigations.
1503 procedure:	No publicity given to Commission's confidential decision unless it is reported to ECOSOC, which rarely happens.
Optional Protocol procedure:	All decisions of a final nature (views on the merits and decisions declaring a petition inadmissible) made public.

Impact of procedure:

World Bank procedure:	Considerable.
1503 procedure:	Generally considered poor.
Optional Protocol procedure:	Considerable.

Composition of implementing bodies/term of office:

World Bank procedure:	Panel of three experts. Term of office: five years (non-renewable).
1503 procedure:	Four different bodies consisting of 26 experts and 53 Government representatives (Sub-Commission and its Working Group on Communications; Commission on Human Rights and its Working Group on Situations). Term of office: four years for expert bodies (renewable); three years for Government representatives (renewable).
Optional Protocol procedure:	Human Rights Committee consisting of 18 experts (including its Working Group on Communications and Special Rapporteurs). Term of office: four years (renewable).

Secretariat staff:

World Bank procedure:	Executive Secretary, Assistant Executive Secretary and two other staff (i.e. four staff in all).

1503 procedure:	Two to three professionals (assigned to other duties as well) and one general service staff (i.e. four staff in all).
Optional Protocol procedure:	Two to three professionals (assigned to other duties as well) and one general service staff (i.e. four staff in all).

Handling of cases (duration of proceedings):

World Bank procedure:	Speedy before the Panel; less speedy before the Board.
1503 procedure:	Slow.
Optional Protocol procedure:	Slow.

Frequency and duration of meetings:

World Bank procedure:	Panel meets whenever required (upon decision of President) for as long as required each time.
1503 procedure:	Each of the four implementing bodies meet once a year (Working Group on Communications for two weeks, Sub-Commission for one to two days, Working Group on Situations for one week and Commission for one to two days).
Optional Protocol procedure:	Working Group on Communications three times a year for one week each time, followed by three to four days of plenary meetings of Committee each time.

Transparency/Confidentiality:

World Bank procedure:	All deliberations (by Panel/Board of Directors) take place in closed meetings – neither petitioner nor borrowing country present.
1503 procedure:	All deliberations at all stages take place in closed meetings – petitioner never present, but Government representative invited to be present at closed meetings of Commission (final stage).
Optional Protocol procedure:	All deliberations (by Committee/Working Group on Communications) take place in

	closed meetings – neither petitioner nor State party concerned present.
Follow-up:	
World Bank procedure:	Board oversees implementation of action ordered.
1503 procedure:	Non existent.
Optional Protocol procedure:	Active follow-up by Human Rights Committee.

We will now briefly elaborate on the basic features listed in the table above, addressing mainly the strengths and weaknesses that emerge.

Legislative basis:
The World Bank procedure and the 1503 procedure are based on resolutions, of the Board of Directors and ECOSOC respectively. Accordingly, they can be changed, modified or discontinued by the establishing bodies at any time. This may be seen as a weakness. As to the World Bank procedure, however, one would think that the relative ease with which the procedure can be modified will be used in a positive sense, by strengthening rather than weakening it, and that that is the purpose of the ongoing review.

Well meaning actors under the 1503 procedure have repeatedly voiced concern about its various inherent weaknesses (e.g. the slow pace of its implementation, lack of transparency and lack of standing of the petitioners during the proceedings). Any attempts at streamlining the procedure or making it more efficient have, however, met with total lack of political will. In recent years, it has been voiced by many that the procedure has run its useful course, that its all-embracing cloak of confidentiality in fact serves to hide serious violations which would otherwise be debated under public procedures (the so-called "special procedure") and that it should therefore be abolished. It has also been pointed out that more efficient complaints mechanisms governed by international treaties now exist.

The Optional Protocol procedure, being treaty based, is by its nature more stable than a resolution based procedure. This may be seen as a strength. Surely, the procedure will not disappear, but the cumbersome way of amending an existing treaty, followed by the process of acceptance by the States parties, may be an obstacle to bringing about desirable improvements. As the caseload increases, it might for example be desirable to provide for the Human Rights Committee to operate in panels. This, however, could hardly be done without a treaty amendment, not to speak of the possibility of making the final decisions on the merits binding on States parties.

Target of petition procedure:
The World Bank procedure certainly distinguishes itself from all other international or regional petition procedures in that the complaint is directed at the Bank itself instead of a Government or government authority. This self-imposed scrutiny, i.e. whether the Bank's own policies and procedures have been observed and adhered to in the design, appraisal and/or implementation of Bank financed projects, is unique. No other UN institution or agency has, so far, subjected itself to an accountability mechanism of this nature. While the wall of immunity has been broken, it remains to be seen whether other institutions or agencies follow suit. So far, only Governments have been the targets of complaint mechanisms. It is a legitimate question, however, whether the World Bank procedure does not indirectly target the borrowing Governments as well (the procedure does not, so far, apply to private sector projects). No doubt, the petitioner is more inclined to focus on the harm or perceived harm done by Government action or inaction than on World Bank policies and procedures. It must however be the goal of the relevant Bank policies and procedures to ensure that the interests and the rights of the inhabitants of borrowing countries are not unduly infringed, i.e. that the projects are "Panel proof", to use a World Bank expression.

As under all other international and regional petition procedures, complaints under the 1503 and Optional Protocol procedure are directed against Governments.

Nature of allegations examined:
To merit an investigation by the World Bank Panel, the allegations must be deemed (by the Board of Directors) to raise issues of a "serious" breach of the Bank's policies and procedures. While it is obvious that non-serious or frivolous complaints (which tend to flood most if not all complaints mechanisms) do not merit consideration, the qualification of "serious" violations, as a prerequisite for an investigation, lends itself to an unclear subjective assessment. How grave does an alleged breach have to be to be considered "serious" by the Board of Directors? It can probably be expected that any Bank financed project may adversely affect the interests of some individuals, notwithstanding the intended beneficial effects for the community as a whole. But, how many have to be adversely affected and how gravely, before the case can be made that Bank policies and procedures have ben seriously violated?

A similar dilemma arises under the 1503 procedure. A situation to be considered on the merits is that which reveals "a consistent pattern of gross and reliably attested violations of human rights". What is the difference between a "pattern" and a "consistent pattern"? How serious does a violation have to be to be considered "gross"? How well substantiated does an allegation have to be to qualify as "reliably attested"? How many ponderables make up the imponderable? At the end of the day, this may depend on the whims of a political yardstick, which is as unpredictable as the weather.

The Optional Protocol procedure is simpler in this respect. A claim, reasonably substantiated for the purpose of admissibility, shall be examined on the merits if it appears to raise an issue under any of the individual rights protected by the Covenant.

Knowledge of procedure, availability and accessibility of the law:
In order to be effective, a petition procedure must be known to the would-be petitioner and the relevant procedural and substantive law must be easily available and accessible to him. How well known are the procedures at issue and how accessible is the law to the would-be petitioners? As to the 1503 procedure, it can be confirmed that the existence of the procedure is well known to many active human rights NGOs in consultative status with ECOSOC, as well as a fairly large number of other human rights organizations. They have easy access to and are well aware of the contents of the Universal Declaration of Human Rights. Irrespective of whether they have confidence in the effectiveness of the procedure, most of the useful input intended for the procedure is received from these organizations. The situation is different when it comes to individuals. The majority of those, who happen to write to the UN about their human rights concerns (alleged victims of human rights violations and others) in the hope that the Organization will not turn a deaf ear to their pleas, do not appear to have any prior knowledge of any UN procedure for dealing with complaints about human rights violations. While they may have heard of the Universal Declaration of Human Rights, more often than not it is not easily available to them and often, at least, not in the local languages of would-be petitioners. Its contents are known to relatively few. After the celebration of the fiftieth anniversary of the Universal Declaration of Human Rights this is not an encouraging situation.

As to the Optional Protocol procedure, at the time of writing applicable to all individuals in 92 countries, it must be admitted that its existence appears to be practically unknown to most. The conclusion to be drawn is that the International Covenant on Civil and Political Rights and the Optional Protocol are not easily accessible to would-be petitioners and that, consequently, their contents are by and large unknown. (No communication has been received against over one third of the States parties to the Optional Protocol). In short, limited knowledge of the existence of UN procedures and limited access to the relevant law are the most serious weaknesses in their application. The author of this paper believes that a lesson is to be learned from this dismal situation in the review of the World Bank procedure.

How accessible and how well known is the Panel procedure to the would-be petitioner? The Panel's own Operating Procedures (explaining the basic features of the procedure) are available in English, French, Portuguese and Spanish and may be obtained from the Public Information Centres of the World Bank in Washington D.C., London, Paris and Tokyo (i.e. four locations, all in highly developed industrialized countries which are hardly likely to become frequent borrowers). Although the same information about the basic features of the procedure is available on the Internet, one must conclude that it is by and large unknown. What about the World Bank's policies and procedures – how accessible are they and how well known? Most of these policies and procedures, said to number over 400, including the Constituent Agreement of the World Bank, policy papers from the Board of Directors and operational policies and procedures of the Management containing instructions to the staff, exist in English only. They were published in 1994 (thanks to the initiative of Mr. Ibrahim Shihata, the Bank's General Counsel).[1] This publication, in one language, can certainly not be expected to cater to the needs of would-be petitioners in all parts of the world. Although it has been submitted by World Bank authorities that it only takes an E-mail request to Headquarters to obtain the Bank's policies and procedures, it must be assumed that this forest of law is not only practically unknown to the world, but will remain so, even with a publicity effort of major proportions. A "best effort" in this regard would perhaps be the translation of the policies and procedures into the main official languages of borrowing countries (this would apply to the Panel's Operating Procedures as well) and dissemination of the same as widely as possible (perhaps with the help of local NGOs and community associations). The difficulty, however, in making the policies and procedures easily available to would-be petitioners will probably remain the basic weakness of the Panel procedure.

In view of the general lack of knowledge of existing machineries, practical measures have been resorted to in order to remedy the situation. Under the 1503 procedure, it is in fact the Secretariat of the implementing bodies that identifies the specific provisions which, based on the narrative of the petition, have allegedly been violated. Invariably, the same applies to the Optional Protocol procedure, i.e. when the petitioner either does not mention the Covenant or invokes the wrong provisions. The Human Rights Committee has accepted in practice that the relevant provisions at issue will be identified for the petitioner, if the description of the facts is clear enough. Th same method appears to be used in the Panel procedure when it comes to identifying the World Bank policies and procedures at issue. The knowledge of the respective

---

1 The World Bank Inspection Panel (New York: Oxford University Press, 1994).

Secretariat and implementing bodies substitutes for the lack of knowledge of the petitioner.

Form and language of petition:
All three procedures dealt with in the present paper have the common feature that petitions (requests, complaints, appeals, communications) must be in writing. Apart from that, none of the procedures lays down a specific form to be followed by petitioners. A model form, however, exists for the World Bank procedure and the Optional Protocol procedure which petitioners may use, if they find it helpful. The working language of the World Bank Panel is English, but petitioners who submit their requests directly themselves (i.e. not through a representative) may use their local language. In the latter instance, the World Bank provides translation into English, but acceptance and consideration by the Panel is unavoidably delayed.

As regards the UN procedures the situation becomes more complex. The working languages of the UN Secretariat are English and French, while the working languages of the implementing bodies are normally English, French and Spanish. The official UN languages are, however, six (Arabic, Chinese, English, French, Russian and Spanish). The implementing bodies expect the Secretariat to process and to place before them, at least in *their* working languages, any communication, irrespective of the original language. This is based on the view that it is in the nature of a petition procedure, if it is to be available and effective, that a petitioner be allowed to write in a language with which he or she feels comfortable. Under the 1503 procedure this may mean practically any language and as regards the Optional Protocol procedure communications may be expected to be received in some 40 or more languages used in the States that, so far, have ratified or acceded to the Optional Protocol. How does this work in practice? Not well, to say at least. Up to the mid-eighties, the few professional staff assigned to processing incoming petitions received a crucial support from the Languages Service of the UN, which provided summary translations of any communication received in a language which the assigned staff did not cope with. This crucial support service was discontinued in the mid-eighties when a political crisis, called financial crisis, hit the Organization, resulting in drastic reduction of staff. The Languages Service no longer had the capacity to provide summary translations of incoming mail. All attempts since then to persuade the budgetary authorities to restore this support have ben unsuccessful. As a result, a large number of communications are either filed away without any action, or are returned to the authors with the explanation that, regretfully, the staff does not understand them. So much for the seriousness with which the Organization treats individual petitioners at large. In a effort to reduce the impact of this deficiency, unpaid interns, selected on the basis of their language skills, have been brought in to do summary translations.

Who can file a petition (standing of petitioners):
Under the Panel procedure, any group of two or more directly affected persons (or persons likely to become directly affected) who claim that "their rights or interests" are being violated (or are likely to be violated) by the Bank may file a request for investigation. They may have formed an organized group for that purpose (association, organization etc.) but that is not necessary. The requirement of "two or more" (probably intended to give the impression that the procedure does not deal with "individual" complaints) appears to be somewhat artificial. It would hardly be difficult for any single individual wishing to file a Request to find another person, similarly affected (e.g. spouse, neighbour, friend) to co-sign the Request, and the requirement is met. For the purpose of admissibility, they simply have to make a prima facie case of the claim that they are or would be directly affected. It appears from the Panel's Operating Procedures that Requesters have standing as a party to the dispute.

In addition to affected individuals, it is envisaged that an Executive Director of the Bank may also initiate a request "in special cases of serious alleged violations". This is remarkable (i.e. that the Bank can initiate a complaint against itself) but the likelihood of that happening may be remote.

Under the 1503 procedure, "standing" (on the face of it) is wide open. It is an actio popularis mechanism, open to all individuals, groups or organizations, whether affected or not, who claim to have "direct and reliable knowledge" of the alleged violations. On closer look the authors have no real standing under procedure. They are simply regarded as a source of information who, at most, get an acknowledgement of receipt of their communication, but play no further role. Furthermore, the majority of them do not appear to have any "direct" knowledge of the events complained about. This applies in particular to those who participate in orchestrated mass write-in campaigns and to the thousands of people in all parts of the world who urge the UN to do something about serious violations reported on a day-by-day basis in the mass media. (Communications based on mass media reports are, in fact, inadmissible).

Standing under the Optional Protocol is similar to that under the World Bank procedure. All individuals (submitting a communication on their own or together with other affected in the same manner), who claim to be victims of violations of the individual rights protected by the International Covenant on Civil and Political Rights, have standing, as a party to the dispute and enjoy equality of arms vis-à-vis the State party complained against.

Permissible representation:
Under the World Bank procedure a petitioner may be represented by a local representative. Only in exceptional cases (i.e. when the Panel receives "clear evidence" that no one in the country in which the project is located is capable of representing the petitioner adequately or in an appropriate manner (?!)) is non-local representation permitted. Apart from the near impossibility of submitting "clear evidence" that no one alive in the country concerned has the required skills and capacity, the rule on permissible representation is unduly restrictive and onerous. Considering the specialized skills required for a successful application of the procedure, i.e. knowledge of World Bank policies and procedures, it is not likely, as indicated above, that these skills are widely possessed for the time being. It is more likely that relatively few professionals, world-wide, would specialize in World Bank policies and procedures, their application and interpretation. It is difficult to understand why such expert representation should be excluded on the ground of residence (not necessarily nationality). Whatever the motivation behind the restriction, it appears unreasonable. This issue, I believe, should be reconsidered in the review process.

Under the 1503 procedure, no restrictions on representation exist. The same is true for the Optional Protocol procedure. It is noteworthy, that petitioners under the latter procedure are invariably represented by practising lawyers in other countries, among other reasons, because very few in the legal profession have specialized in the field.

Other remedies to be exhausted first:
Before filing a request under the World Bank procedure, the prospective petitioner must first turn to the Bank's Management, ask it to deal with the problem and seek its reaction thereto. The Panel's Operating Procedures do not explain further the nature and scope of these prior contacts, but apparently, the Panel must assess whether Management's reaction has been satisfactory or not before it decides whether or not to deal with the request. Other remedies (i.e. domestic remedies) do not have to be resorted to, since the complaint is directed against the Bank itself, not the borrowing country. It should be borne in mind, however, that the allegations directed against the Bank may be that it has been remiss in its obligation to require others (e.g. the borrowing country) to act in accordance with its policies and procedures. At any rate, a request filed under the Panel procedure cannot preclude recourse to domestic remedies (whether simultaneous or not) e.g. to seek judicial orders to cease and desist or in respect of claims of compensation for damage suffered by the affected persons.

Under the 1503 procedure domestic remedies have to be exhausted first "unless it appears that such remedies would be ineffective or unreasonably prolonged"[2]. The internationally recognized domestic remedies rule is reasonable under a procedure dealing with individual complaints. Under the 1503 procedure, which does not deal with individual cases *per se*, but rather consistent patterns of gross violations affecting a large number of persons over a protracted period of time, it has turned out to be impractical. Consistent patterns of violations (invariably reflecting government policies and practices) would simply not exist, if domestic remedies were effective. On the other hand, the normal requirement of prior exhaustion of domestic remedies works well under the Optional Protocol procedure. There too, however, the obligation only applies in respect of effective remedies and only in so far as the remedies are not unduly prolonged. The case law of the UN Human Rights Committee amply clarifies the scope and perimeters of this rule.

Timeliness:
Under the World Bank procedure a request is inadmissible if it is filed after the closing date of the loan/credit financing the project in question or when 95% or more of the loan/credit has been disbursed. In other words, the procedure applies to on-going projects only, not projects that are completed or near completion. This limitation is understandable. While a project is in progress, the Bank may still be in a position to take corrective measures and remedy mistakes made. *Post facto*, this may not be feasible. No matter, therefore, how serious the impact of a Bank-financed project turns out to be, for example 5 or 10 years after its completion, the procedure does not apply, irrespective of whether the policies and procedures of the Bank were adhered to or not at the time of design, appraisal and implementation of the project. During that time, however, which undoubtedly extends for years in most cases, prospective petitioners would have ample time to raise their grievances with Management and, thereafter, file a request for investigation.

Under the 1503 procedure, a communication must be filed "within a reasonable time after the exhaustion of domestic remedies" (Sub-Commission resolution 1(XXIV), op. cit). Normally, as explained above, it would have little practical purpose to try to count from the time of exhaustion of domestic remedies. In reality, the issue boils down to assessing what would be considered "reasonable" in the particular circumstances of the situation. On the one hand, if the situation complained of still persists, it may not matter how many years ago the specific events complained of started, if they form part of a continuing pattern. On the other hand, if the situation complained of no longer

[2] See the admissibility criteria set out in resolution 1(XXIV) of the Sub-Commission on Prevention of Discrimination and Protection of Minorities, 13 August 1971.

exists (i.e. the consistent pattern no longer continues, but belongs to the past) it may not be considered "reasonable" to deal with the situation at all, even if the complaint describes recent events. For example, when a democratically elected Government replaces a dictatorial regime and puts an end to policies of violation, arbitrary detention, torture and killings, the UN Commission on Human Rights would no longer consider it timely to deal with the matter under the 1503 procedure. In this respect it may be said that the 1503 procedure, like the World Bank procedure, deals with current situations not past situations. At the end of the day, the time-factor is not determinative, the change in the situation is. Out of over one million communications channelled into the 1503 procedure since 1970, only a few have been rejected as out of time. These have related to events that took place prior to the founding of the United Nations (including during the Second World War).

There is no time-limit for the submission of complaints under the Optional Protocol (cf. the six months time-limit under the European Convention on Human Rights). The competence of the Human Rights Committee, therefore, to receive and consider communications under the Optional Protocol about alleged violations of the International Covenant on Civil and Political Rights, is limited only, *ratione temporis*, by the date of entry into force of the instruments for the State party concerned. At one point or another the question may arise whether an amendment to the Optional Protocol is needed to preclude claims relating to events that took place a long time ago. (In respect of the earliest ratifying or acceding States claims can already be over 20 years old). Failing the enactment of a time-limit clause, the Committee might sooner or later have to resort to declaring communications inadmissible on the ground of abuse of the right of submission when the events complained of (acts or omissions) allegedly took place a long time ago, e.g. 30, 40 or 50 years ago.

Stages of procedure:

Under the World Bank procedure, the preliminary review of a request for investigation (carried out by the Panel or a Panel member designated by the President and leading to a recommendation to the Board of Directors as to whether an investigation should be carried out) may be seen as the pre-admissibility stage. The decision of the Board then determines whether the case is closed, or whether the Panel is authorized to proceed with an investigation. This is akin to a decision on admissibility, i.e. whether an examination on the merits of the claim should be carried out or not. It may be seen as a weakness, that the independent body of experts, the Panel, is not vested with the authority to decide whether a request warrants an investigation. Its recommendation may carry considerable weight, but appears to the little more than an advisory opinion. The decision making rests with the Board. It may accept or reject the Panel's recommendations, including ordering an investigation when the Panel has recommended that no further action should be taken. Subject to the Board's decision, an investigation then takes place. Again, the President designates one or more Panel members to take primary responsibility for the work under a broadly based authority to use such working methods as may be considered appropriate, including meetings with all concerned, public hearings, visits to the project site (with the consent of the borrower), broad powers to seek and receive oral and written submissions from all relevant sources (including independent experts and NGOs), hiring of consultants and unrestricted access to the Bank's files. The end result is a Panel *report* with conclusions and findings, submitted to the Board of Directors. Here again, the Board decides what action, if any, shall be taken by the Bank in the light of the Panel's conclusions and findings. As at the admissibility stage, political control rests with the 24 Executive Directors also at the merit stage. It must be assumed, however, that the Panel's conclusions and findings are taken seriously and that there is a genuine will to demonstrate that the machinery is effective.

Under the 1503 procedure, screening of communications takes place at two levels, i.e. in the Sub-Commission's Working Group on Communications and in the Sub-Commission itself. Three affirmative votes (i.e. three out of five) are needed at the Working Group level for any communication to reach the second stage. Example: If two members vote in favour of a proposal to elevate a particular communication to the Sub-Commission, one member votes against and two abstain, that is the end of that. The communication is "dropped" (rejected), no matter how serious it is and no matter how well substantiated it is. A small fraction of thousands of communications reviewed each year passes the 3-vote test and reaches the Sub-Commission for a second round of screening. In the Sub-Commission, a majority vote is needed (of those present and voting) for a "situation" to be referred by to the Commission on Human Rights for examination on the merits. After the Sub-Commission started to vote by secret ballot under the 1503 procedure some years ago, "situations" that merit referral to the Commission stand a better chance than before of being so referred. Preliminary consideration on the merits takes place in the Commission's 5-member Working Group on Situations, which adopts (by majority vote) and places before the Commission "recommendations" (in the form of a draft resolution) on the course of action to take in respect of each particular "situation". Consideration on the merits then takes place in the 53-member Commission, ending with the adoption of a confidential decision (in the form of a resolution) made known only to the Government of the country concerned. Compared with the World Bank Panel procedure, this is a long, drawn out and cumbersome process.

Under the Optional Protocol procedure the admissibility stage involves the Human Rights Committee's Special Rapporteur for New Communications, the Committee's Working Group on Communications and, in cases declared inadmissible, the Committee itself. The Working Group can declare communications admissible (by unanimous decision) but decisions declaring communications inadmissible can only be taken by the Committee in plenary. That is often a waste of time and effort. Many communications suffer from an obvious inadmissibility ground (e.g. *ratione temporis* or because domestic remedies have clearly not been exhausted). In such clear cases, the Committee's Working Group, or even the Special Rapporteur for New Communications, should have the authority to declare communications inadmissible. A request for a review of such decisions by plenary could be allowed. The merit stage involves the Working Group (preparation of draft Views to be placed before plenary) and the Committee (consideration of draft Views), which adopts its Views by majority decision. Individual members can file separate opinions, concurring or dissenting.

Consultations during procedure:
Under the World Bank procedure, the Panel consults the borrower and the Executive Director representing the borrower country at both stages of the procedure. In addition, the Panel has access to all Bank staff and to all relevant Bank records anc consults as need be with the Director General, Operations Evaluation Department and the Internal Auditor. Written legal advice in respect of the Bank's rights and obligations is sought from the Bank's Legal Department. Obviously, the Panel has also access to the petitioner in the information gathering process. Accordingly, the Panel procedure envisages extensive consultations on the various aspects of the Request under consideration.

Under the 1503 procedure, consultations are most often limited to offering the Government concerned an opportunity to provide written replies and observations to the allegations made. A dialogue with the Governments concerned only takes place if the Commission decides to designate an Independent Expert to establish "direct contacts" with the Government and the people of the country concerned (between sessions) and to report back to the Commission at the following session. This method of implementation (which requires a rather high degree of political support in the Commission) has been used in respect of 8 of the 75 country situations examined since the procedure became operative in the early seventies.[3] The presence of Government representatives at the very meeting when the Commission adopts its confiden-

---

[3] In 5 other country situations the Commission has requested the Secretary-General to assign a similar role to a special representative (of the Secretary-General).

tial decision on a given country situation can hardly be described as "consultations".

Under the Optional Protocol procedure, consultations are limited to seeking written information and/or observations as required from both parties. Up to the adoption of the Committee's Views on the merits there are no other "consultations". However, the Committee has established an interesting follow-up mechanism to ascertain how and to what extent States parties, which are found to be in breach of a Covenant provision, give effect to its Views. Direct consultations, including country visits, have taken place under that mechanism (see under Follow-up below.).

In situ investigation:
Under the World Bank procedure in situ visits have become normal practice at both stages of procedure.

Paragraph 6(b) of the 1503 procedure envisages in situ investigation by ad hoc committees if the Commission on Human Rights deems that course of action warranted. This, however, appears to be a dead letter. No ad hoc committee of investigation has ever been appointed under the procedure. Instead, the Commission has on a number of occasions designated an independent expert to visit the country concerned and to report back to the Commission.

In situ investigations are not envisaged under the Optional Protocol and the procedure is conducted purely in writing.

Participation by third parties:
Under the World Bank procedure, any member of the public may provide the Inspection Panel with supplementary information that he/she believes to be relevant to the evaluation of the Request. Such supplementary information should not, however, exceed 10 pages (not counting supporting documentation which may be enclosed).

Third party participation is neither permitted under the 1503 procedure nor the Optional Protocol procedure. However, under paragraph 5 of the 1503 resolution, the Sub-Commission may consider "other relevant information" in addition to communications and the Government replies relating thereto. In fact, the Sub-Commission has once purported to take into account "other relevant information". In 1979, a confidential report prepared by a group of eminent African lawyers under the auspices of the Organization of African Unity (OAU) was "added" (in spirit) to the dossier on the country concerned which was referred to the Commission, although no Sub-Commission member had actually seen or read the report. Its existence was simply known. Through its contacts, the Secretariat managed to obtain a copy of the report prior to the

Commission session. This was made known to the Commission members, but no one bothered to ask for it.

Final action of implementing body:
Under the World Bank procedure, both the Panel recommendation (at the admissibility stage) and the Panel report (following investigation on the merits) are submitted to the Board of Directors for action. In other words, the Panel never has the last word. As mentioned above, the inability of the Panel to decide on its own whether an investigation takes place, or not, is probably seen by many as an intrinsic weakness in the procedure. Notwithstanding, the Panel's recommendation and its report (if the Board approves an investigation) are communicated to the petitioners and both are made public. There is therefore no secrecy about the outcome of the Panel's work, irrespective of any action by the Board. The petitioners are made aware of the nature of the Panel's recommendation and, in case an investigation is carried out, whether or not the conclusions and findings of the Panel reveal a breach by the Bank of its policies and procedures. In the absence of consensus, the minority views are also included.

Under the 1503 procedure, the final outcome is normally a confidential decision of the Commission which is communicated only to the Government concerned, not to the petitioners. (As explained above, they are regarded as a source of information, and no more, and therefore have no standing). Only on rare occasions has the cloak of confidentiality been lifted. This happens only, if the Commission makes a recommendation to its parent body, the Economic and Social Council (paragraph 8 of resolution 1503).

Under the Optional Protocol procedure all decisions of a final nature, i.e. decisions declaring a communication inadmissible and Views on the merits, are adopted by the Human Rights Committee. If a breach is found, the Views state which steps should be taken by the States party concerned to remedy the violation. In the absence of a consensus, individual opinions (concurring or dissenting) are appended to the Committee's Views.

Publicity:
Under the World Bank procedure, a notice that a Request has been registered and all subsequent notices and documents issued by the Panel in the conduct of its mandate (including recommendations and reports) are made public. The principle of transparency prevails in the procedure and is commendable.

Under the 1503 procedure, it is the other way around. The principle of secrecy is almost all-embracing. Apart from the few exceptions referred to under 14 above, only the names of the countries under consideration at the Commission level are made public.

The situation is markedly better under the Optional Protocol procedure. All decisions of a final nature (decisions declaring communications inadmissible and the Committee's Views on the merits) are made public.

Impact of procedure:
The purpose of the World Bank Panel procedure is to provide an independent forum through which directly affected persons can request the Bank to act in accordance with its policies and procedures, i.e. to correct mistakes that allegedly have been made or to prevent a threatened occurrence of such mistakes. Logically, one would expect that remedial action would be taken once the Panel through its fact-finding investigation has concluded that non-compliance has taken place or would take place without corrective measures. What is perhaps the most interesting feature resulting from the operation of the procedure is the willingness of the Bank Management to act at an earlier stage. In almost all cases where investigation has been recommended by the Panel, Management has placed remedial action plans before the Board of Directors before an investigation has taken place. As has been observed by a Panel member, Management tends to jump in with a rapid development of a remedial action plan, once a request for an investigation has been received or when the Panel places its recommendation before the Board. There are those who view this turn of events with concern, questioning what happens to consultations, if the Board approves a remedial action plan at the time when the Panel places before it a recommendation for investigation, or even earlier. The author of this paper is inclined to consider it a remarkable success that the mere submission of a Request may trigger corrective measures to remedy mistakes in respect of ongoing projects. One would assume that the sooner corrective measures are taken, the better. One may also assume that the earlier a mistake or potential mistake is detected, the less costly it will be to correct. If a remedial action plan is put in place and persuades the Board that an investigation is no longer warranted, the existence of the procedure has already had an impressive impact. After all, it is a recognized goal of Management to be "Panel proof".

The 1503 procedure can certainly not boast of rapidly developed remedial action plans and its overall impact can hardly be rated above poor. Nevertheless, it has forced the Commission on Human Rights to give some consideration to the human rights situation in some 75 countries, some of which would have otherwise escaped scrutiny altogether. Governments are under pressure to demonstrate willingness to cooperate and the level of cooperation with the Commission has generally increased, at least in terms of the quality of the written replies and observations which they place before it under the procedure. Instead of categorical denial of any wrongdoing (which was the rule in the early years of the operation of the procedure) Governments are now more inclined to demonstrate that positive measures have been taken or are being taken to improve the situation under consideration. This hardly explains the fact, however, that the Commission has decided not to take any action in more than half of the country situations referred to it by the Sub-Commission as appearing to reveal a consistent pattern of gross and reliably attested violations of human rights. If the majority of the Government representatives sitting on the Commission do not find it politically expedient to proceed, the matter is dropped, irrespective of how grave the situation is and how thoroughly substantiated the dossiers before the Commission are.

An element most often forgotten or unnoticed is the positive impact that the mere transmittal of a communication to the Government concerned may have. All communications destined for pre-screening by the Sub-Commission's Working Group on Communications are transmitted by the Secretariat to the Governments concerned well in advance. This routine Secretariat action, in particular in individual cases, has had positive results through the years in a considerable number of cases. Thus, by correcting wrongdoing in individual cases and submitting a corresponding reply to the allegations made, the Government concerned satisfies the Working Group on Communications which, accordingly, takes no further action. Hundreds of letters addressed to the Secretariat by grateful petitioners, whose problems have been solved, demonstrate that their petitioning the United Nations has had the desired impact. Admittedly, the success rate is however low.

The impact of the Optional Protocol procedure must be rated as considerable. Giving effect to the Views of the Human Rights Committee in cases where a breach of a Covenant provision has been found, States parties have amended laws found inconsistent with the Covenant, compensation has ben offered to the victims, sentences have been commuted and victims have been released from imprisonment or detention. States parties have also offered compensation during the course of the proceedings to remedy past wrongs. Increasingly, the Committee's case law is being cited in important judgements of national courts and by scholars and researchers of international human rights law.

Composition of implementing bodies/term of office:

The World Bank Inspection Panel consists of three independent development experts (Inspectors), nominated by the Bank's President and appointed by the Board of Directors for one non-renewable term of five years. One of the experts severs as Panel Chairman.

In comparison, the UN machineries are heavier, in particular the cumbersome machinery under the 1503 procedure where four bodies are involved, consisting of 26 experts and 53 Government representatives whose term of office can be renewed without limitation in time. The 26 human rights experts of the Sub-Commission (five of whom serve concurrently on its Working Group on Communications) are nominated by Governments and elected by the Commission on Human Rights for a term of four years at a time. Some of the members have served for more than 25 years. The Commission on Human Rights consists of the representatives of 53 States, elected by the Economic and Social Council for a term of three years at a time, renewable ad infinitem. Representatives of five Commission members (one from each geographical region) serve concurrently on the Commission's Working Group on Situations, for renewable one year terms at a time, ostensibly in their individual capacity. While some regions try to rotate members on the two working groups, it appears that specific countries in other geographical regions have staked out working group seats as their private fiefdoms. This does not inspire confidence in their independence. To the innocent bystander it also looks odd when the same person represents his Government on the Commission and serves as an expert on the Sub-Commission.

The Human Rights Committee consists of 18 experts, nominated by Governments that have ratified or acceded to the Covenant (but not necessarily the Optional Protocol) and elected by meetings of the States parties to the Covenant for renewable terms of four years. (One Committee member served uninterrupted from 1977 (first session) through 1998). Five members serve at the same time on the Committee's Working Group on communications (for one session at a time). There has been a reasonable rotation of working group members through the years. Most if not all Committee members have so served at one time or another. From 1977 to date, almost all Committee members have been lawyers.

Secretariat staff:
From the outset, the staff of the World Bank Inspection Panel has consisted of an Executive Secretary, an Assistant Executive Secretary and two other staff members. In the ongoing review of the Panel procedure it must be assumed that provisions will be made for an adequate increase of staff, commensurate with the workload. The Bank would be well advised to avoid the UN practice of almost starving existing petition procedures out of existence by failure to provide adequate supporting staff.

Under existing UN petition procedures, the staffing situation has gradually deteriorated since the mid-eighties. The core problem is the starvation budget doled out by the Member States to the UN Secretariat, resulting in the sad role of the Budget Division of dividing too little amongst too many. Budgetary constraints have dictated a drastic reduction of posts Secretariat-wide. For the human rights programme of the Organization a recent restructuring of the Office of the High Commissioner for Human Rights (formerly Centre for Human Rights) has compounded the problem by eliminating the core unit that previously serviced the petition procedures. It may not take a cynic to conclude that these mechanisms are simply not meant to work efficiently. In the unlikely event that the Budget Division would actually propose an increase in resources for petitions procedures, more likely than not such a proposal would be rejected by the all-powerful Advisory Committee on Administrative and Budgetary Questions (ACABQ) – a standing committee of the General Assembly consisting of 16 Government representatives. What finally reaches the General Assembly (Fifth Committee) for approval every other year is a Pandora's box called Proposed Programme Budget (for a given biennium). What is cynical about the Proposed Programme Budget is the ritual statement issued in the name of the Secretary-General to the effect that the proposed allocation of the Organization's resources is sufficient to implement fully all mandated programmes and activities. This statement does not even pass the giggle test.

Some 15 years ago, the daily work under the 1503 procedure was carried out by five to six professional officers and three to four general service staff. In 1998, the fiftieth anniversary year of the Universal Declaration of Human Rights, this work is assigned to one full-time officer and two part-time officers (i.e. officers assigned to other demanding and time-consuming duties at the same time) and one general service staff. The procedure does not even pretend to function normally any longer, and a large number of communications are filed away annually without being attended to.

Ten years ago, with 45 States parties to the Optional Protocol, the Human Rights Committee started to warn (in its annual report to the General Assembly) that work under the Optional Protocol was deteriorating because of lack of staff. At that time, three to four lawyers and two to three general service staff were assigned to the procedure. In 1998, ten years later, with 92 States parties and on ever growing workload, two lawyers (one of them funded for two years by a voluntary contribution from a Government, not the UN) are assigned to the procedure full-time and one part-time (i.e. assigned to other duties as well). They are assisted by one general service staff. Some of the basic secretariat functions under the procedure have been discontinued and hundreds of potential Optional Protocol cases wait unattended to for a year or more because of lack of staff.

Handling of cases (duration of proceedings):

With a view to expediting the handling of Requests, the Panel's Operating Procedures lay down stringent time-limits, in particular in the early phases of the proceedings. At the time of registration, a request is brought to the attention of the Bank's Management which has 21 days to comment thereon. (Some further time may be allocated, if the Panel seeks further clarifications from Management or affords the Requester an opportunity to comment thereon). As a rule, however, the Panel is to make its recommendation to the Board of Directors within 21 days after receipt of the Management's response (whether or not the additional clarification or information is received). If the Panel decides that a preliminary study is needed (normally including an in situ visit) for making an informed recommendation to the Board, the three week time-limit may be extended to eight weeks (exceptionally more, with the Board's approval). This means, that the Panel's recommendation should normally reach the Board within 11 weeks from the date of registration of the Request and, exceptionally, somewhat later. This is an impressive speed for the Panel to establish a prima facie case and base its recommendations thereon. The speed of the next phase, i.e. the Board's consideration of the Panel's recommendations and action thereon is less impressive. This phase does not appear to be subject to any time-limit. In fact, it has be lamented by Panel members that it has taken the Board up to 13 to 14 months to act. One wonders what the Board is waiting for in the meantime. A remedial action plan from Management? At any rate, without justification, a delay of 13 to 14 months in this phase seems excessive compared with the swiftness of the first phase.

Should the Board so approve, the third phase, the Panel's investigation, ensues. Although the operating procedures do not dictate a time-limit for the conclusion of an investigation, the Requests so far dealt with on the merits demonstrate the Panel's ability to work expeditiously. Once the Panel's investigation Report is submitted to the Board of Directors and to the President of the Bank, deadlines apply again. At this time, Management has six weeks to submit its own report to the Board in response to the Panel's findings. This triggers the fourth and the final phase in the determination of the fate of a Request, i.e. consideration by the Board of Directors of the Panel's report and Management's report in response thereto. The Operating Procedures are silent about how long the Board can engage in the consideration of the two reports placed before it, but stipulate that within two weeks after the Executive Directors consider these reports, the Bank shall inform the Requester of the results of the investigation and the action decided by the Board, if any. In short, the Panel and Management shall act swiftly, the Board can take its time without any time-limits. On balance, however, and in comparison, with UN petition procedures, the World Bank inspection procedure operates relatively fast.

The 1503 procedure is a long drawn-out machinery, with inherent delays at various phases. Communications are received by the Secretariat on a day by day basis and transmitted to the Governments concerned for reply. The first screening body (the Sub-Commission's Working Group on Communications) meets during the latter half of July each year and considers communications received since its last session and transmitted to the Governments concerned at least 12 weeks prior to its meeting. Example: Any communication received and transmitted to the Government concerned during the last week of April 1998, or later, will wait for screening until the Working Group's meeting in July 1999. Accordingly, the information screened can be up to 15 months old when it is considered by the Working Group. In the event that the Working Group transmits in 1999 a communication received in late April 1998, and in the event that the Sub-Commission decides to transmit the same to the Commission on Human Rights, as appearing to reveal a consistent pattern of gross and reliably attested violations of human rights, the Commission would receive the dossier at its March/April session in the year 2000, i.e. two years after the situation was brought to the attention of the United Nations. In the meantime, there is no authority for the Secretariat or the implementing bodies to solicit up-to-date information from the authors. Should they, unsolicited, submit further information about the same situation at a later stage, that information would be regarded as a new communication which, depending on the date of receipt, might be reviewed by the Working Group in July of the year 2000 to reach the Commission, through the Sub-Commission, in March/April 2001. And so on, and so on. This is an inbuilt weakness in the procedure, which repeatedly permits the Governments concerned to argue that the dossier before the Commission is obsolete. The Commission also takes its time in the consideration of a particular situation and is known to have kept the same situation pending before it for up to six to eight years, without doing much more. Unless the dossier is so poor that it should never have reached it in the first place, a country situation is, in fact, only removed from the Commission's 1503 list in the following three circumstances: (a) The majority finds it politically expedient to drop the matter, irrespective of the gravity of the situation; (b) The majority musters the political courage to elevate the debate from the confidential 1503 procedure to a public procedure; (c) A democratically elected Government has replaced the former repressive Government which was responsible for the massive violations complained of, or other positive developments have resulted in a marked improvement in the situation.

Procedurally, the Human Rights Committee should be in a position to adopt its Views in a given Optional Protocol case within a year or two after it has been transmitted to the State party for reply. In reality, however, the duration of the process is most often considerably longer, or up to four to five years. Firstly, the Committee devotes only a relatively small part of its meeting time to Optional Protocol work, while most of its time is devoted to the consideration of State reports under a periodic reporting system established by the Covenant. This reduces the Committee's capacity to deal expeditiously with cases. Secondly, failure of the parties, one or both, to meet established deadlines for the submission of requested information or clarifications invariably results in delays in the proceedings. Thirdly, the principle of equality of arms dictates that each party be afforded the opportunity to comment on any submission from the other. Repeatedly, one party or both appear to have used, or abused, this principle for no apparent reason other than delaying a decision. By making a further submission, sometimes repeatedly, (purporting to provide additional facts, more detailed clarifications or even new allegations) at a time when the case would otherwise be ripe for decision, the submitting party triggers the requirement of forwarding the new submission to the other party for comments, thus delaying a decision to the Committee's next session. Fourthly, as indicated under 18 above, insufficient Secretariat support has delayed and will continue to delay the Committee's work under the Optional Protocol until the workforce is substantially increased.

Frequency and duration of meetings:
The Inspection Panel's Operating Procedures do not refer to the frequency and duration of Panel meetings. One must assume, however, that the President (who works on a full-time basis) can call meetings at short notice whenever required and that the duration of meetings each time is dictated by the workload. The tight deadlines in the early stages of the proceedings would appear to necessitate prompt attendance to each Request once registered. In this sense, the Panel can be seen as a standing body meeting whenever required.

Each of the four bodies involved in the 1503 procedure meets once a year. The Sub-Commission's Working Group on Communications meets for two weeks during the latter half of July, screens literally thousands of communications and makes a selection to pass on to the Sub-Commission. The Sub-Commission meets for four weeks in August and devotes one to one and a half days to the consideration of communications, which is one of about 20 substantive items on its agenda. During this day and a half, the Sub-Commission determines which particular country situations to refer to the Commission on Human Rights for consideration. The Working Group on Situations meets for one week, prior to the Commission's annual six weeks session held in March/April, studies the dossiers received from the Sub-

Commission, as well as the dossiers which the Commission may have decided to keep pending before it at the previous session, and prepares recommendations for the Commission on the course of action to take in respect of each country situation. The dossiers, including written observations from the Governments concerned and reports of Independent Experts, if any, normally amount to some 700 to 800 pages or more. Consideration of communications under the 1503 procedure has been a sub-item of one of over 20 substantive items on the agenda of each six weeks annual session of the Commission. For this sub-item the Commission has normally allocated one day, or one and a half at the most. During these few working hours (six to nine) the Commission is supposed to have a serious substantive debate on the information contained in the voluminous country dossiers, listen to statements made by the representatives of the countries concerned and act on the recommendations received from the Working Group on Situations, or act on any other proposal tabled by members during the debate. It is not uncommon that some 7 to 10 country situations are dealt with in this manner within the time span of less that 10 hours. The restricted time devoted to consideration of communications at the Sub-Commission level and country situations at the Commission level limits the seriousness of the debate.

Prior to each session of the Human Rights Committee, its Working Group on Communications meets for one week to consider Optional Protocol cases. Apart from declaring cases admissible, it prepares and places before the Committee a considerable number of draft inadmissibility decisions and draft Views on the merits. The Committee itself meets three times for three weeks per year, amounting to 45 working days. Out of these, it devotes seldom more than three to four working days per session to the consideration of Optional Protocol cases, i.e. some 9 to 12 working days per year. Obviously, the limited time allotted to Optional Protocol work affects the Committee's capacity to deal expeditiously with cases. Nevertheless, consideration of the cases is serious and professional and the Committee has produced an impressive body of case law. From the beginning (1977) up to and including its sixty-fourth session in October/November 1998, 844 cases had been placed before the Committee with the following results:

(a) Concluded by adoption of Views on the merits: (with violations found in 236 cases)	308 cases
(b) Declared inadmissible:	248 cases
(c) Discontinued or withdrawn:	125 cases
(d) Not yet concluded: (including 46 cases declared admissible)	163 cases

Transparency/Confidentiality:

All three procedures dealt with in the present paper have the common feature that all meetings of the implementing bodies are closed. In that sense the proceedings are confidential. Under the World Bank procedure, however, there is a commendable degree of transparency at the various phases in the handling of a Request. Thus, the Panel's Register, recording all actions taken during the processing of a Request, as well as the dates on which any documentation or notification is received by or sent from the Panel, is public. The contents of a notice that a Request has been registered (including the name and location of the project complained about, the name of the Requester (unless anonymity is sought) and a brief description of the matter complained of), and the contents of all other notices or documents issued by the Panel in the course of the proceedings "will be available to the public", as worded in paragraph 65 of the Panel's Operating Procedures. After the Board of Directors has considered the Panel's recommendation as to whether or not an investigation is warranted, the Request itself, the Panel's recommendation and the Board's decision is made public. Upon completion of an investigation and consideration by the Board of the Panel's report thereon and Management's response thereto, the report, the response and the Board's decision are released to the public. What remains confidential are the actual deliberations at the Panel's meetings and the deliberations at the Board meetings. All results are made public. Remarkable transparency, that could be copied by others.

Under the 1503 procedure there is hardly any transparency whatsoever at any stage in the procedure. As dictated by paragraph 8 of the 1503 resolution, it is strictly confidential. The Working Group on Communications, the Sub-Commission and the Working Group on Situations cannot disclose any of its activities, and the Commission on Human Rights has chosen to be stifled also, by almost consistent non-use of the exception in paragraph 8, permitting it to make its decisions public in the form of recommendations to its parent body, the Economic and Social Council. Through an odd coincidence, the Commission has, however, released each year since 1978 the names of the countries considered by it under the 1503 procedure.[4] The cloak of confidentiality is by many seen as the most serious weakness of the 1503 procedure.

---

[4] In 1978, a notorious African dictator promised to cooperate with the Commission under the confidential 1503 procedure on condition that the name of his country would not be mentioned under the public procedure for dealing with violations of human rights. The Commission accepted the condition, but to make it less evident it agreed that there should be no discussion of any of the 1503 countries under the public violations item that followed the 1503 item. That is why the names of the 1503 countries had to be read out to the participants (Observers, NGOs etc.) at the public meeting that ensued. This became a practice, but the gagging order only lasted for two years.

Apart from the parties being informed of any action taken during the course of the proceedings and the transmittal of any written submission from either party to the other, the proceedings under the Optional Protocol are confidential. The register of the Human Rights Committee is not made public, its working documents are kept confidential and the parties are requested not to give publicity to their submissions before the Committee has reached a final decision (declaring the case inadmissible or adopting its Views on the merits). Once a decision of a final nature is reached and has been transmitted to the parties, the rule of confidentiality is lifted. Final decisions are publicly available and the Committee's case law is issued in its annual report to the General Assembly. The parties are no longer required to refrain from giving publicity to the submissions which they made or received in the course of the proceedings. In short, the proceedings are confidential, but the results are made public.

Follow-up:
The Operating Procedures of the World Bank's Inspection Panel do not envisage any further action by the Panel after an investigation has taken place and a report thereon submitted to the Board. The Panel has at that time concluded its work. It would appear self-evident that the Board has an obligation to ensure that any action ordered by it to remedy non-observance is carried out by Management. On occasions, the Board has however assigned a supervisory role to the Panel when a remedial action plan is offered by Management without an investigation.

The same country invariably stays on the Commission's 1503 list for a number of years (is "kept under review"). But once it has been deleted from that list (i.e. the Commission decides to "discontinue consideration of the matter"), there is no follow-up.

The Optional Protocol does not spell out any mandate for the Human Rights Committee to take follow-up action once its Views under article 5(4) of the Protocol have been transmitted to the parties. The Committee has determined, however, that, in cases where a breach of the Covenant has been found, it has implied powers to ascertain what steps have been taken by the State party concerned to remedy the violation. For that purpose, the Committee includes a statement in its Views to the effect that it "wishes to receive from the State party, within 90 days, information about the measure taken to give effect to the Committee's Views". Further, the Committee has since 1990 designated one of its members to act as a Special Rapporteur on follow-up of Views, whose function is, systematically, to solicit information from States parties on the measures taken by them in relation to Views finding violations of the provisions of the Covenant. The Special Rapporteur reports to the Committee and a detailed chapter on the results of his work is included in the Committee's annual report. There is no doubt that the follow-up mechanism enables the Committee to better evaluate the effects of its work under the Optional Protocol and contributes to its effectiveness.

CONCLUSIONS

The World Bank's Inspection Panel is not a decision making body, but carries out important fact-finding functions reported to the Board of Directors in the form of recommendations and findings. Its work has considerable impact and adds a dimension to the network of international mechanisms for the promotion and protection of human rights. The procedure is relatively swift and its transparency is commendable. Compared with other international petition procedures, its strengths would appear to outnumber its weaknesses. The unnecessary restriction on permissible representation constitutes a weakness that should be eliminated. It has no place in the procedure.

Other apparent weaknesses are more difficult to remedy. These are the same as those that hamper effective and efficient use and application of other petition procedures, i.e. limited knowledge of the existence of the procedure and limited availability and accessibility of the law (the Bank's policies and procedures). Even if a "best effort" publicity campaign is undertaken, this deficiency will probably remain a permanent weakness in the World Bank procedure.

It is to be hoped that the World Bank procedure will avoid the other serious weakness that has frustrated UN petition procedures for many years, i.e. the inability of the budgetary authorities to understand, or their intentional unwillingness to recognize, the need for adequate resources to permit efficient servicing of the procedures in question.

The work of the Inspection Panel has enormous potential and deserves to be followed with keen interest by the international human rights community for years to come. The World Bank is to be congratulated for the bold, innovative step it has taken by establishing the procedure.

ILO Supervision and the World Bank Inspection Panel

Lee Swepston[*]

I should start by saying that the ILO and the World Bank have been discussing for about the last 18 months questions of mutual concern relating to the need for the Bank to take into account basic principles of the ILO – and the UN system – on four subjects: freedom of association and protection of the right to organize, and freedom from forced labour, child labour and discrimination. These discussions are continuing, and may have made some progress. There have also been discussions, at the instigation of the International Federation of Building and Wood Workers, one of the ILO's trade union constituents, about how to ensure the inclusion of basic workers' rights concerns in the World Bank's own procurement contracts.

The ILO and the United Nations are the two primary standard-setting and supervisory bodies in the UN system. There is a close relationship between ILO and UN standards: to put it very simply, the UN sets the broad standards of human rights conduct that apply universally; while the ILO adopts standards that go much more deeply into the narrower range of subjects which are within its mandate. An example relates to the excellent UN Convention on the Rights of the Child, which contains only a few lines on child labour. The ILO, on the other hand, has adopted 11 Conventions on minimum age for admission to employment or work, and a number of others on various other aspects of the question – and will shortly adopt another on the most intolerable forms of child labour. These standards examine in depth the questions touched upon lightly in the UN Convention, and form an international reference for those who want to examine how they can implement the UN Convention's strictures against economic exploitation of children.

The ILO has developed the highest number of standards in the system, with 184 Conventions to date; and the most elaborate and precise supervisory system, which will be explained in a few moments.

* Chief, Equality and Human Rights Coordination Branch, International Labour Office, Geneva. This article is an adaptation of the presentation made to the meeting, and has kept the same basic form

How does all this relate to the work of the World Bank and the other international financial institutions, and in particular to the work of the Inspection Panel and the similar institutions being developed by the Inter-American and Asian Banks?

The World Bank is prohibited from concerning itself with "political" questions, which often is taken to mean that it cannot deal with human rights. However, its operations have a significant effect on the implementation and enjoyment of human rights. This is particularly so as the implementation of the projects funded by the World Bank, and the implementation of its procurement agreements, invariably involves the use of labour in the countries concerned, sometimes in massive numbers. There is thus a close link between ILO standards and the operations of the World Bank and the others.

Another factor is that some countries – in particular the United States, but it is not the only one – are bound by their own internal law to take account of "internationally-recognized workers' rights" or similar concerns, when approving Bank-funded activities.

So far the Inspection Panel has investigated between one and three cases, depending on which of the figures we have heard discussed this past few days is accurate. These have concentrated on environmental, resettlement and indigenous questions so far. Even with the few cases mentioned during this meeting which have been submitted to the Panel, at least five countries have been mentioned with which the ILO has active supervisory concerns under two important ILO Conventions which nevertheless are rather marginal to its main work: the Indigenous and Tribal Peoples Convention, 1989 (No. 169) and its predecessor instrument of 1957, No. 107. However, other concerns are likely to surface in the work of the Inspection Panel in coming years, that might concern for instance forced labour, discrimination, child labour, and other principles of the ILO which also find their place in the policies and procedures of the World Bank. Thus we are likely to have much more contact on these subjects in the future, and the relationship between the work of the Inspection Panel and the ILO is likely to remain close.

Another concern – and this must be both said and understood very cautiously – is that there are aspects of the policies and procedures of the World Bank, and of those of the regional Banks, that bear a close resemblance to the more "conventional" standards, in both senses of that term. The Bank's policies are considerably more constraining because they can be imposed on borrowing countries by contract and enforced by financial penalties; though they are of narrower application than ILO standards which apply to the entire country and not only to a given project. Bank policies influence government behaviour. They are now subject to a kind of supervisory process. In addition, the "1,500-lb. Gorilla" syndrome must be taken account of: while the ILO and the UN must rely on persuasion, publicity and leverage for their policies to prevail, the World Bank does not have to bargain for its views to be taken into account, for reasons we all know. Yes, we are all aware that the World Bank's share of international investment in development has diminished, but it remains an immensely powerful voice, often able to fix conditionalities of which the rest of the international system remains innocent.

Finally, we all know by experience that things go wrong in the implementation of technical cooperation projects. It has happened to all of us, the ILO, the UNDP, the Banks – it is quite normal and must be expected, though regretted and fought against. It happened to the ILO in earlier years, and of course it still does. Any time a project is set in motion and then overseen from a distance, child labour, discrimination, forced labour and many other phenomena may occur in its implementation. Now that the Inspection Panel has been created, the only surprise is that so few cases have been submitted. The World Bank took one set of measures to cope with this by installing the Inspection Panel. The ILO took another by establishing a close operational link between the standards its own International Labour Conference has adopted, and all technical assistance activities carried out by the ILO. There is a requirement in the ILO that all operational activities arise out of its standards, and that no ILO activities will violate these standards.

SUMMARY OF ILO ACTION ON THE SUPERVISION OF INTERNATIONAL LABOUR STANDARDS

The ILO has been adopting standards – Conventions and Recommendations – since 1919, and there are now 184 Conventions on a variety of subjects. While the discussion in the expert meeting focussed on human rights, a number of other subjects are essential to the effective realization of these rights, such as labour administration, promotion of employment, and many others. There are some 6,500 ratifications of these instruments, creating a vast web of common obligations around the world on matters within the ILO's mandate.

The ILO recognized early in its history that it had to supervise the application of these standards in some detail, or its standard-setting work would be in vain. It therefore has developed an extensive supervisory system.

The ILO's supervisory machinery has evolved over time from the foundations laid down in the Constitution, and from the functions assigned by the Conference and the Governing Body. The various bodies and functions outlined below form a unified whole. For those more familiar with the procedures of the United Nations, this is in fact one of the distinguishing characteristics of the ILO system, that all Conventions are supervised under the same system by the same bodies.

When a Convention has been ratified, a State is required under article 22 of the ILO Constitution to submit periodic reports on its law and practice under the Convention. Reporting periods have been modified on several occasions, and reports are now due at intervals of two years (for fundamental human rights instruments) or five years (all others), though reports can be requested more frequently if necessary. Note that the ILO receives nearly 2,000 reports each year. The rate of reporting is about 65% before the annual session of the Committee of Experts (see below), rising towards 90% by six months after the session.

In the case of non-metropolitan territories (NMTs), States are required under article 35 of the Constitution to report as under article 22, on the application of Conventions which they have declared applicable to these territories. There are about 1,000 declarations of application to NMTs.

States are required under article 23, para. 2, of the ILO Constitution to communicate copies of their reports to the most representative organizations of employers and workers in their countries, and these organizations may comment on these reports. This is because governments are often economical with the truth when reporting to international bodies, especially on human rights. In fact, everyone familiar with international supervisory mechanisms knows that governments are apt to say that the overall picture is excellent, and any details of inconsistency with international obligations are mere statistical errors. The ILO currently receives workers' or employers' comments on over 20% of governments' reports each year, and this helps keep the record straight, and governments honest. It is a built-in NGO verification system, from which the ILO benefits enormously.

The Committee of Experts on the Application of Conventions and Recommendations is the ILO's principal supervisory body. It was created in 1926 by the International Labour Conference, holding its first meeting in 1927, to examine the reports submitted by governments and by employers' and workers' organizations under articles 19, 22 and 35 of the Constitution. It is a body of 20 independent legal experts, appointed by the Governing Body on the nomination of the Director-General, which meets once a year in Geneva. It issues a report which consists of:

- a General Report, with the text of its Observations, published in report III (1A) to each annual session of the Conference (usually some 500 pages of comments – a copy was circulated for information at the meeting); and

- a General Survey, published in Report III (1B), summarizing the reports received under article 19 of the Constitution on unratified Conventions and on Recommendations.

The Committee of Experts also adopts Direct Requests, which for reasons of economy are not printed and published; they are sent directly to governments but are not put before the Conference. The Observations and Direct Requests are published in the annually-updated ILOLEX data base on CD-ROM (and soon "on-line" at the ILO's web site[1]), and it is planned to include also the General Surveys in future editions.

One of the standing committees of the International Labour Conference at its annual session, is the tripartite Committee on the Application of Conventions and Recommendations. It discusses the report of the Committee of Experts, and usually calls before it the representatives of about 30 governments whose situation is mentioned in the Experts' report, to examine their situation more closely. These discussions can be very tense, but government representatives almost always accept these invitations. In the last two years, for instance, there have been discussions with Myanmar on forced labour and freedom of association, Nigeria on trade union rights, and Iran on discrimination. The reports of this committee include a virtually verbatim record of the discussion. they are public information, and may be used as such – and thus, like all the ILO supervisory material, are available to the World Bank and its Inspection Panel.[2]

COMPLAINTS PROCEDURES

Article 24 of the ILO Constitution provides for a "representation" to be made "by an industrial association of employers or of workers that any of the Members has failed to secure in any respect the effective observance within its jurisdiction of any Convention to which it is a party". If it considers that the representation is receivable, the Governing Body usually establishes a tripartite committee from among its members to examine the representation and to make any recommendations it may consider appropriate. Whereas for many years there were few representations received, the ILO is now receiving 10 or more a year in some years.

1 At http://www.ilo.org. ILOLEX also includes a great deal more valuable information for anyone interested either specifically in the ILO, or in the setting and implementation of economic, social and cultural rights in the international system. It may be ordered from the International Labour Office, Geneva.

2 Published in the *Record of Proceedings* of each annual session of the Conference, as well as on ILOLEX.

The Constitution also provides, in article 26, that "Any of the Members shall have the right to file a complaint with the International Labour Office if it is not satisfied that any other Member is securing the effective observance of any Convention which both have ratified". The Governing Body may, and usually does, refer complaints to a Commission of Inquiry, composed of three independent persons. "The Governing Body may adopt the same procedure either of its own motion or on receipt of a complaint from a delegate to the Conference." Commissions of Inquiry usually hold hearings and make on-the-spot investigations before making their conclusions and recommendations. There is one such Commission of Inquiry now in operation, examining the application of the Forced Labour Convention, 1930 (No. 29), by Myanmar.

Special complaints procedures on freedom of association deserve special mention, as a unique ILO supervisory method. The Committee on Freedom of Association (CFA) is a tripartite committee of the Governing Body, established by agreement with the United Nations' Economic and Social Council (ECOSOC) in 1950. It may examine complaints from workers' and employers' organizations that member States of the ILO are not respecting basic principles of freedom of association. These complaints may be examined whether or not the country concerned has ratified the ILO's Conventions on the subject, as the procedure is based on constitutional principles. If the country has ratified the Conventions, the Committee's conclusions are followed up by the Committee of Experts.

The Fact-Finding and Conciliation Commission on Freedom of Association was also created by agreement with ECOSOC, at the same time as the Committee on Freedom of Association. It may examine the same kind of complaints as the CFA, but to do so requires the consent of the government concerned. It may also examine complaints of violations of freedom of association against non-member States of the ILO – and has on several occasions – when such complaints are forwarded to it by the United Nations and the country consents. Panels of the Commission are formed of three independent experts appointed by the Governing Body.

Reports on unratified Conventions and on Recommendations. The ILO does not examine reports only on ratified Conventions. Under article 19(5)(e) and (6)(d) of the Constitution, the Governing Body may request reports from each member State on "the position of its law and practice in regard to the matters dealt with in the (Convention or Recommendation), showing the extent to which effect is given, or is proposed to be given, to any of the provisions of the (Convention or Recommendation)". In the case of Conventions, the State shall also indicate "the difficulties which prevent or delay the ratification of such Convention." These reports are examined by the Committee of Experts on the Application of Conventions and Recommendations, and form the subject of a "General Survey" which is examined each year by the Conference.

In addition, under a procedure adopted in 1996 by the Governing Body, States which have not ratified one or more of the ILO's fundamental Conventions (Nos. 29 and 105 on forced labour, Nos. 87 and 98 on freedom of association, Nos. 100 and 111 on discrimination, and No. 138 on minimum age for employment or work) are asked under article 19 of the Constitution to report at four-yearly intervals on the obstacles to ratification. These reports are also examined by the Committee of Experts, in connection with the current campaign for the ratification of these fundamental instruments.

Finally, at the moment there is discussion going on of the possibility of the ILO adopting a declaration of fundamental rights which arise from the fact of membership in the Organization. This is to be supplemented by a follow-up mechanism which would allow examination of the situation of individual countries, but the form and contents of both the Declaration and the procedure have not yet been decided. This will be discussed at the November 1997 Governing Body of the ILO, and may be on the agenda of the International Labour Conference in 1998.

CONCLUDING REMARKS CONCERNING THE INSPECTION PANEL AND GENERAL INTERNATIONAL HUMAN RIGHTS LAW[3]

As indicated above, the Inspection Panel so far has trodden very close to subjects already being dealt with under standards and the ILO supervisory procedures. This should be no surprise, as the international development agencies are all dealing with similar problems. Indeed, as many human rights problems arise directly from poverty, exclusion and exploitation, it is not surprising either that both development and supervisory concerns should deal with the same situations.

It was also indicated above that World Bank policies had aspects of international standards. In fact, they are often derived from international standards, and herein lies a problem. Whereas international human rights conventions are carefully negotiated and different interests taken into account, and then are subject to ratification before becoming binding on States, the World Bank's Operational Guidelines and other policy documents are the fruit of staff work and are submitted to the political bodies of the Bank only for approval. As was stated by the Vice-President of the Bank during the expert meeting, this may make the World Bank the most effective implementation

---

3 This part of this article picks up remarks made during the expert meeting, not necessarily at the time the ILO supervisory procedures were discussed.

agency for human rights in the United Nations system, because it extracts from human rights standards what is useful and is able to work for the implementation of these principles with a certain force that other parts of the system lack.

Nevertheless, this has its drawbacks. It is a matter of concern – and, I think, legitimate concern – if the staff of any agency rewrites international human rights standards to its own specifications, and then applies them in that form rather than in the form in which they were adopted. It is a matter of even more concern if that agency then examines the implementation of those standards through its own projects, as it understands them and without reference either to the original standards themselves or to the way they have been supervised by the international bodies established for that purpose. This is particularly of concern if the country concerned has ratified those standards, and is being encouraged, or allowed, to violate them.

This is not to say that this is necessarily happening, but rather to state that it should be avoided. As indicated, the World Bank Inspection Panel is likely to encounter problems in the future of child labour, discrimination, forced labour and violations of freedom of association in the implementation of its projects. This is not blameworthy, it is inevitable, and it is a matter of congratulations to the Bank that it has recognized that problems will arise and is prepared to deal with them. But – and here is the problem of consistency of international law – what will be the effect if the World Bank decides that a form of discrimination prohibited under the International Covenant on Civil and Political Rights and the ILO's Discrimination (Employment and Occupation) Convention, 1958 (No. 111), both ratified by a country in which the Bank is working, are in fact in line with the Bank's own operational guidelines and therefore not to be discouraged?[4] This is the question around which the

[4] This is not so farfetched an example. In 1996 the ILO learned that the Office of the UN High Commissioner for Refugees had participated in the forced repatriation of 200,000 refugees from Bangladesh to Myanmar, on condition inter alia that they *not be required to perform more than four days of forced labour a month.* This was in direct violation of the ILO's Forced Labour Convention, 1930 (No. 29), ratified by Myanmar and the subject of fierce ILO criticism. The UNHCR said when this was brought up, that this was in accordance with the UNHCR's own standards, and therefore the implementation of other UN-system standards was not relevant.

expert meeting danced, and which we firmly hope will be the subject of future meetings hosted by the Raoul Wallenberg Institute, as well as of continuing dialogue within the UN system.[5]

[5] Just as these comments were being prepared for publication, a speech was given to the Third Committee of the UN General Assembly by Ms. Mary Robinson, new High Commissioner for Human Rights, in which she stated:

> "I will also encourage a closer link between the recommendations of UN human rights experts (of the treaty bodies and the mechanisms of the Commission on Human Rights) and the work of agencies and programmes of the UN system, including the World Bank and the IMF, in order to give the promotion and protection of all human rights even more practical applications in our daily work." (14 November 1997, intervention to the Third Committee of the General Assembly, taken from the United Nations home page.)

Protecting Rights under the EU's Aid Programme – The Need for a Dedicated Complaints Mechanism for Non-European Citizens

Patricia Feeney[*]

Negotiations underway concerning the future of the Lomé Convention – EU's aid and trade agreements with developing countries in Africa, the Caribbean and the Pacific (the ACP States) provides Member States and the Commission with an opportunity to rectify the lacuna that currently exists in the protection offered the intended beneficiaries of its development cooperation programme. The EU is virtually the only major multilateral aid agency which has not yet established a complaints mechanism to enable people who allege that they have suffered material harm as a result of an aid programme to have a fair and reasonably independent hearing. In other important respects the European Commission's development guidelines have lagged behind other institutions such as the World Bank, partly as a result of a shortage of staff with the appropriate skills. The Commission has for example been much slower to adopt and implement social and environmental guidelines. Although an Environmental Impact Assessment Manual was prepared by Commission's Directorate General for Development (DGVIII) in 1993, it did not become mandatory until 1996. Those EIAs which were undertaken by the Commission were found to have a number of common deficiencies: these included limited consultation with stakeholders and intended beneficiaries. Many environmental projects, which started before 1992 were designed without any form of consultation and even today "a substantial proportion of environmental projects do not appear to take the views of local communities into account during design and preparation."[1] In most of the financing proposals evaluation reports show that gender perspectives have been neglected.[2] The concept of

---

* Rights and Accountability in Development Project, Refugee Studies Programme, Queen Elizabeth House, University of Oxford.

1 ADE "Evaluation of EU Aid to ACP Countries Managed by the Commission" Phase 1, Final Report, July 1997

2 See BMB,"Institutional Appraisal and Development Methodology Programme Phase One", April 1995, evlaution report drawn up on behalf of the Commission of the European Communities; and, "Assessment of WID/Gender policies of the Community and its member states and

participation with local beneficiaries has also been missing: the Commission itself has acknowledged that collaboration with decentralised actors only rarely took place "upstream" since the administrations themselves – the EU or recipient governments – were responsible for the decisions on programme planning and design. In addition the Commission's programmes have rarely been subjected to rigorous scrutiny. The concerns of Member States have focused on the need to keep external spending within agreed budget ceilings rather than on the quality of the aid on offer. This neglect has been compounded by the relative lack of interest demonstrated by members of the European Parliament: "Few decision-makers actively sought impact information. EC aid management has been much more driven by resources than by objectives both at the level of the Commission and the level of ACP countries."[3]

The National Indicative Programmes, NIPs, drawn up by the European Commission and the recipient governments, form the largest portion of aid to the ACP countries. They are five year agreements which set out development priorities, define the areas of co-operation, earmark projects and programmes and set a timetable for implementation. However access to the Commission's preliminary Country Strategy Papers and the final NIP has been extremely restricted. As a member of European Parliament commented, "So far, indicative programmes have been treated virtually as state secrets. They must become joint commitment programmes to be discussed and concluded with all the operators concerned".[4] At the UN's Commission on Sustainable Development the EU has championed the establishment of national judicial and administrative channels to enable affected parties the opportunity of seeking redress from decisions that are socially and environmentally harmful or which violate human rights (in line with Principle 10 of the Rio Declaration). But what about the damage wrought on people's lives by its own aid programme? In its development co-operation activities the EU has not taken a lead in offering the right to a fair hearing and redress to non-EU citizens whose lives may have been damaged by its projects and programmes.

---

of their implementation by the different administration", 1/10/94 – Colombo D; and "Inventory of Environment and Tropical Forests Programmes – Final Report March 1996", ERM; and ADE "Evaluation of EU Aid to ACP Countries Managed by the Commission" Phase 1, Final Report, July 1997.

3 ADE, "Evaluation of EU Aid to ACP Countries Managed by the Commission" Phase 1 Final Report, July 1997.

4 Wilfried Martens, MEP Draft Report to the European Parliament on the Future of Lomé, p. 23.

DISPUTE MECHANISMS UNDER THE LOMÉ CONVENTION

Since 1980 successive Lomé Conventions have incorporated principles committing the EU to upholding the basic rights of individuals and to protecting the environment.[5] Lomé III stipulated that, development cooperation in ACP-States should promote the social and economic 'well-being of their population'; 'the satisfaction of their basic needs'; 'the enhancement of people's capacities'; and 'respect for their dignity'. Provision should be made for the cultural and social implications of aid to be taken into account at all stages of the operations and for local people's participation in project design and implementation so that their basic needs are met. It is further stipulated that project appraisal must consider 'the effects expected from the ... social ... and environmental viewpoints'. Lomé IV, covering the period 1990-2000, reinforces the message: cooperation through development 'shall help abolish the obstacles preventing individuals and peoples from actually enjoying to the full their economic, social and cultural rights'; and 'priority must be given to environmental protection'.

But there is no clear indication about what should happen when these principles are not upheld. Firstly, under Lomé III, disputes between an ACP-State on the one hand and Member States or the Community on the other over both the application or interpretation of the Convention are resolved by referral to the Council of Ministers or, if necessary, through arbitration. Should a party then fail to take the measures required for the implementation of the arbitrator's decision, no explicit sanctions are detailed under Lomé III; however, and in the extreme, either the Community or the ACP-State may denounce the Convention. Secondly, the Convention specifies how disputes between an ACP-State and contractor should be resolved. Similar provisions exist under Lomé IV, and indeed were extended after a mid-term review.[6]

Two points need to be made about these provisions in respect of remedial action. Firstly, there is an implicit assumption – despite the formal power of both the Community or an ACP-State to invoke remedial measures – that any failure to meet the principles in the Convention will be on the part of the ACP-State and not on the part of the Community. After all, 'denouncement' of the Convention only makes sense as sanction when it is applied against an ACP-State. Such dual standards further the cause of those who argue that conditionality is incompatible with the desire for greater ownership of the development process. A growing number of development and environmental NGOs believe

---

5 The Lomé Convention determines the principles and instruments of development cooperation between the EC and African, Caribbean and Pacific (ACP) States. It is now under its fourth revision and draws the bulk of its financing from the European Development Fund (EDF).

6 Lomé IV was revised at a meeting in Mauritius on 4 November 1995.

that the Commission must also look to itself and its own obligations in upholding the principles of the Convention. Secondly, because channels of remedial action are limited to redressing disputes and failures of obligation between the Community and an ACP-State, people adversely affected by projects and programmes have no direct means of redress or compensation under the Convention. In short, if the Commission fails to fulfill its own obligations under the Convention, and as a consequence the basic rights of local residents are undermined in the implementation of a project or programme, then there is currently no clear-cut provision for them to take the matter up directly with the Community.

There is, however, a provision in the latest Lomé IV Convention that builds on a previous article in Lomé III and can reasonably be interpreted as applicable to both the Community and ACP-States in the redress they offer to people adversely affected by a project. Article 10 is unequivocal in determining that action should be taken:

> The Contracting Parties shall, each as far as it is concerned in the framework of this Convention, take all appropriate measures, whether general or particular, to ensure the fulfillment of the obligations arising from this Convention and to facilitate the pursuit of its objectives. They shall refrain from any measures liable to jeopardize the attainment of the objectives of this Convention. [Emphasis added]

Yet, despite this obligation, no specific measures of redress for third parties have been codified in any detail under the Lomé Convention. Unless Member States rectify this situation and set up an accountable chain of responsibility, the principles espousing human rights and poverty alleviation at the level of the individual and the local community in the Convention amount to little more than empty rhetoric. The EU has acknowledged that shared responsibility in managing aid between the Commission and the beneficiary countries has been a source of confusion and delay. "Despite improvements made in successive conventions, all evaluation studies show the cumbersome joint management system has hampered the effectiveness of aid".[7] Oxfam has suggested that one way of translating the principles of transparency, accountability and participatory development into specific action would be in setting up an effective complaints mechanism. The current situation imposes an inordinate burden on project affected people.

JOINT MANAGEMENT OF THE AID PROGRAMME

One of the characteristics of the Lomé Convention is its commitment to joint management: this means that there is a complex chain of responsibility for

[7] EU Commission "Policy Guidelines for future EU-ACP relations" October 1997.

project preparation, appraisal and approval. It is the joint responsibility of the Commission and the ACP government to appraise projects, to ensure that they meet all the criteria and principles under the Convention. The effectiveness of projects should include an assessment of their likely social and environmental impacts. Final approval of the Financial Proposal which forms the basis of the Financing Agreement rests solely with the Union. During the implementation stage both the Commission and the ACP government have a duty to supervise the project. Under both Lomé III and Lomé IV, a National Authorising Officer appointed by the government of each ACP State is responsible for the execution of operations and for making adaptation arrangements on technical and economic grounds [Article 227, Lomé III].[8] However, the Commission-appointed Chief Authorising Officer is ultimately responsible, subject to the powers exercised by the National Authorising Officer, for managing the European Development Fund's resources and ensuring the proper execution approved operations [Article 226, Lomé III and Article 311, Lomé IV]. Furthermore the Commission is represented in each ACP-State by a delegate who shall work in close co-operation with the National Authorising Officer; shall be kept informed of the adaptations made during the execution of operations; and shall make sure that EC-funded projects are executed correctly from the financial and technical angles.[9] Lomé IV requires the delegate to maintain close and continuous contact with the National Authorising Officer for the purpose of analysing and remedying specific implementation problems. There is a provision under both Lomé III and IV for the periodic evaluation of ongoing projects through joint progress reports, and again, the EC delegate must co-operate with the national authorities and must draw up reports on the outcome of such evaluations.[10] At the end of each year there is a requirement under Lomé IV that the delegate submits a progress report on projects and programmes to the ACP State and the Community.[11]

---

8 The Community's responsibilities in respect of contracts are codified in Articles 225(2), 226(2), 228(3). Lomé IV further specifies that all contracts financed from the resources of the EDF must be governed by the Convention in accordance with regulations adopted by the Council of Ministers (see Articles 305, 306, 325). Under Lomé IV, the role of the NAO is clarified in Article 313.

9 Article 228, Lomé III.

10 Article 224(1)(a) and Article 228(6), Lomé III; see also Articles 320 and 321(1)(b) and Article 317(1) Lomé IV.

11 Article 318 (b) Lomé IV.

LIMITED ACCOUNTABILITY

If these supervisory mechanisms fail to detect and correct problems as they arise, there are additional safeguards. The Development Finance Cooperation Committee, which is a subsidiary body of the Council of Ministers, already has powers to examine specific problems at the request of the Community or the ACP States. While it can study problems of implementation "with a view to facilitating the removal of any difficulties" there are few examples where people whose rights have been adversely affected by a project have succeeded in having their complaint heard at this level.[12] Despite its formal powers, the Council of Ministers has on occasion sought to disclaim all responsibility for the EDF programme on the grounds that its has delegated- decision making authority to a subsidiary body, the EDF Committee: "the management of the European Development Fund is conferred to Commission in its own responsibility (see Article 9 of Financial Regulation 91/491/EEC of 29 July 1991 applicable to development finance cooperation under the Fourth ACP-EC Convention, OJ No L 266, 21.9. 1991, p.1) Financing proposals relating to projects of less than MEC 2 are approved by the Commission. For projects above this threshold, the Commission is assisted by the so-called 'EDF-committee', which is a committee under the auspices of the Commission (Articles 21 and 25 of Internal Agreement 91/401/EEC on the financing administration of Community aid under the Fourth ACP-EC Convention, OJ No L 229, 17.8. 1991, p. 288). The Council not being involved in the management of the European Development Fund is therefore not in a position to take any position on the content of the complaint in question'.[13] This response would appear to conflict with the obligation set down in Article 324, Section 6 of the ACP-EEC Convention which requires the Council of Ministers to examine 'at least once a year whether the objectives of development finance cooperation are being attained and 'examine the general and specific problems resulting from the implementation of that cooperation'.

Given the relative weakness of the European Parliament (for example, in the case of the non-budgetised aid the European Parliament has no formal control over the European Development Fund) there is no means of ensuring that the political institutions take up the exhortations in the Maastricht Treaty to respect human rights.[14] Under the Lomé Convention, decisions on whether to finance specific projects are taken by the EDF Committee, which is composed of senior civil servants from Member States. Control of the

---

[12] Lomé Convention Articles 193 and 216(2).

[13] Letter dated 19 March 1997 from G. Zalm, Council of the European Union to Mr Jacob Soderman, European Ombudsman re: complaint no 983/29.10.96/ABU/KDENYA/BB.

[14] Article F1 of the Treaty of Union.

Communities' finances is the responsibility of the Court of Auditors which reviews all EU expenditure, including the cost effectiveness of the Commission's development and humanitarian work. The Court of Auditors' reports which have been critical of the aid programme have been influential in changing spending priorities and improving accounting procedures. As an institution, however, it is less successful in following up problems with specific projects.[15] [Oxfam, for example, received no formal response to a letter sent in September 1996 to the Court of Auditors requesting it to examine the issue of substantial cost overruns in the Kenyan Northern Corridor Road project and the repeated failure of the EC Delegation and Project Team in Uganda to submit audited accounts and to implement recommendations in the 1991Auditor's Report to improve supervision of the Natural Forest Management and Conservation Project.]

While the Parliament's Development and Cooperation Committee has the power to raise concerns about implementation of the EDF programme and to question Commission officials, the level of detailed knowledge about specific projects and programmes that is required inevitably puts even the most conscientious MEPs at a disadvantage. Since 1981 the European Parliament's rules of procedure have allowed for the setting up of ad hoc committees of inquiry. Article 138c of the Maastricht Treaty strengthened this provision allowing the Parliament to establish a temporary inquiry committee "to investigate alleged contraventions or maladministration in the implementation of Community law". There is also an entitlement for both citizens and any person resident in or having their office in a Member State to petition the European Parliament (Article 138 d Treaty of Union). Community Institutions are also subject to the jurisdiction of the newly created Ombudsman (Article 138 e Treaty of Union) who is appointed by the European Parliament. The Ombudsman may examine cases of maladminstration on the part of Community institutions by which is meant administrative irregularities or omissions, abuse of power and negligence. The institutions must supply information on request and give access to files, except where grounds of security are pleaded. At the conclusion of the investigation the Ombudsman is to send a report to the European Parliament and to the institutions under investigation and the complainant is to be informed of the outcome. The Ombudsman also presents

---

15 In April 1991 the Court of Auditors noted that a decision to drop an energy subcomponent of the Ugandan Natural Forest Management and Conservation Project (approximately 18 per cent of the total project budget) and to retain the funds in the NFMCP had not been referred to the eDF Committee, authorised by the Chief Authorising Officer in Brussels, or reflected in an amendment to the Financing Agreement. No action was taken to regularise the position after the Court of Auditors report. Although weaknesses in monitoring the donor co-ordination were identified in the 1991 Court of Auditors report to specific action was taken by Brussels or the EC Delegation in Kampala to strengthen the systems. See LTS Evaluation paras 4.74 and 4.76.

an annual report to the European Parliament. But once again the Ombudsman may only receive complaints of maladministration by Community Institutions from the same category of persons who may submit petitions.

THE RESTRICTED POWERS OF THE OMBUDSMAN

In January 1997 a complaint filed by a Kenyan MP, Mr Paul Muite, was rejected by the Ombudsman. He had written on behalf of several thousand poor people living on the outskirts of Nairobi who had been struggling for over six years to obtain compensation for damages incurred during an EDF-financed road rehabilitation project for the Westlands-St Austin and Kabete-Limuru roads. A parallel complaint concerning the same project, the Great Northern Corridor Road Project in Kenya, filed by an EU citizen was however considered admissible and (at the time of writing) is still under consideration.[16] But at the end of this protracted process, even if the Ombudsman finds that the Commission had been negligent, while he is entitled to make recommendations to institutions of the European Community, he has no formal powers to ensure that remedial action is carried out. The problems residents of Gitaru and Rungiri have experienced and continue to face resulted from the design of the highway and the manner in which the construction work was carried out. A quarry and stone-crushing plant was located in the vicinity of their homes and farmland. Residents suffered a decline in their living standards, their basic right to physical and mental health was violated and many now suffer permanent damage to their lungs as the direct result dust inhalation. In short, people in both communities have been impoverished as a result of the road construction.

Under Lomé III the Commission had joint responsibility to appraise the project and final responsibility for approving the Financial Proposal, which formed the basis of the Financing Agreement. A social and environmental assessment should have been carried out and alternative solutions should have been examined. Despite repeated complaints from the residents about the impact of the project during implementation, the EC took no action to remedy the situation.[17] Some of the residents attempted to file claims in the Kenyan Courts against the contractors, FEDIMP (a Nairobi based company in which the Italian holding now known as IMPREGILO was a prominent stakeholder

[16] See Complaint by Mrs Ann Barbara Usher to the European Ombudsman, Ref: 983/29.10.96/ABU/KENYA/BB.

[17] Oxfam Policy Department "A Profile of European Aid II: Northern Corridor Transport Project. Adverse Social and Environmental Impacts caused by the Rehabilitation of the Westlands-St Austin and Kabete-Limuru roads, Kenya" September 1996.

at the time). But as of February 1998 very few of the claims had been settled and their cases will soon be time-barred. The poverty of the residents means even when legal representation is given pro bono and when lawyers agree to defer fees in exchange for a share of any settlement, filing fees are prohibitive and calculated as a percentage of the amount, so the more that is claimed in damages, the higher the fee. Attempts to reach an out-of-court settlement have also stalled.

OTHER ROUTES FOR OBTAINING REDRESS

In the absence of an effective complaints mechanisms a sustained high profile – and adversarial – campaign may be the only means of securing a remedy when the EU's aid programme goes wrong. Between 1990 and 1993, more than 130,000 people were evicted – some forcibly – from forest areas in Uganda, as part of the European Commission's (EC) Natural Forest Management and Conservation Project. The project was designed to assist the Ugandan Forest Department to clear the forests of encroachers. The most violent evictions occurred in April 1992, when some 35,000 people were evicted from the Kibale Forest Reserve and Game Corridor. There were reports of serious human rights violations during the evictions, including beatings and rape. A number of people died as a direct result of the manner in which the evictions were carried out: some were burnt to death in their homes or died from physical exhaustion after running away, panic-stricken, into the bush to escape the police. Many people reported that their personal belongings, tools, and livestock were looted, their homes and crops and store grains were destroyed. Pregnant women forced to flee miscarried, some later died. No provision had been made to resettle the families and those evicted were left destitute, begging along the roads with no food or shelter. There was a public outcry in the country and President Museveni directly intervened, promising those who had been evicted the chance to resettle in another part of the country.

After the evictions thousands of displaced people had to resort to squatting in shopping centres or working as farm labourers inexchange for space for their temporary shelters. Some worked as sharecroppers or as cheap labour for local landowners. Those who attempted to return to their plots of land and collect food from their stores were allegedly beaten by guards. Those who moved to the neighbouring district of Kasese found themselves in an even more desperate state: with water and food in scarce supply they could only find some temporary base along the railway line in appalling conditions. They even faced the ultimate indignity of having nowhere to bury their dead. There is no accurate record of how many people – but the old, the young and vulnerable like pregnant women succumbed in these first few terrible months. They remained in these conditions until September 1992 when finally efforts were made by the Government to resettle them in Bugangaizi, in the District of Kibaale.[18]

At almost no stage of implementation of the project did senior staff members of either the World Bank or EC question the compatibility of the Ugandan government's evictions policy with existing World Bank guidelines or with the underlying principles of European aid. The issue never appears to have been raised at any of the donor coordination meetings. In February 1990 for example, the Bank's supervision mission, disregarding World Bank policy, commented that the EC programme "has made significant achievements in removing encroachers from the high forest ..." Although when it first approved the project, the EC had no formal guidelines on involuntary resettlement, by 1992, the time of the Kibale evictions, the EC had adopted and was bound by OECD Guidelines on Involuntary Displacement and Resettlement (OCDE/GD 201).[19]

Any project may have unforeseen consequences, despite best efforts at thorough preparation, consultation with local people and careful monitoring during implementation. In the case of the EC's forest project in Uganda both the preparation and the supervision were deeply flawed; and there was never any attempt to consult local people living in the forests and national parks. Efforts to bring the matter to the attention of Commission's made little headway. It took over a year even to get the issue investigated. It was in October 1992 that Oxfam first raised its concerns about the situation of the people evicted from the Kibale forest with the Commission which were. In December 1993 pressure from Member States and MEPs had led to the World Bank and EC sending a joint mission to investigate the situation in Bugangaizi. Senior officials in DG VIII, the EC's Directorate for Development Cooperation had publicly promised that some remedial action would be taken to ameliorate the situation of the settlers.[20] The World Bank had also agreed in principle to make IDA funds available for key areas such as water supplies, roads, and health care once the EC had had identified the needs. In mid 1994 the EC commissioned a feasibility study to draw up a development programme for Bugangaizi, which was to benefit both

---

[18] Kibaale District, which includes the sub-county of Bugangaizi in which those displaced were resettled, is distinct from the Kibale Forest and Game Corridor where the evictions occurred despite the close similarity of the names."

[19] "All involuntary resettlement should be conceived and executed as development programmes, providing sufficient investment resources and opportunities for resettlers to share in project benefits. Displaced people should be i) enabled to reconstruct a land-based or employment-based productive existence; ii) compensated for their losses at replacement cost; iii) assisted with the move and during the transition period at the relocation site; and iv) assisted in their efforts to improve their former living standards and income earning capacity, and production levels, or at least to restore them."

[20] Information Memo to the EDF Committee, 20 October 1993.

the settlers and the impoverished host community.[21] But by the middle of 1995 these plans were quietly shelved by the Commission. In May 1996 when the Commission presented to the EDF Committee its Cooperation Strategy paper, outlining its funding priorities for Uganda's next National Indicative Programme, there was no reference to a rehabilitation programme for the Bugangaizi settlers. As a last resort Oxfam and two Ugandan NGOs representing the settlers, URDT and the Bugangaizi Settlers Committee, jointly submitted a complaint to the UN Committee on Economic, Social and Cultural Rights requesting it to decide on "the advisability of international measures" taken by the World Bank and the EC in respect of the Kibale Forest evictions.[22] The submission argued that, since the Government of Uganda had ratified the Covenant, and given that many of the rights within the Covenant had been, and continued to be violated, as a result of the failure of the donor agencies to prepare, implement and supervise the project adequately or to take remedial measures to rehabilitate those people who were evicted, then the role of the donor agencies fell within the scope of the Committee's powers to assist other UN organs in deciding on the advisability of international measures.[23] Oxfam's version of events in the Kibale Forest was substantiated by a long-overdue, officially commissioned Evaluation Report, which concluded that the costs of the resettlement of settlers evicted from the forest should have been borne by the project.[24]

ARBITRARY DECISION ON REMEDIAL ACTION

But finally it was pressure from MEPs that broke the deadlock. In October 1996, after a number of MEPs had taken up the cases, and in particular after the intervention of Mrs Glenys Kinnock, MEP, the Commission while denying any formal liability for the problems arising from its aid programme in

---

[21] See Bugangaizi Community Development Programme Proposal and LTS Evaluation Report Annex 12 para 8.12 which states that 'In November 1994 the consultants recommended a project covering education, health, roads and water, with an estimatd total cost of Ush 2,873 million (approximately 2.5 MECU). This programme would have gone a long way towards meeting the needs of the settler and host communities'.

[22] Oxfam, Ugandan Rural Development and Training Programme (URDT) and the Bugangaizi Resettlers Association "Submission to the Committee on Economic, Social and Cultural Rights" Oxfam Policy Department, April 1996.

[23] A letter from Philip Alston, Chairpeson of the Committee on Economic, Social and Cultural Rights dated 24 June 1996 to M. Joao de Deus Pinheiro, Commissioner – DGVIII commented that 'The Committee has reviewed the materials contained int he submission referred to and considers that the relevant information would, if accurate, raise significant questions as to the conformity of the project with the Convenant'.

[24] LTS International Edinburgh "Evaluation of the EDF-Funded Natural Forest Management and Conservation Project – a component of the World Bank Forestry Rehabilitation project, Uganda (1988-1995) Volume 1, para 9.30.

Uganda and Kenya, offered to finance a cluster of micro projects for the affected communities. In each case, the Commission specified a ceiling of 300,000 ecus although no attempt was made to assess the level of losses incurred or the nature of the damages suffered by the complainants.[25] Oxfam Kampala agreed to work with the settlers and help them draw up a project proposal which would focus largely on their needs for safe water and education. But while Oxfam has expressed appreciation for the EU's willingness to support a community project, it sees the limited funding available as a key constraint in providing much-needed infrastructure work, which would greatly improve the quality of life for not only the settlers but also the impoverished, host community in Bugangaizi.[26] In Nairobi, more than 18 months later, agreement has been difficult to reach among the various groups of beneficiaries so little progress had been made in drawing up project proposals.

Conclusion

Both the Ugandan and Kenyan cases have highlighted the need for the EU to have an independent complaints mechanism – similar to the World Bank's Inspection Panel – so that those people who have a bona fide complaint about inadequate preparation, appraisal and supervision of an EU financed project or programme, or alleged violations of the principles of the Maastricht Treaty and revised Lomé Convention, could be assured of a fair and prompt hearing. Contingency funds should be available to compensate those people adversely affected – without having to resort to a complex government negotiations or waiting, sometimes years, for the next round of aid programming. In the public debate launched in 1997 by the Commission around its Green Paper on the future of its cooperation agreements with ACP countries, a growing number of European development and environmental NGOs have urged EU governments to give priority consideration to the establishment of such a complaints procedure. As the MEP, Mrs Kinnock, writing about the Kenyan

[25] The LTS Evaluation Report casts light on the discrepancy between the level of actual losses incurred by the people evicted from Kibale and the level of "compensation" on offer. It estimated that the value of the agricultural income lost in the first year after the evictions was about $2.04 million. Most of the people resettled in Bugangaizi lost at least one year's agricultural production. "Even on the assumption that among the evicted households production levels after three years recovered to two-thirds of the pre-eviction levels this implies a continuing annual loss of $0.68 million, which probably understates the losses".

[26] To put the 300,000 ecu community development project in perspective it is worth noting that in 1992/3 when approximately 15,000 people were resettled at Bugangaizi, Oxfam and other NGOs, with support from the British Government, provided $1.4 million of emergency assistance. The Government of Uganda provided $0.6 million.

and Ugandan cases) has pointed out "many of the problems we are now dealing with could have been minimised if complaints had been thoroughly examined and acted upon sooner". In her view a complaints mechanism could help the Commission and MEPs assess grievances at a much earlier stage. "If after an inquiry complaints were considered to be well-founded, the complaints committee could make recommendations to correct damage to the local community. This procedure would obviously only be used in cases where problems have arisen and the EC Delegation and the alleged affected parties have been unable to resolve the matter through the normal channels".[27]

Unlike the World Bank, which enjoys immunity from legal action before national courts except where this is explicitly waived, the EU does offer one other potential avenue for project affected people to seek redress.[28] Article 215 of the Maastricht Treaty entitles even non EU citizens to file a complaint before the European Court of Justice (which overseas the proper application and interpretation of Community law) and seek to recover damages caused by Community institutions or "by its servants in the performance of their duties". But all litigation is lengthy, costly and complicated and this perhaps explains why to date no cases concerning the Commission's development cooperation programme have been filed.

One of the inherent weaknesses of existing grievance procedures is the fact that the Commission, in its anxiety to avoid any suggestion of formal liability, usually restricts remedial action to community-wide, small-scale development projects. Individual or household compensation is almost never an option. Development literature is replete with examples of how cash payments are an inappropriate method of compensation, however there are clear equity problems with the current "community" solutions. First of all there are huge opportunity costs for a community in drawing up project proposals which meet the Commission's stringent requirements. In order for them to do so almost inevitably requires support from an established intermediary, which has the effect of transferring responsibility for solving the problem from the Commission to an NGO. These remedial actions tend to become bogged down in wider government-EU aid negotiations and project cycles. In the Uganda case, for example, the Commission insisted that since it had no contingency funds to draw on remedial action would have to wait for the next round of (the 5-yearly) national indicative programming. In the Kenyan case, those affected by the road construction were not a homogeneous or readily identifiable

---

27 Letter to Steffen Smidt dated 13 November 1996.

28 The World Bank's immunity is based on customary international law which affords immunity to all public international organizations, at least for their non-commercial activities. The principle is codified in the 1947 Convention on the Privileges and Immunities of the Specialized Agencies of the UN.

group. In these circumstances the Commission's insistence that remedial assistance could only be provided once the diverse, shifting and fragmented population living in the Nairobi suburbs had produced a cluster of interlocking micro projects was unrealistic. Secondly, community solutions are by their nature non-specific, which leaves open the possibility that the proposed remedies may not address or correct the residual harm suffered by particular, vulnerable individuals or households. The building of a school, for example, though desirable to the majority of people in a community, may not be of any direct benefit to an elderly widow bereft of adequate shelter or means of support. Thirdly, in the absence of base line data, the lengthy delays that almost invariably occur between the damage being inflicted and obtaining the agreement from the Commission that it will finance some mitigatary measures means that the task of identifying those who have suffered the greatest physical or economic losses becomes more difficult and contentious. Finally, neither the World Bank's Inspection Panel nor the European Ombudsman are empowered to make recommendations. This means that final discretion for determining the level and nature of any remedial action rests in the hands of the aid managers who may have been, at least in part, responsible for the original damage. In such a process the needs and views of the injured parties are easily sidelined.

One of the most tangible indications of the EU's determination to overcome past difficulties in the effectiveness of its aid and its willingness to incorporate principles of transparency and accountability into its own operations would be the establishment of a complaints mechanism which recognizes the rights of non-EU citizens. If the EU is genuinely interested in fostering participative approaches then it should acknowledge that the traditional closed governmental circuits that have typified its deliberations and decision-making processes will have to be opened up not only to EU citizens but to a wider public, including the intended beneficiaries of its development cooperation.

List of Participants

EXPERT MEETING ON WORLD BANK'S INSPECTION PANEL
LUND 1997-10-23–25

Mr. Eduardo G. Abbott
The World Bank

Mr. Gudmundur Alfredsson
Raoul Wallenberg Institute

Mr. Richard Etter Bissell
The World Bank

Ms. Laurence Boisson de Chazournes
The World Bank

Mr. Emmanuel V.O. Dankwa
African Commission of Human and Peoples' Rights

Mr. Mac Darrow
European University Institute in Florence, Italy

Mr. Koen Davidse
The World Bank

Mr. Dominick Devlin
International Labour Organization

Mr. Stefan Emblad
Swedish Ministry of Finance

Ms. Patricia Feeney
Policy Department at OXFAM, United Kingdom

Mr. Rolf Folkesson
Swedish International Development Co-operation Agency (Sida), Sweden

Mr. Kåre Frydenlund
Norwegian Ministry of Foreign Affairs

Mr. Michelo Hansungule
Raoul Wallenberg Institute

Ms. Ruth Jacoby
Swedish Ministry for Foreign Affairs

Mr. Rahmatullah Khan
Centre for Studies in Diplomacy, International Law and Economics, School of International Studies, India

Mr. James MacNeill
The World Bank

Ms. Eugenia McGill
Asian Development Bank

Ms. Gay Miller
Inter-American Development Bank

Mr. Göran Melander
Raoul Wallenberg Institute

Mr. Jakob Möller
UN Centre for Human Rights (retired)

Mr. Francois Pagé
The World Bank

Ms. Jan Piercy
The World Bank

Mr. Murilo Portugal
The World Bank

Mr. Rolf Ring
Raoul Wallenberg Institute

Ms. Katrine Schjoenning
Danish Ministry of Foreign Affairs

Ms. Sabine Schlemmer-Schulte
The World Bank

Mr. Ibrahim Shihata
The World Bank

Mr. Surendra Singh
The World Bank

Mr. Ingemar Ståhl
Faculty of Law, Lund University

Ms. Jennifer Sullivan
International Finance Corporation

Mr. Lee Swepston
International Labour Organization

Mr. Jerzy Sztucki
Raoul Wallenberg Institute

Ms. Sia S. Åkermark
Åbo Academy University Institute for Human Rights, Finland

Secretariat

Ms. Britta Dyrendahl
Ms. Susanne Malmström
Ms. Ingela Ståhl

Index